1985

The Living Lyre in English Verse

The Living Lyre
in English Verse

from Elizabeth through the Restoration

Louise Schleiner

University of Missouri Press
Columbia, 1984

Library of Congress Cataloging in Publication Data

Schleiner, Louise.
The living lyre in English verse from Elizabeth through the
Restoration.

Bibliography: p.
Includes index.
1. Songs—England—16th century—Texts—History and
criticism. 2. Songs—England—17th century—Texts—
History and criticism. 3. Music and literature.
I. Title.
ML2831.S3   1984   784.3'00942   84–2206
ISBN 0–8262–0441–4

Portions of this book were originally published in somewhat
different form in the following journals: "Herrick's Songs and the
Character of *Hesperides*," *English Literary Renaissance* 6 (1976):
77–91; and "Jacobean Song and Herbert's Metrics," *Studies in
English Literature* 19 (1979): 109–26. A version of the chapter
on Crashaw was originally published in *Essays on Richard Crashaw*, edited by Robert M. Cooper (Salzburg: University of Salzburg, 1979), pp. 145–68. All are used with the permission of the
original publishers.

Preface

ὡς καὶ ἐμοὶ τόδε ἔργον ἀέξεται, ᾧ ἐπιμ⟨ι⟩μνω

. . . as even this my work prospers, which I keep doing.

Eumaios the Swineherd

he scholarly preface has well-defined conventions apt for parody. A recent author warmly thanked his former colleagues at the place where he had not received tenure for not having helped him with his book by the absence of scholarly interchange in their department. He supposed the book would be the worse for it if they had. And he warmly thanked his state welfare agency for financial support toward the book's preparation. Such wit could be merely facetious, but if a preface is intended to suggest the context and mood of a piece of scholarship, it has its place.

The present book has grown along with my children for the past ten years. The hours spent on it had mostly to be bought or pilfered from time for other doings; thus they had some of the aura of "things forbidden" and were greatly enjoyed. Besides the scholarly acquaintances who helped me through conferences, correspondence, and inspiration, among others Earl Miner, John Shawcross, Claude Summers, Edward Doughtie, James Winn, Christopher Hatch, Elise Jorgens, Daniel Donno, and my former teachers Andrew Sabol and Barbara Lewalski, I thank Kern Holoman and other musicians who performed old songs for me, babysitters who gave their good time for poor pay, my long-suffering typist Alice Henin, close friends who shored me up and shared their own rich interests with me, and my husband, who saw to it that his extended research opportunities in several far-flung libraries became mine too, and who happily spent major portions of our income on my research and writing costs. I owe special thanks to the staff people of the Huntington and Herzog August libraries, both of them "earthly paradises" for scholars.

L. S., Davis, California
September 1983

Contents

Introduction

his book reads Elizabethan to Restoration lyric poetry from the perspective of the age's vocal music. It is not a work of musicology, though musicians can find here much to interest them. I have aimed for appreciative reading of poems, with each reading inspired by music or musical contexts; occasionally I discuss nonmusical elements of the poems as well, in spelling out the musically inspired interpretations. Readers who dip in and peruse, say, only the Cowley chapter need to read first the account of methodology and specially defined terms comprising pp. 4–11.

Chapter I begins examining the changing interaction between English lyric verse and music through the Elizabethan era and seventeenth century by means of a concept of three modes of lyric, conceived as adjoining segments on a spectrum of utterance types: simulated verbal song, simulated declamation or oratory, and simulated conversational speech. Such distinctions have been used by many critics of the period's poetry, without being systematized as they are here. These modes, defined in terms of syntax, diction, meter, and rhetorical devices, are valuable for the study of musical-poetic interaction because they help us trace two phenomena: the preferences in lyric verse of composers and writers of contrafacta texts (texts to fit preexisting music), and the uses of and allusions to song in the work of major poets, even in works not specifically intended for musical setting. Having proposed this framework, Chapter I examines Elizabethan verse experimentation, primarily in three representative figures, Sidney, Thomas Watson, and Shakespeare (in the sonnets). It concludes by considering some influences of Continental music and verse forms and some musical dimensions of the English attempts at quantitative verse.

Each of Chapters II–VI discusses song mode and/or song allusion and influence in the work of a major poet, beginning with George Herbert. Tracing

1

the nexus of song influence and major lyric poetry, I have followed the prints in the snow wherever they led. What the poets make of song in their lyric verse varies greatly from one to the other, and such analysis contributes to our understanding of their characteristic styles and voices, revealing new dimensions in their poetry. After Herbert, the remaining chapters treat Herrick, Crashaw, Milton, and Cowley. Chapter VII surveys stylistic changes through the seventeenth century in both lyric and song and examines the changing interaction between the two. It analyzes the text and music together in two representative songs: by Jonson/Ferrabosco and Dryden/Purcell.

Music did not influence all the poets in the same fashion. Each drew upon his musical knowledge and experiences, as listener or amateur performer, in his own way. Thus the chapters vary considerably in approaches and conclusions. Herbert, Sunday lutenist and singer of his own lyrics, was greatly influenced by lute songs in his prosody and stanza forms. Herrick, song lyricist par excellence and favored poet of Caroline song composers, can be seen moving toward speech-mode lyric in his revisions for *Hesperides*. Crashaw, translator of songs in his youth, displays a habit of musical allusion for particular effects in his mature odes. Milton, organist, reader of music theory, collaborator with Henry Lawes, and fan of music drama, found in Italian dramatic song the proper rhythmic milieu and musical justification for his ebbing and flowing monodies, choral odes, and epic inset lyrics. Cowley, in his anacreontics, Pindaric odes, and occasional odes, worked into a vein of "grand lyric" perfectly attuned to the interests and musical resources of the best Restoration composers.

Despite this diversity of approach, the overview of these several studies allows us to follow in some detail through the century the relationships between stylistic changes in vocal music and those in English lyric poetry. In this endeavor the idea of the three modes of lyric supplies a set of coordinates by which to plot what poets and composers at different times thought lyric verse should be and what they thought music should do with it in song. In such a study covering the whole century we can take into account a dimension of poetic composition that until very recently has been ignored in diachronic literary-historical work, though it is often considered with reference to individual poems and poets.

In certain passages I have necessarily assumed for my readers some musical education, such that they know time and key signs, can read a melody line in treble or bass clef, and can understand common terms like *leading tone*, *cadence*, and *sequence*, as well as the triadic nature of chords and the relationship of major and relative minor keys. (Diatonic harmony was just coming to full clarity in this era.) People with less musical knowledge than this will read most of the book without difficulty and I hope with profit, though they may want to skim over the passages directly analyzing music. This is not a book for the "fit audience though few" of the musically trained: all are welcome.

A Note on the Music Examples

Each chapter includes at least the treble and bass lines of one complete song or monody (pp. 43, 66, 79, 92, 144, 171, 200). By reading and humming through this set, one may do a quick minicourse in the changing song styles of the century and the kinds of lyric verse associated with each. I have modernized spelling in the lyrics for the reader's ease in sight singing.

The other music examples are excerpts, only so much of a given song as is needed for what I am discussing. These are generally a bit longer than musicologists' customary examples because multilined passages of poetry are at issue and need to be seen in the song treatment.

I.   Three Modes of Lyric among the Elizabethans

Song and Three Modes of Lyric

bout relations between poetry and music in sixteenth- and seventeenth-century England much is known to us: song lyrics have become available in their musical contexts.[1] Wilfred Mellers has shown us how to analyze words and music together in songs of the time.[2] Gretchen Finney and John Hollander have described musical influences on poetry, and more recently Elise Jorgens has done the reverse.[3] Musical imagery in poetry has been explained.[4] We have studies of figures important for the topic of literary-musical relations, such as Thomas Wyatt, Thomas Campion, Ben Jonson, and Henry Lawes.[5] And Ian Spink's *English Song, Dowland to Purcell* describes very well the particular composers'

1. See especially E. H. Fellowes, ed., *English Madrigal Verse: 1588–1632* and *The English School of Lutenist Song Writers*, ser. 1 and 2; Alfred Einstein, "The Elizabethan Madrigal and 'Musica Transalpina'"; Joseph Kerman, *The Elizabethan Madrigal*; Germaine Bontoux, *La Chanson en Angleterre au Temps d'Elisabeth*; and Edward Doughtie, ed., *Lyrics from English Airs.*

2. Wilfrid Mellers, *Harmonious Meeting: A Study of Music, Poetry and Theatre in England, 1600–1900.*

3. Gretchen Finney, *Musical Backgrounds for English Literature, 1580–1650*, primarily on Milton; John Hollander, *Vision and Resonance: Two Senses of Poetic Form*; and Elise B. Jorgens, "On Matters of Manner and Music in Jacobean and Caroline Song," which reappears in her *The Well-Tun'd Word: Musical Interpretations of English Poetry, 1597–1651.*

4. See especially John Hollander, *The Untuning of the Sky: Ideas of Music in English Poetry, 1500–1700.*

5. See Winifred Maynard, "The Lyrics of Wyatt: Poems or Songs, I & II"; Miles Kastendieck, *England's Musical Poet, Thomas Campion*; Edward Lowbury et al., *Thomas Campion, Poet, Composer, Physician*; Walter Davis, Introduction to *The Works of Thomas Campion*; David A. Richardson, "The Golden Mean in Campion's Airs"; Mary Chan, *Music in the Theatre of Ben Jonson*; Willa Evans, *Ben Jonson and Elizabethan Music* and *Henry Lawes: Musician and Friend of Poets.*

4

styles and merits, with occasional perceptive comments about the verse they set. Despite this wealth of information and insight, there is still much to be told about the interaction of English poetry and music from Elizabethan to Restoration times.

So far our survey of the changing relations between the two arts in the period has been Bruce Pattison's *Music and Poetry of the English Renaissance*, which concludes that music and poetry, having enjoyed a close, fruitful interaction through the late sixteenth and early seventeenth centuries, then went their separate ways:

> The madrigal had allowed musical ingenuity free play, but criticism of counterpoint and the new attention to monodic music could logically lead only to a sovereignty of speech rhythms over musical values. The Italians had tried to stylize natural speech into recitative: only thus could literary values be further applied to music. The Italian declamatory style had already made some impression on the English airs . . . The leading composers of the next generation, the brothers Lawes, applied the declamatory style to the setting of lyrics . . . But there was no future for music along his [Henry Lawes's] lines. Instrumental composers were busy creating a technique that owed nothing to poetry . . . If music had reached a point at which it could not profitably gain much further from literary inspiration, poetry was developing in a way that left the musician little scope. The lyric was ceasing to trouble about singing qualities and appealing to the reader. [John Donne broke] with the traditional values of lyric poetry [and] initiated a separation between music and poetry that widened as the seventeenth century advanced. (pp. 197–98, 200)

Pattison has usefully synthesized many widespread impressions,[6] but perhaps the image of the sibling arts going their separate ways after Donne has lulled students of literature into ignoring some important musical dimensions of English poetry through the seventeenth century.

The stylistic interaction of poetry and vocal music in seventeenth-century England is of interest to both literary and music historians, but has more potential interest for the former, since seventeenth-century English music between the lutenists and Purcell is relatively little regarded, while lyric poetry of the same era includes works of timeless importance. What was involved in the changes of lyric style from Sidney to Dryden? I want to show that song setting, through its interaction with lyric poetry, played a part in these stylistic changes, and further that many poems have dimensions we will miss unless we are aware of their musical contexts, their musically influenced features of rhythm and verbal pattern, and their musically allusive effects.

It has been usual to say that much Elizabethan lyric poetry was smooth and songlike, with end-stopped lines and regular caesuras, while that of

---

6. John Stevens, *Music and Poetry in the Early Tudor Court*, pp. 33–35, has stressed that the Elizabethan union of poetry and music was a humanist reunion of the two, which had been professionally separate since the thirteenth century.

Donne and increasingly of later poets was dominated by speech rhythms. Donne's lyrics, says Pattison, have an "affinity with dramatic blank verse. The line is no longer the rhythmical unit. Speech periods are freely counterpointed on the metrical base . . . Many of Donne's lyrics begin with a stanza freely constructed from the natural prose rhythm of passionate speech."[7] Similar distinctions between what might be called song mode and speech mode in English lyric have been formulated by several scholars, for example Catherine Ing, Joseph Summers, and Edward Selig.[8]

The distinction is extremely useful and must be extended and more precisely defined for the present study. First, Donne on his own did not invent the lyric mode based on speech rhythms. Certainly the Elizabethans, if not even earlier Tudor poets,[9] were already working on it, being quite willing to experiment with speech rhythms, just as they did with shaped verse, classical meters, stanzaic patterns, contrafacta verse for foreign music, and anything else that occurred to them. We must start with the Elizabethans. Second, there are many lyrics, especially as the seventeenth century progresses, which, in the rhythms and suggestions of their language, remind us neither of song nor of conversational speech but more of some form of oratory or declamation—speeches, proclamations, sermons, formal circulating epistles, the tragedian's set piece or indeed much of dramatic blank verse—language for public occasions. Thus if we think of lyric modes in terms of the kind of language use implied as a model, we should add to *song* and *speech* a third mode, *declamatory* or *oratorical*, the fruit of a pervasive verbal model in an age of intense political and religious controversy, when people relied on speeches, proclamations, and sermons for information and for clues to politic choices. Yvor Winters offhandedly reflects his perception of these modes, saying that songlike lyrics were "written as if intended to be set," that Donne's lyrics sometimes sound like "petulant conversation," and that Milton's lyric language is "primarily that of oratory."[10]

Song, speech, and declamation, as lyric modes, are not boxes into one of which every lyric may be put, but rather segments of a spectrum that shade into each other, within each of which various shadings exist. Many lyrics are of mixed mode in these terms, and none the worse for being so. But most poets, in their lyric verse, incline toward one of them—Donne toward colloquial speech, Shakespeare toward declamation, Campion or Herrick toward song—not that Donne and Shakespeare could not write excellent songmode lyrics when they pleased. Herbert, despite being a preacher and uni-

---

7. Pattison, *Music and Poetry*, p. 199.

8. Catherine Ing, *Elizabethan Lyrics*, pp. 143–45; Joseph Summers, *George Herbert: His Religion and Art*, pp. 157, 165–70; and Edward Selig, *The Flourishing Wreath*, pp. 51–54.

9. Stevens, *Music and Poetry*, p. 148, citing E. K. Chambers, contests Pattison's view and finds that Wyatt was the innovator in this respect.

10. Yvor Winters, *Forms of Discovery*, pp. 36, 76, 119. The three modes bear no relation to the categories of "plain" vs. "ornate or Petrarchan" lyric.

versity orator, usually divided his time in his English poetry between speech and song modes. Milton, the superb rhetorician and pamphleteer, as a lyricist naturally inclined to the declamatory—by that time for musical as well as rhetorical reasons, as we shall see.

The use of *declamatory* for the third lyric mode must be correlated with the term's musical meanings. First, declamatory recitative is the most speech-like or least melodious form of recitative in music drama or other musical-dramatic contexts. A second usage, among British music historians (for example, Henry Davey and Percy Young), refers to English monody of the mid-seventeenth century in its various forms, which sometimes approaches true recitative, in some works intermingles near-recitative and more melodious passages, and in others strikes a vein of declamation midway between air and recitative. As texts for such "declamatory song," composers did not always take what I call declamatory lyrics, but they had developed the style specifically in the process of coping with the challenges of setting speech and declamatory lyric. *Declamatory* as applied to lyric derives from the model of spoken declamation—from stage, pulpit, soapbox, or lectern—as do the two musical meanings. In short, not all declamatory song texts are declamatory lyrics, but many are, and with good reason.

One assumes that composers usually prefer to set lyrics in song mode: smooth, audibly patterned lyrics with mostly end-stopped lines and certain kinds of imagery and argument suitable for the reduced comprehensibility of words in song. (This is the assumption behind Pattison's statement that seventeenth-century lyrics "left the musician little scope" because they neglected "singing qualities.") But as Jorgens and other scholars have shown, Caroline composers deliberately developed a compositional method apt for setting metrically rough lyrics in speech rhythms and declamatory lyrics with extended periods, predominant enjambment, and elaborate syntax. The process occurred naturally as English musicians imitated Continental monody, but it was also influenced by the shift in dominant poetic styles toward speech and declamation. Later, after declamatory composers had done all they could to represent and interpret such lyrics (with limited musical success), poets began devising new styles of lyric—especially in the ode or "grand lyric"—that would be amenable to the styles of vocal music developed in the Restoration. We must examine this interaction of the arts more closely, and the idea of modes of lyric based on implied language models provides terms for exploring composers' options, choices, and word-setting methods.

The present scheme is of course not the first effort to define modes of seventeenth-century English poetry. Modal definitions can be based on different considerations, depending on what one means to explore. Earl Miner's private, social, and public modes, for example, are based on the relationship that obtains between the speaker and the implied audience in a poem.[11] Or John Shawcross's deliberative, forensic, and epideictic modes, deriving from Aristotle's *Rhetoric*, are based on the intent of the poetic speaker with respect to the subject matter, whether the intent is, for example, to persuade to action.[12] Or Walter Davis's idea of Campion's "epigrammatic mode" defines that poet's dominant style by reference to a generic subcategory.[13] The present scheme of song, declamatory, and speech modes is based on the consideration of what sort of everyday language use is evoked or imitated by the poem as recited aloud. Does its language, in rhythm, syntax, diction, and prevalent kinds of rhetorical structures, remind us of someone singing or chanting? Or of conversational speech between lovers or coworkers? Or does its language evoke the sound of a bishop's circular letter, an actor's soliloquy, or the ringleader's speech for a peasant revolt? To take a term from the aesthetician Susanne Langer, is it *virtual* song, speech, or declamation?[14]

Taking hints from many commentators who have used similar distinctions, we may compile the following lists of traits that tend to predominate in song, declamatory, and speech modes of poetry.

song	declamation	conversational speech
metrical smoothness	moderately smooth meter	relative metrical roughness
inclination to short-lined meters (tetrameter, trimeter, ballad measure, intermixed dimeters) for flexibility with motion and pauses	inclination to long-lined meters (pentameter, alexandrines), for scope of expansive periods	tetrameter most common, downplaying or submergence of metrical units
frequent end-stopped lines	much enjambment of sentences, but seldom within phrases or between subject and verb, or verb and complement	frequent enjambment, even within clauses and phrases (call this *strong enjambment*)[15]
short, uninterrupted syntactic units; frequent exclamations and questions	long, smooth syntactic units, with much parallelism, subordination, and use of conjuncts and disjuncts	prominent syntactic unit the single independent clause, often interrupted by parenthetical insertions (speechlike improvisations)

11. Earl Miner, *The Metaphysical Mode from Donne to Cowley*; *The Cavalier Mode from Jonson to Cotton*; and *The Restoration Mode from Milton to Dryden*.

12. John Shawcross, "The Poet as Orator," pp. 5–36.

13. Davis, Introduction, p. xxi.

14. See Susanne K. Langer, *Feeling and Form* and *Problems of Art*. Langer's idea is that each of the arts creates a particular kind of *virtual* experience for its audience in imitation of real experience. Thus the mode of music is virtual experienced time passage, that of painting virtual space, that of literature virtual memory of experienced events.

15. I have adopted the term from Jorgens's *Well-Tun'd Word*, where it appears several times.

prominent (foregrounded) patterns of repeated sounds and rhythms, often over scope of whole stanza or poem; rhyme prominent	no long-scope patterns of repeated sounds or rhythms; frequent patterns of repeated grammatical structures; rhyme generally submerged or not used	no long-scope sound or rhythmic patterns, rhyme submerged
frequent use of other rhetorical "figures of sound" as well as rhyme (anaphora, anadiplosis, polyptoton, alliteration, etc.)	considerable use of both "figures of sound" and "figures of sense" (i.e., phonological patterning and lexical cohesion)	occasional use of "figures of sense," seldom of "figures of sound"
frequent liquid consonants	liquid and single consonants preferred	frequent "hard" consonants and consonant clusters
diction highly conventional, formal to moderately formal, treating conventional themes	diction from formal to middle level, depending on desired tone	diction from middle level to informal/colloquial, depending on implied dramatic situation
conventional imagery of simple, sensory impressions, frequent appeal to smell, taste, and hearing, as well as sight	images apt to be conventional, but tend to careful and original elaboration, often into extended metaphor or illustrative anecdote	imagery apt to be idiosyncratic, or ironic (sometimes a distortion of conventional imagery); frequent elliptic or compressed imagery

The idea of speech, song, and declamatory modes of lyric poetry was first proposed by Russian formalists. Osip Brik argued that syntax must be considered in descriptions of poetic rhythm, which is a far more complex phenomenon than traditional metrics can describe, even with the idea of standard levels of deviation from norms.[16] As Victor Erlich summarizes the concept: "The term [rhythm] encompassed both the organization of the quantitative elements (pitch, stress, length) [depending on the given language and era] and the use made of the quality of the individual speech sounds, or verbal orchestration [for example, alliteration, assonance, and so on], as well as . . . phrase melody."[17] Boris Ejxenbaum in *Verse Melodics* (1922)[18] said that the uses and relative prominence of these rhythmic factors vary from one type of verse to another. As Erlich summarizes Ejxenbaum's argument,

16. See Osip Brik, "Contributions to the Study of Verse Language," and Jurij Tynjanov, "Rhythm as the Constructive Factor of Verse," in *Readings in Russian Poetics*, ed. Ladislav Matejka and Krystyna Pomorska; and Victor Erlich, *Russian Formalism, History-Doctrine*, pp. 212–29.

17. Erlich, ibid., p. 222.

18. Boris Ejxenbaum, *Melodika stixa* (Petrograd, 1922). Apparently this work as a whole has not been translated into a western European language. For a brief account by Ejxenbaum of his three lyric modes, see "The Theory of the Formal Method," *Readings in Russian Poetics*, pp. 22–26.

Depending on the esthetic "orientation" of the poem, each of the three elements of rhythm can assume the status of the underlying principle of verse structure. Starting from his assumption, Ejxenbaum set out to examine the relative importance of phrase melody in three styles which he discerned in Russian lyrical poetry—the rhetorical or declamatory, the conversational, and the melodic or "singable" (*napevnyj*) styles. In the first type, . . . phrase melody is clearly a secondary phenomenon, an "accompaniment to, or a by-product of, the logical canon." In the second, . . . Ejxenbaum noted a tendency to emulate the variety and mobility of colloquial intonations. But it is only in the "singable" verse, asserted the critic, that we have to do with a consistent artistic exploitation of phrase melody—a "full-fledged system of intonation (*intonirovanie*), comprising the phenomena of melodic symmetry, repetition, crescendo, cadence, etc."

In the melodic style, Erlich's summary continues, "intonational patterns were emphasized by means of such devices as inversion, lyrical repetition or refrain, [and] the *'reprise'* (the repeating of a question within a stanza)."

For me the idea of song, declamatory, and speech modes of lyric verse arose from reading sixteenth- and seventeenth-century English verse and commentary on it. Ejxenbaum drew his examples from nineteenth-century Russian poetry. Yet the schemes are very similar. In the chart above, as with the Russian formalists, aspects of poetry that have traditionally received separate treatment (imagery, diction, syntax) are intermingled with considerations of meter and rhythm. If one defines lyric modes as forms of virtual utterance, all the features of their everyday models must be included in the account; thus poetic meter, phonemics, syntax, and semantics will be interrelated. In this effort I have mainly used the terminology of traditional grammar and rhetoric since it is close to the mentality of the poets being studied, only occasionally supplementing it with terms from modern linguistics.[19]

To make the idea of these modes concrete, consider three relatively pure samples, from the 1590s or the turn of the century.[20]

> Come away, come, sweet love,
> The golden morning breaks;
> All the earth, all the air
> Of love and pleasure speaks.
> Teach thine arms then to embrace,
> And sweet, rosy lips to kiss,
> And mix our souls in mutual bliss.
> Eyes were made for beauty's grace,
> Viewing, rueing love-long pain,
> Procured by beauty's rude disdain.
> (from John Dowland, *First Book of Songs or Airs*, 1597)

19. Such terms are either from Randolph Quirk and Sidney Greenbaum, *A Concise Grammar of Contemporary English*, or Elizabeth Traugott and Mary Pratt, *Linguistics for Students of Literature*.

20. "Come away, come" is cited from Fellowes, *English Madrigal Verse*; Sonnet 33 from *The Riverside Shakespeare*, ed. G. Blakemore Evans et al., as subsequent Shakespeare sonnets will be; and part of "The Good-morrow" from *Poems of John Donne*, ed. H. J. C. Grierson.

Full many a glorious morning have I seen
Flatter the mountain tops with sovereign eye,
Kissing with golden face the meadows green,
Gilding pale streams with heavenly alcumy;
Anon permit the basest clouds to ride
With ugly rack on his celestial face,
And from the forlorn world his visage hide,
Stealing unseen to west with this disgrace:
Even so my sun one early morn did shine
With all-triumphant splendor on my brow,
But out, alack, he was but one hour mine,
The region cloud hath mask'd him from me now.
    Yet him for this my love no whit disdaineth:
    Suns of the world may stain, when heaven's sun staineth.
          (Shakespeare, Sonnet 33)

I wonder by my troth, what thou, and I
Did, till we lov'd? were we not wean'd till then,
But suck'd on country pleasures, childishly?
Or snorted we in the seaven sleepers den?
T'was so; But this, all pleasures fancies bee.
If ever any beauty I did see,
Which I desired, and got, t'was but a dreame of thee.

And now good morrow to our waking soules,
Which watch not one another out of feare;
For love, all love of other sights controules,
And makes one little roome, an every where.
        (Donne, "The Good-morrow," lines 1–11)

Sidney, Watson, and Shakespeare

The three modes are not indicators of whether a given poem was specifically meant to be sung. As John Stevens says, be a poem never so songlike, we cannot know that it was for a song unless the poet says so or sets it.[21] We can say whether it is "virtual" song: whether it evokes a sense of singing.

In Elizabethan times, such song-mode verse was regarded as the most suitable kind for setting. Thus there are many contemporary settings of the *Astrophil* songs, but hardly any of texts from Spenser's lyrics, which incline mainly toward declamation. And many humanists even believed that because song verse was, as Sidney's Arcadian shepherd Dicus said, "just appropriated to musicke," it was the highest kind of poetry, "since verses had ther chefe ornament, if not eand, in musicke."[22] Dicus added that one could hear in such verse a "secret musicke, since by the measure one may perceave some verses running with a high note fitt for great matters, some with a light foote fit for no greater than amorous conceytes." The sounds of the verse

21. Stevens, *Music and Poetry*, pp. 28–29.
22. *The Poems of Sir Philip Sidney*, ed. William A. Ringler, Jr., pp. 389–90. This passage was omitted from later copies of the *Old Arcadia*.

may suggest music, and even a certain musical mood. This "secret music" is what I mean by virtual song in lyric. Similarly, Puttenham observed that poets could make their verse "many wayes passionate to the eare and hart of the hearer," so that it would "counterfait the harmonicall tunes of the vocal and instrumentall musickes." [23]

Although in the *Apology for Poetry* Sidney repeated the ancient commonplace (the poet "commeth to you with words set in delightfull proportion, . . . prepared for the well inchaunting skill of Musicke" [24]), in the debate of Dicus and Lalus the doctrine that such musicality is the highest quality in verse is in effect refuted. For Lalus had the last say, arguing that poets did not need to make poems especially apt for music since music was the servant of poetry, not vice versa, [25] that the pleasures of poetry were superior to those of music, "for by one the eare only, by the other the mind was pleased" (see *Paradise Lost* II, 555), and that "rimers" or poets in vernacular traditions were superior to those who, imitating the ancients, sought to write quantitative verse. As Lalus notes, the English quantitative verse was more difficult for musicians to set than the "rimer's" work, since the quantitative poet had "no care of the accent . . . which the rimer regardeth." The drift of the debate is not that quantitative verse is necessarily bad but that rhymed accentual verse is just as good for reading, better for musical setting, and not obliged to concern itself with musical demands and possibilities.

The songs of *Astrophil and Stella* (to adopt William Ringler's spelling), intermingled among the sonnets, are clear-cut song-mode lyrics. If Sidney could make Lalus argue against the necessity of writing songlike lyrics, he certainly knew how to do so himself when he wished to. The songs of *Astrophil* contrast sharply with the sonnets, in which we see Sidney well on the way to speech-mode lyric, though most of them should be described as borderline between declamation and speech mode. To begin applying the lyric modes, let us look at this contrast in *Astrophil*. Then, to move to a lesser poet but no less eager experimenter than Sidney, we may examine some pieces by Thomas Watson. The two of them will supply our initial sample of Elizabethan lyric forms at a most innovative stage.

By the time Sidney wrote *Astrophil* in 1582 he had several years of verse experimentation behind him. In the eclogues, songs, and sonnets of the *Old*

---

23. George Puttenham, in G. Gregory Smith, ed., *Elizabethan Critical Essays*, 1:88.

24. Ibid., 1:172.

25. Sidney would have been thinking of such humanist statements as that of Barthélemy Aneau in his *Quintil Horatian*: "il n'est pas en usage que les poëtes composans chansons se assujectissent à suivre la musique; ains au contraire les musiciens suyvent la lettre & le subject (qu'ils appellent) à eux baillé par les poëtes" (cited in G. Thibault, "Musique et Poésie en France au XVIᵉ Siecle Avant les 'Amours' de Ronsard," *Musique et Poésie au XVIᵉ Siecle*, ed. Jean Jacquot, p. 85). On the musical humanists' inclination to subordinate music to poetry, see James Winn, *Unsuspected Eloquence: A History of the Relations between Poetry and Music*, pp. 171–80.

Arcadia and the *Certain Sonnets* he had worked at length with two kinds of verse experiment which, as influences on English prosody, require further study by literary scholars and will be taken up later in the present chapter: verse in classical meters and contrafacta verse (verse written to fit preexisting music).

My comments in the following pages are based on the view that the quantitative experiments had two beneficial results, one positive and one negative. First, they brought into English many musically suggestive rhythmic figures, mostly iambic-anapestic or trochaic-dactylic combinations, and thus enriched the poets' stock of possibilities for verbal song. For as Hollander noted of these verses based on an arcane, inaudible system, the listener's "ear inferred that all sorts of accentual patterns it heard were indeed intended to be systematic."[26] And second, as in the Spenser-Harvey argument over carpénter versus cárpenter, the quantitative verses helped to make poets keenly aware of their own speech by showing them what would *not* work in English verse. This led them to reflect on the phonetic and morphological qualities of English,[27] its consonant clusters, monosyllables, stress patterns, and relative lack of inflectional syllables, and thus doubtless improved their ability both to reproduce speech rhythms in verse and to create audibly patterned songlike verse when they wished.

As Sidney did in the *Certain Sonnets*,[28] many poets wrote contrafacta verses to fit Continental tunes. The benefits of such work would show up in their later success with song mode: from musical definition of a rhythmic line they learned to think of the verse line as a rhythmic unit capable of greatly varied structural definition, not limited to set patterns, neither of native English metrics nor of stress-adapted classical metrics. And again, for the developing use of speech rhythms, this ability to recognize and imitate patterns of musical rhythm was negatively useful in teaching poets what does not sound like natural speech because it is too conspicuously patterned.

26. *Vision and Resonance*, p. 66. See also Hallett Smith, *Elizabethan Poetry*, pp. 270–72.

27. Ringler, *The Poems*, p. 391, prints, from a manuscript of the *Old Arcadia*, Sidney's formulation of ten rules for quantitative verse (or see Ringler's "Master Drant's Rules"); for Campion's ideas on quantitative metrics see *Observations in the Art of English Poetry* (1602). Derek Attridge in *Well-weighed Syllables: Elizabethan Verse in Classical Metres* explains the metrical speculations of many Elizabethans and how they applied the rules of position, penultimate syllable, digraph, vowel before vowel, and precedent for English quantitative verse.

28. Ringler, in his commentaries on the lyrics, mentions the tunes Sidney listed for them, identifying only "Wilhelmus van Nassau," the Dutch national anthem. Sidney names for both #3 ("The fire to see my wrongs for anger burneth") and #4 ("The Nightingale, as soon as April bringeth") the tune of "Non credo già che più infelice amante"; for #6 ("Sleep, baby mine") the tune of "Basciami vita mia" (Pattison, *Music and Poetry*, p. 179, points out a tune of this name—but Ringler says there are several, and we don't know which was meant); for #7 ("O fair! O sweet! when I do look on thee") the tune of "Se tu señora no dueles de mi"; for #23 ("Who hath his fancie pleased") "Wilhelmus van Nassau"; for #24 ("Who hath ever felt") "The smokes of melancholy"; for #26 ("No, no, no, no, I cannot hate my foe") a Neapolitan song beginning "No, no, no, no"; and for #27 ("All my sense thy sweetnesse gained") "a Neapolitan villanell." See also Frank Fabry, "Sidney's Poetry and Italian Song-Form."

While I would not claim that the sonnets of *Astrophil and Stella* are entirely in speech mode, Sidney there demonstrates his ability to write it and to use it to good poetic effect. As Ringler says, in *Astrophil* Sidney "allowed the rhythms of speech to have an increasing part in introducing variations in the fixed [metric] pattern." [29]

> Your words my friend (right healthfull caustiks) blame
>   My young mind marde, whom *Love* doth windlas so,
>   That mine owne writings like bad servants show
> My wits quicke in vaine thoughts, in vertue lame:
> That Plato I read for nought, but if he tame
>   Such coltish gyres, that to my birth I owe
> Nobler desires.
>   (*Astrophil and Stella*, #21, lines 1–7)

Here we see the salient features of speech mode: frequent metrical irregularity of heavy stress (yoúng mínd márred, bád sérvănts, wíts qúick, váine thóughts, ówe / Nóblĕr dĕsíres); strong enjambment across basic clause structure (subject-verb-complement); frequent parenthetical insertions interrupting the grammar of the clauses (my friend, right healthful caustics, like bad servants—such insertions are characteristic of a speaker, thinking of things to add while a sentence is in progress); consonant clusters (caustics blame, writings like, coltish gyres); absence of any noticeable "figures of sound" (anaphora, anadiplosis, and so on). The ending of this sonnet, with its ironic evaluation of the friend's advice ([you] dig deep your wisdom's mine), also well illustrates speech lyric:

> Sure you say well, your wisdome's golden mine
> Dig deepe with learning's spade, now tell me this,
> Hath this world ought so faire as Stella is?

Or later we hear Astrophil beg for news of Stella in convincing speech, beginning "Be your words made (good Sir) of Indian ware, / That you allow me them by so small rate?" He goes on to chide his informant:

> When I demaund of *Phenix Stella's* state,
> You say forsooth, you left her well of late.
> O God, thinke you that satisfies my care?
>   I would know whether she did sit or walke,
> How cloth'd, how waited on, sighd she or smilde,
> Whereof, with whom, how often did she talke,
> With what pastime, time's journey she beguilde,
>   If her lips daignd to sweeten my poore name.
> Say all, and all well sayd, still say the same.
>   (# 92, lines 7–14)

The jerks and starts, the exclamations (O God! Say all!), the casual sniff of speech parody in "You say 'Forsooth, you left her well of late,'" and the

---

29. Ringler, *The Poems*, p. lv.

other speechlike qualities here make us perfectly imagine the anxious questioner plying his nonchalant visitor for news.

This, like several of the other most speechlike sonnets, is immediately followed by one of the eleven interspersed songs of the sequence.[30] Whether consciously intended or not, the contrast is effective (see also #63 followed by song #1, and #86 followed by the cluster of songs #5–9). The sonnet "When I demand" (#92, above) is followed by song #10, which turned out to be the most popular of the *Astrophil and Stella* songs among composers, set by William Byrd, Robert Dowland, and John Ward.[31]

> O dear life, when shall it be
> That mine eyes thine eyes shall see,
> And in them thy mind discover
> Whether absence have had force
> Thy remembrance to divorce
> From the image of thy lover?
> (st. 1 of 8)

As Ringler says, Sidney had tried out this seven-syllable accentual trochaic line in *Certain Sonnets* #7, #26, and #27, all contrafacta of Spanish and Italian songs, and "aside from one isolated exception," this was the first appearance of the meter in English[32]—a noteworthy innovation since it proved so valuable to later lyricists, especially Campion and Jonson.

In the structure of his songs Sidney departs from the usual thematically repetitive organization of many song lyrics, whereby each stanza is a relatively independent unit repeating the theme of the song and potentially omissible in performance. Instead, most of Sidney's songs depict carefully developed structures of thought from beginning to end, often with a narrative strand, such that no stanza can be omitted. As parts of the sonnet sequence, the songs were probably not meant actually to be sung, but to be read and to evoke a sense of singing.

In "O Dear life," smooth trochaic meter, end-stopped lines, liquid consonants, conventional images of the lovers' interlocked eyes and the "faire wonders" of the lady's body, standard love song rhymes (discover-lover, pleasure-treasure)—these things create the feel of flowing song until, by the end of the fourth stanza, we are feeling properly serenaded and ready for the song to end. Suddenly, we are jolted, metrically and semantically, by the final line, addressed to personified "Thought" (fantasy) as "he" is exploring the secrets of the beloved body: "take with thee / Strength of liking, rage of

---

30. Ringler assumes that the placement of the songs in *Astrophil and Stella* was Sidney's doing, although some manuscripts have them collected at the end. He posits three now-lost copies (X, Y, and Z) of Sidney's holograph, two of which had the arrangement we know from the Countess of Pembroke's edition (1598), while the third collected the songs at the end.

31. Ringler lists these settings: William Byrd, in *Songs of Sundrie Natures*, 1589; Robert Dowland, in *A Musicall Banquet*, 1610; John Ward, *The First Set of English Madrigals*, 1613.

32. Ringler, *The Poems*, p. 427.

longing." From that point the song swells in erotic intensity to a remarkable penultimate stanza ("Think, think of those dallyings") which bursts out of the metrical frame on all sides:

> Think of that most grateful time
> When my leaping heart will climb
> In thy lips to have his biding,
> There those roses for to kiss
> Which do breathe a sugared bliss,
> Opening rubies, pearls dividing.
>
> Think of my most princely power
> When I blessed shall devour
> With my greedy licorous senses
> Beauty, music, sweetness, love,
> While she doth against me prove
> Her strong darts but weak defences.
>
> Think, think of those dallyings
> When with dovelike murmurings,
> With glad moaning, passed anguish,
> We change eyes, and heart for heart
> Each to other do depart,
> Joying till joy makes us languish.
>   (stanzas 5–7 of 8)

The final stanza then dispels the fantasy ("O my thoughts, my thoughts surcease!"). As in the well-known song #8, "In a grove most rich of shade," Sidney has used song mode, by contrast with the sonnets (sometimes speech-like, sometimes declamatory), as a suitable dream medium where Astrophil can enact the sexual fulfillment that Stella will never allow to become reality. In the process, the songs have become poorly suited to stanzaic singing. Not that music cannot evoke and dramatize erotic climax. It can—but not suddenly in the fifth repetition of a stanzaic tune.

If Sidney could differentiate speech and song so well and could so effectively use the contrast, a less successful poet can also show us something about the Elizabethans' developing facility with various modes of lyric verse. Thomas Watson, the lugubrious neo-Latin poet and translator from Greek, French, and Italian, published a "sonnet" sequence, the *Hekatompathia* or *Passionate Century of Love*, in 1582, the same year when Sidney was apparently writing *Astrophil*. Besides these Petrarchan "passions" in an eighteen-line form, Watson is noted for his *Italian Madrigalls Englished, not to the sense of the originall dittie, but after the affection of the noate* (1590), which helped bring the madrigal to England. These contrafacta texts for madrigals mostly by Luca Marenzio reveal the musical side of Watson's verse experimentation and are quite different from his early love lyrics.

Watson's works may well puzzle modern readers. In the *Hekatompathia*[33]

---

33. Thomas Watson, *The Hekatompathia*, facs. ed. S. K. Heninger, Jr.

the love "passions" are all introduced by pedantic prose commentaries on their sources, doubtless written by the author himself though cast in the third person. While Astrophil's love for Stella sounds utterly convincing, Watson's "passions" persuade us frequently that his pains and his mistress are indeed, as his preface and Protrepticon admit, "but supposed" or "warmed up at a pretended fireplace" (*mentito me tepuisse foco*—with a pun on *tepere*, to be warm, to be in love). Writing love poems to an imaginary lady was a common amusement, but it is odd that Watson's erudition should, for a decade and a half, pour itself out in the suffering of imaginary love pains, drawn from five languages and in a multiplicity of forms and genres. For Watson's sorrows did not end with the *Hekatompathia*. He was known to his contemporaries as weeping Amyntas grieving for his lost Phyllis because of his Latin pastoral poem of that name, in hexameters. *Amyntas* (1585)[34] was translated into English hexameters by Abraham Fraunce, a version published in 1586. A set of sonnets of a suffering lover, *The Tears of Fancie* (1593), ascribed to "T. W." and very much in Watson's vein, may also be considered his.[35] And even the texts he devised for Marenzio's madrigals, many almost unrelated in sense to their Italian originals, are mostly elegies or love laments. There is a certain intensity and strength in some of Watson's verse, suggesting not love but the power of a melancholic (we would say neurotic) obsession with death and imaginary rejected love.[36]

Watson's pedantic experiments,[37] as S. K. Heninger noted,[38] probably

34. Thomas Watson, *Amyntas*, and Abraham Fraunce, *The Lamentations of Amyntas*, ed. Walter F. Staton, Jr., and Franklin M. Dickey (1585; Chicago: University of Chicago Press, 1967).

35. Identification of *The Tears of Fancie* as Watson's in the Stationer's Register has turned out to be one of the Collier forgeries (see Franklin M. Dickey, "Forgeries in the Stationer's Register"). But Watson's authorship of the *Tears* is strongly indicated anyway. It was published by Christopher Marlowe, a friend of his. It bears the appearance of a posthumous publication (no dedication or commendatory matter), which it would have been for Watson. It is ascribed on the title page to "T. W." and no other candidate for its authorship has been advanced. And two of its poems are in the rare eighteen-line form of Watson's earlier sequence. Furthermore, anyone who will read both it and the *Hekatompathia*, considering characteristic tone and favorite devices, will have little doubt that it is his. On Watson see Mark Eccles, *Christopher Marlowe in London*.

36. In a Bodleian copy of the *Hekatompathia* (Malone 311) is a sheet cataloguing works that had originally belonged to an earl of Northumberland, including one "On Waters and Fountaines" by Thomas Watson, a translation of Bernard Palissy's *Of Waters and Fountains* (1580). Perhaps as a study in his favorite hyperbolic imagery of tears and fountains, Watson translated this engineering treatise on transporting water supplies.

37. Sidney may be poking fun at Watson in *Astrophil and Stella* #15:

You that do search for every purling spring,
Which from the ribs of old Parnassus flows,
And every flower, not sweet perhaps, which grows
Near thereabouts, into your posey wring;
Ye that do dictionary's method bring
Into your rimes, running in rattling rows . . .

38. Heninger, Introduction to *Hekatompathia*, p. v.

served as a handbook for English poets on the devices and conceits of Continental poetry. The *Hekatompathia* is sometimes remembered for its rather mechanical structural devices, such as acrostics, shaped verse, or the extended anaphora of the correlative verse sonnet quoted by Kyd and Shakespeare, "In time the Bull is brought to weare the yoake" (#47).[39] But in fact such poems comprise only a small proportion of it. A more typical one, exhibiting Watson's learned allusions, smooth meter, end-stopped lines, "figures of sound" ("joys enjoy their end"), and songlike three-stanza structure, is #71:

> Alas deere *Titus* mine, my auncient frend,
> What makes thee muse at this my present plight,
> To see my woonted ioyes enjoy their end
> And how my Muse hath lost her old delight?
>   "*This is the least effect of Cupids dart,*
>   "To *change the minde by wounding of* the heart.
> *Alcides* fell in loue as I haue done,
> And layd aside both club and Lions skinne:
> *Achilles* too when he faire *Bryses* wunne,
> To fall from warres to wooing did beginne.
>   Nay, if thou list, suruey the heau'ns aboue,
>   And see how *Gods* themselues are chang'd by *Loue.*
> *Ioue* steales from skies to lye by *Loedaes* side;
> *Arcas* descendes for faire *Aglaurus* sake,
> And *Sol*, so soone as *Daphne* is espied,
> To followe her his Chariot doth forsake:
>   No meruaile then although I change my minde,
>   Which am in loue with one of heau'nly kinde.

Comparing this with Astrophil's expostulation with the critical friend that was cited earlier, we see in Watson's sonnet a mixed mode of song and declamation such as he found in his favorite Italian models, chiefly Petrarch and Serafino, whose poems were still being set by the best Italian composers.

But when Watson attempts the dialogue-sonnet in his eighteen-line form, something different results:

> Come gentle Death; who cals? one thats opprest:
> What is thy will? that thou abridge my woe,
> By cutting of my life; cease thy request,
> I cannot kill thee yet: alas, why soe?
>   Thou want'st thy Hart. Who stoale the same away?
>   *Loue*, whom thou seru'st, intreat him if thou may. . . .
>   Why then, whats thy request? that thou [Love] restore
>   To me my hart, and steale the same no more.
> And thou, O Death, when I possesse my *Hart,*
> Dispatch me then at once: why so?
> By promise thou art bound to end my smart.

---

39. As Heninger says (Ibid., p. xi), lines from the poem appear in *The Spanish Tragedy* (II.i.3–10) and in *Much Ado about Nothing* (I.i.263).

Why, if thy Hart returne, then whats thy woe?
　That brought from colde, It neuer will desire
　To rest with me, which am more hote then fire.
　　　　　(#54, lines 1–6, 11–18)

In the speaker's urgent cries and the brief answers of Death and Love, stresses become much more frequent and the meter less regular, with the result closer to speech rhythms than in most of Watson's poems. Several statements cannot be accommodated by the line unit, and strong enjambment results: "that thou restore / To me my heart" and "It never will desire / To rest with me." Line 14 is deliberately shortened by a foot, as befits its request for haste: "Dispatch me at once." As Watson explained in his preface, "it is nothing *Praeter decorum* for a maimed man to halt in his pase." Halting along indeed, the sonnet uses staccato speech rhythms. Thus while Watson was mainly disposed to song and declamation, the dialogue form could lead him close to speech mode.

In the *Tears of Fancie* (1593), Watson achieved a less wooden poetic voice and more convincing formal mastery, this time in "quatorzains" (except #49 and #59—see n. 35), the now-usual fourteen-line sonnet form. The verse is smooth and in many passages evocative of song, displaying Watson's exceeding fondness for figures of sound. But it is also declamatory; he has learned to build longer verse sentences with careful parallelism, more matter, fewer filler words, and a kind of relentless pace suited to his melancholy vein. A good example is #58, where the wounded deer, traditional emblem of melancholy,[40] is doubled by a bleeding ostracized bird to image the speaker's malaise.

When as I marke the ioy of euery wight,
Howe in their mindes deepe throbbing sorrow ceaseth
And by what meanes they nourish their delight,
Their sweete delight my paine the more increaseth.
For as the Deare that sees his fellow feede,
Amid the lusty heard, himselfe sore brused:
Or as the bird that feeles her selfe to bleede,
And lies aloofe of all her pheeres refused.
So haue I found and now too deerely trie,
That pleasure doubleth paine and blisse annoy.
　　　　　(*Tears of Fancie*, #58, lines 1–10)

The smooth meter, lengthy regular periods, formal diction, and rhetorical figures of sound (such as anadiplosis: "nourish their delight, / their sweet delight my paine")—these traits show Watson close in mode to the mixed declamation and verbal song of Spenser's lyric verse, though without its metaphoric and conceptual intricacy.

---

40. On the weeping deer as emblem of melancholy see Winfried Schleiner, "Jaques and the Melancholy Stag."

Similarly, #40 of the *Tears* depicts with considerable force a smoothly social but inwardly miserable melancholic:

> The common ioye the cheere of companie,
> Twixt myrth and mone doth plague me euermore:
> For pleasant talke or musicks melodie,
> Yelds no such salue vnto my secret sore.
> For still I liue in spight of cruell death,
> And die againe in spight of lingring life:
> Feede still with hope which doth prolong my breath,
> But choackt with feare and strangled still with strife,
> Witness the daies which I in dole consume,
> And weary nights beare record of my woe:
> O wronge full world which makst my fancie fume,
> Fie fickle Fortune fie thou art my foe.
> O heauie hap so froward is my chance,
> No daies nor nights nor worlds can me aduance.

Here the latter portion of the sonnet (lines 4–14) suggests many a love song of the time, with figures of repetition, alliteration, direct address to Fortune, and smooth meter, rippled only by the choriambic rhythmic variation common in songs on "Fíe, fìcklĕ Fórtŭne." Thus after a relatively declamatory opening quatrain, the rest of the sonnet is more songlike.

A final example from Watson's *Tears of Fancie* (#22) will illustrate his practice of the last technique I listed in the chart of lyric modes as especially characteristic of declamatory lyric: extended metaphor. "Where in" here is to be read "Wherein" ("Wherein an arbour . . . / Did boast his glorie . . . / For in his shadie boughs my Mistress slept"). The periods ending quatrains 1 and 3 must be ignored.

> I saw the object of my pining thought,
> Within a garden of sweete natures placing:
> Where in an arbour artificiall wrought,
> By workemans wondrous skill the garden gracing.
> Did boast his glorie glorie farre renowned,
> For in his shadie boughs my Mistress slept:
> And with a garland of his branches crowned,
> Her daintie forehead from the sunne ykept.
> Imperious loue vpon her eielids tending,
> Playing his wanton sports at euery becke,
> And into euerie finest limb descending,
> From eies to lips from lips to yuorie necke.
> And euerie limbe supplide and t'euerie part,
> Had free accesse but durst not touch her heart.

Octave and sestet each form one sentence, with the subsidiary syntactic units neatly fitted into single lines or the final couplet, and with a high degree of metrical smoothness. The traditional, usually static image of love's enticing force emanating from the lady napping in a bower has been activated, turned into a lively vignette, by the motion of Cupid fondling, one by one, the lady's exquisite parts.

The improved combination of song and declamation in the *Tears* of 1593 is just what one could have expected Watson to achieve through his varied experiments. The contrafacta verses for his *Italian Madrigalls Englished* (1590) had required him to develop a rhythmic flexibility not evident in the *Hekatompathia*, for in the madrigals he had to supply lines of varying length and syncopated rhyme, suitable for internal breaks or pauses at just the right places, as demanded by the phrasal repetitions in the voice parts.[41] Joseph Kerman faults Watson for not closely translating Marenzio's texts,[42] but as Watson's title states, he was usually not doing a translation and in some cases achieved something better. The four best texts rhythmically are the very ones later chosen by the English madrigal composers Wilbye, Bateson, and Vautor for resetting to new music, namely "O merry world," "Alas, what a wretched life," "Alas, where is my love," and "Unkind, O stay thy flying."[43] Watson's lyrics were widely enjoyed in England and inspired further contrafacta texts for Marenzio's madrigals.[44]

Corresponding syllabically with their Italian counterparts, the last three of these four are in the common loose canzone form of Italian madrigals: a stanza of indefinite length (seven to twenty lines), "freely combining seven- and eleven-syllable lines with no set rhyme scheme (typically one line, such as the first, does not rhyme at all) and usually ending with a couplet and a final eleven-syllable line for epigrammatic point."[45] "Alas, what a wretched life," when examined along with Marenzio's music and the original text of Petrarch, illustrates Watson's "Englishing" process. The text translates somewhat as follows (I include the opening lines from Petrarch, omitted from Marenzio's text):

[Amor, quando fioria	[Love, when my hope, and
mia spene e'l guidardon di tanta fede	the guerdon of such faithfulness, was flowering,
tolta m'e quella ond'attendea mercede.]	she from whom I hoped for mercy was taken from me.]

41. Joseph Summers in *George Herbert: His Religion and Art* (pp. 228–29n) suggests that rhyme on lines of unequal length be called "rhyme syncopation," though Albert M. Hayes had earlier named it "counterpoint" in his "Counterpoint in Herbert."

42. Kerman observes that only three of his texts "can properly be called translations," while eleven rely to some extent on the Italian and twelve are "effectively independent poems" (*The Elizabethan Madrigal*, p. 60).

43. See *English Madrigal Verse*, pp. 307, 19, 263, 308 for the songbook sources of these settings.

44. Chr. Ch. MS. 720 preserves a sacred text for the most popular of these madrigals, "Zephirus Breathing" (Marenzio's "Zefiro torna"), beginning "What shall we render to the Lord for all his love." Chr. Ch. MSS. 750–53 have several contrafacta identified with Watson's titles, such as "O Lorde view my wofull plighte" to the music of "Farewell, cruel and unkind" ("Veggo dolce mio bene").

45. Kerman, *The Elizabethan Madrigal*, p. 28.

Ahi dispietate morte, ahi crudel vita	Ah pitiless death, ah cruel life
l'una m'ha posto in doglia	the one has left me in pain
e mie speranze acerbamente ha spente,	and harshly extinguished my hopes,
l'altra mi tien quaggiù contra mia voglia,	the other holds me in this world against my will,
e lei che se n'è gita	and her who is departed
seguir non posso, ch'ella nol consente:	I cannot follow, for death would not consent:
ma pur ogni or presente	but still everywhere present
nel mezzo del mio cor madonna siede,	my lady is seated in the midst of my heart,
e qual è la mia vita ella se'l vede.[46]	and what my life is, she sees it herself.
Petrarch	[my translation]

Watson's text (below) is not even a paraphrase, and the implied love situation is significantly altered: instead of his lady's death, the lover is complaining of cruel rejection. Nevertheless, Petrarch's mournful tone and somber rhythms are more convincingly caught through "the affection of the note" in this text than they ever were in Watson's sonnet adaptations of him. The discipline of writing canzone verse for music has forced Watson to a new level of rhythmic skill:

> Alas, what a wretched life is this! | Nay, what a death,
>   Where the tyrant Love commandeth.
> My flowering days | are in their prime declining,
> All my proud hope | quite fall'n, and life untwining;
>   My joys each after other
> In haste are flying, | and leave my heart dying
>   For her that scorns my crying.
> O she from hence departs, | my love refraining,
> From whom, all heartless, alas, | I die complaining.
>   (Fellowes, *English Madrigal Verse*, p. 274)

The lines have irregularly placed caesuras (marked here) to correspond with the music's pauses—in canzone form the music almost always breaks the longer (eleven- or twelve-syllable) lines into two parts, making a caesura at some point from the fourth to the ninth syllable. This flexibility allows the composer, through word repetition and delayed voice entries, to make much or little of each phrase. For the rhythmic unit here is not the line, but the four- to eight-syllable phrase. The irregularly spaced rhyme sounds func-

46. *Petrarch's Lyric Poems*, ed. Robert M. Durling (Cambridge, Mass.: Harvard University Press, 1976), p. 507.

tion as a kind of evocative, rhythmically variable echo of a sound from a few bars earlier, rather than the way they do in isometric verse, as a satisfying, regular drumbeat. This effect became even more distinct in the English contrafacta madrigal texts, where the frequent feminine rhymes sounded mannered and imported, than it had been in the original madrigals. Watson has not attempted to retain Petrarch's rhyme scheme, but has contented himself with couplets. The fact that "other" in Watson's line 5 remains unrhymed while "flying" in the next line becomes an internal rhyme suggests that Fellowes, instead of following the line divisions of the Italian text, should have printed Watson's lines as

> My joys each after other in haste are flying,
>   and leave my heart dying

Watson must have been working from the madrigal score, without a separate text of the poem, and took "posso" for the end of line 5 rather than "gita." The alteration is unimportant, both for the madrigal as sung and for the text read as a lyric. Either way the lines fit the canzone pattern of syncopated rhymes (see n. 41) in interspersed longer and shorter lines.

Madrigals helped to train poets' ears in phrasal rhythms. One might think that since the words become garbled in polyphonic music, madrigal texts have little importance for poetry. But their rhythms must be studied at the level of the individual phrase and from the perspective of the performer singing within the harmonic structure, not from the passive listener's perspective.[47] The single phrase becomes, for composer and singer, a mini-artifact that can be turned many ways, or simply stated and left behind. The bass, let us say, hears the first entry of a phrase in the tenor; its second in the cantus, slightly altered by its new position in the harmonic structure; then comes his own first entry with it; and then after a pause on sustained notes, a final repetition of it. Such a phrase will stay in the singer's memory, its rhythm an established pattern.

A good example is "e qual è la mia vita" ("and what my life is"), the climax of Marenzio's madrigal, which Watson replaces with "From whom, all heartless, alas." Despite the resulting musical lengthening of the first syllable of "alas," Watson's words fit the music better than the original text does at that point, since in Marenzio's text a strong musical accent repeatedly falls on the unimportant article "la."[48]

---

47. Ing stresses the importance of the whole lyric phrase as a unit in rhythmic patterns; see especially *Elizabethan Lyrics*, pp. 121–28. The line shows "an arrangement of stressed and unstressed syllables which could be recognized as making complete phrases capable of repetition and recognizable variation." Hollander (*Vision and Resonance*, p. 30) notes that "subtle variation on the rhythmic intricacies of a line" in madrigals are perceptible to the singers, not the audience.

48. For an edition of Watson's version of the madrigal, see Luca Marenzio, "Alas, what a wretched life," ed. Jessie MacLennan (London: Stainer & Bell, 1965).

from Ahi dispietate morte/Alas, what a wretched life

Petrarch
Thomas Watson
Luca Marenzio

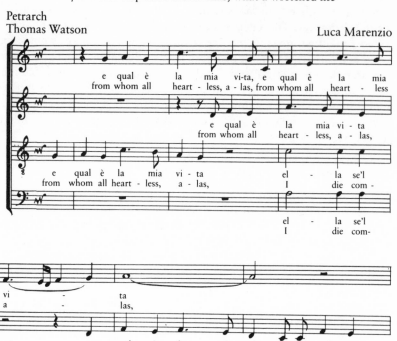

qual è la mia vi - ta el - la se'l ve - de.
whom all heart - less, a - las, I die com - plain - ing.

ve - de, el - la se'l ve - de.
plain - ing, I die com - plain - ing.

e qual è la mia vi - ta el - la se'l ve - de.
from whom all heart - less, a - las, I die com - plain - ing.

la se'l ve - de.
die com - plain - ing.

(measures 32–45)

In such a verse line, musical influence and the influence of classical metric patterns perhaps come together. If one transposes the quantitative hendecasyllabic or "phaleuckiak" line into an accentual pattern with an extra, unstressed initial syllable (thus hypercatalectic), it corresponds to the meter of Watson's line, "From whom all heartless alas I die complaining." Whether Watson was conscious of hendecasyllables here we cannot know, but besides the hexameters of *Amyntas*, he did write Latin verse in asclepiads and hendecasyllables, for example in the *Pompae* and *Themata* accompanying his *Antigone* translation.[49] When he devised English lines to suit the note quantities and rhythms of an Italian madrigal, the classical line patterns in his mind, with their mixtures of spondees and dactyls, would have suggested various possibilities. At any rate, Watson's line makes a fine ending for this madrigal. "Heartless" is especially emphatic, as befits its climactic position in the musical phrase, because it is syntactically ambivalent, seeming to refer to both the cold lady ("whom") and to the lover ("I"), who has lost his heart. What would be a flaw, a "squinting modifier," in prose can work well as a synchysis in *poesia per musica*.

Watson takes various cues from the music. Where the upper three parts take an octave leap downward on "tien quaggiú" in "l'altra mi tien quaggiú contra mia voglia" ("the other [Life] holds me here against my will"), Watson puts the words "quite fallen" at the bottom of the leap, in an effective line, "All my proud hopes quite fallen." Or again, for the sequential stepwise phrase on "e lei che se n'è gita / seguir non posso" ("and her who is departed / I cannot follow"), Watson puts the chasing effect of the closely spaced voice entries and sequential phrases into the words: "My joys each after other / In haste are flying."

49. Kerman (*The Elizabethan Madrigal*, p. 10) speculates that Watson wrote some quantitative English verse.

from Ahi dispietate morte/Alas, what a wretched life

(measures 20–24)

Watson knew Petrarch's lyric, even if he was not consulting it as he devised his text; the lost flowering hope of the lines omitted from Marenzio's text becomes "My flowering days are in their prime declining," and the departed lady of Petrarch again "departs," but here literally rather than euphemistically; thus the poem has been metamorphosed from Petrarch's lament for the dead Laura into a lament for Watson's favorite persona, the weeping rejected lover. With the music in his ears, he has produced a kind of reflection in song mode on Petrarch's poem, a rhythmically precise and syntactically flexible contrafacta text.

Watson's early attempts at English verse had been awkward and amateurish, now racked on the frame of his chosen eighteen-line form, now stuffed with verbiage to fill it out, often stiffly derivative and syntactically clumsy, sometimes resorting to such bathetic rhymes as "stint I" and "flinty" and to bare lists of mythological characters and tales. Yet unpolished as they were, they exhibited the mode of lyric he would soon learn to practice more successfully, a mixture of song and declamation. In devising replacements for Marenzio's madrigal texts from Petrarch and Serafino, he had the help of music to teach him fluidity, conciseness, and rhythmic subtlety. The *Tears of Fancie* (1593), as we have seen, shows him achieving some measure of these qualities in the sonnet.

Sidney's early *Certain Sonnets* had still been song-mode lyrics, indeed contrafacta. But he and Watson were major influences on the definition of English sonnet form in the 1580s, and as their sonnets moved toward speech or declamation and away from song, so the English sonnet moved. By the 1590s it had left song-mode verse behind. When Shakespeare wrote his sonnets, he laid out the lines of his dramatic blank verse on the sonnet's miniature frame, with results so definitive that the English sonnet has characteristically worked in declamatory mode ever since.

Having considered samples of song and speech mode in Sidney, as well as Watson's mixed mode of song and declamation, we now look at Shakespeare's declamatory mode in the sonnets. It may seem odd to consider Watson and Shakespeare together, but to Gabriel Harvey, surveying the recent English poetic scene from about 1598 to 1600, they were two among others in a list of "owr florishing metricians":

> And now translated Petrarch, Ariosto, Tasso, and Bartas himself deserve curious comparison with Chaucer, Lidgate, & oure best Inglish, auncient & moderne. Amongst which, the Countesse of Pembrokes Arcadia, & the Faerie Queene ar now freshest in request: & Astrophil, & Amyntas ar none of the idlest pastimes of sum fine humanists . . . . The younger sort takes much delight in Shakespeares Venus, & Adonis: but his Lucrece, & his tragedie of Hamlet, Prince of Denmarke, haue it in them, to please the wiser sort . . . . [Sir Edward Dyer's] Amaryllis, & Sir Walter Raleighs Cynthia, how fine & sweet inuentions? Excellent matter of emulation for Spencer, Constable, France, Watson, Daniel, Warner, Chapman, Siluester, Shakespeare, & the rest of owr florishing metricians . . . . God knows what is good for the world, & fitting for this age.

God and Gabriel Harvey. No slouch at recognizing the best productions of his contemporaries, Harvey lists Watson's *Amyntas* (published first in his Latin hexameters, then translated—see above) together with three other works that he says deserve comparison with Petrarch, Ariosto, and Tasso: *Astrophil*, the *Arcadia*, and the *Faerie Queene*.[50] Shakespeare's sonnets, so

---

50. Harvey's marginal note, in a copy of Speght's *Chaucer* (1598), is printed in E. K. Chambers, *William Shakespeare: A Study of Facts and Problems* (Oxford: Clarendon Press, 1930), 2:197–98. Chambers (p. 196) takes the "Amyntas" here to be Fraunce's translation of Tasso's *Aminta*. But Harvey is referring to "owre best Inglish" modern works. Watson's *Amyntas* was highly regarded by his contemporaries.

far as we know, had not been read by Harvey at this time, but they would have confirmed his view of Shakespeare as a notable "metrician." [51]

The following observations about declamatory mode in the sonnets could be illustrated in the most famous of them, but for variety's sake let us take some lesser-known ones. With the exception of the frivolous seduction pieces (perhaps the earliest?) among the "dark lady" sonnets, which are at times colloquial and direct—such as #128 "How oft, when thou, my music, music play'st" or #132 "Thine eyes I love"—with such exceptions, the sonnets, despite being addressed to friend or lady, are not at all in a mode of speech or direct conversation. Rather they show us the poet-lover pouring his devotion, obsession, and/or anguish into miniature, rhetorically intricate pieces, fit to be declaimed from a stage: elegant verbal gifts for the beloved friend or enticing lady when they were actually to be sent, or private, diary-like creations for the poet's own satisfaction when they were not. [52] In either case they show us the master sculptor of dramatic blank verse casting his chiseled pentameter lines into timeless sonnet shapes.

The best remembered of these shapes is the structure of three solid quatrain blocks surmounted by an epigrammatic couplet—the Shakespearean sonnet —made famous by such favorites as #65 "Since brass, nor stone, nor earth, nor boundless sea" or #73 "That time of year thou mayst in me behold." Rhyme scheme, syntax (four-line sentences), parallelism of three equivalent metaphors, and in many cases repeated grammatical structures work together to define these quatrain blocks. But setting off and playing against this most prominent shape are many other forms, made with the same rhetorical tools and materials, and with no less deliberation.

Some structures are adopted from earlier sonneteering practice, such as one of Watson's favorites, the catalog order of parallel items in end-stopped lines:

> Tir'd with all these, for restful death I cry:
> As to behold desert a beggar born,
> And needy nothing trimm'd in jollity,
> And purest faith unhappily forsworn,
> And gilded honor shamefully misplac'd,
> And maiden virtue rudely strumpeted,
> And right perfection wrongfully disgrac'd,
> And strength by limping sway disabled.
>   (Sonnet 66, lines 1–8)

51. They could have been—we do not know how widely they were circulating in manuscript. Meres in 1598 referred to Shakespeare's "sugared sonnets among his private friends," and two of the sonnets appeared in *The Passionate Pilgrim* miscellany (1599).

52. As W. H. Auden notes (*The Complete Signet Classic Shakespeare*, ed. Sylvan Barnet, pp. 1727–28), many of the sonnets do not seem at all the sort of thing the poet could have shown to the friend or lady. But others seem very much designed to be sent, such as #26 "Lord of my love, . . . / To thee I send this written ambassage," or the generation sonnets, or the pleas to be remembered (e.g., #32 "If thou survive my well-contented day / . . . And shalt by fortune once more resurvey / These poor rude lines"), and so on.

Or there is an approximate form of correlative verse in the list-and-relist organization of such sonnets as #77 on the mirror, the sundial, and the commonplace book ("Thy glass will show thee how thy beauties wear"). Or again, #91 "Some glory in their birth, some in their skill" builds its opening list into a first quatrain marked by anaphora ("Some in . . . Some in . . . Some in . . ."), reflects on each of the cherished items in quatrain 2, then reiterates them in succession to constitute the rejection of such values in quatrain 3:

> Thy love is [better] than high birth to me,
> Richer than wealth, prouder than garments' cost,
> Of more delight than hawks or horses be.

Or there is the device of playing on one repeated word throughout the poem (called *anaclasis* or *ploce*), as in #40, where the word *love* in multiple senses is loaded down with all the poet's pain at discovering the friend's betrayal of him with the dark lady:

> Take all my loves, my love, yea, take them all,
> What hast thou then more than thou hadst before?
> No love, my love, that thou mayst true love call,
> All mine was thine, before thou hadst this more.
> Then if for my love thou my love receivest,
> I cannot blame thee for my love thou usest,
> . . . .
> And yet love knows it is a greater grief
> To bear love's wrong than hate's known injury.
>   (lines 1–6, 10–12)

Such devices are no less part of the oratorical mode of this verse in Shakespeare than they were in Watson and other Elizabethans—or in Petrarch and Serafino. In #82 Shakespeare parodied, with a heavy-handed polyptoton on the words *true* and *truly*, the "gross painting" and the "strained touches rhetoric can lend" in a rival poet's verses. But no one ever used such "figures of sound" to more potent effect than he himself did.

Rhetorical devices represent only the surface of Shakespeare's technical achievements with oratorical lyric. We can see in the sonnets four other distinguishing traits of declamatory or oratorical lyric listed in the chart given in the early part of this chapter: extended syntactic units with sentence enjambment; patterns of repeated grammatical structure; formal diction; and extended metaphor, sometimes elaborated even into anecdote. The other traits in the chart are commonly noted features of the sonnets.

The extended periods, within which each line makes a neat subsidiary syntactic unit (so that there is no strong enjambment), the thrice repeated grammatical structure (here set up by the phrase "Against that time") organizing the entire first twelve lines, and the formal (in this case legalistic) diction characteristic of declamatory mode in lyric—all are evident in #49:

> Against that time (if ever that time come)
> When I shall see thee frown on my defects,
> When as thy love hath cast his utmost sum,
> Call'd to that audit by advis'd respects;
> Against that time when thou shalt strangely pass,
> And scarcely greet me with that sun, thine eye,
> When love converted from the thing it was
> Shall reasons find of settled gravity:
> Against that time do I insconce me here
> Within the knowledge of mine own desert,
> And this my hand against myself uprear,
> To guard the lawful reasons on thy part.
>> To leave poor me thou hast the strength of laws,
>> Since why to love I can allege no cause.

The poet is reflecting that, without societal sanction, the love between him-self and the friend is extremely vulnerable. Love for one's wife, brother, child, master—even, to a lesser degree, for one's paramour—is supported by obligations, rewards, punishments, sanctions, built into "the strength of laws" and reinforcing the given relationship. But passionate love between a bourgeois stage actor and a high-ranking young nobleman, even if it be not actively sexual, has no place in the social fabric of law and custom. Indeed the "strength of laws" operates to block off such a connection, however much literati might eulogize male friendship. The poet takes the law's own highly formalized language to compile a probatory weight representing the negative societal sanctions under which, he fears, the friend's love for him must soon give way: the poet's "defects," in the absence of any binding obli-gation, will soon not be tolerated; the friend's love will then "cast his utmost sum," that is, make a final "audit" and demand payment; it will be forced to this audit by "advised respects," solid social considerations based on the "settled gravity" of a man in his position; the poet will now "insconce" himself as a defendant fortified against this coming result of the "lawful rea-sons on thy part" for giving up their love: he will settle out of court in ad-vance, since for their love he "can allege no cause." The formality and cumulative weight of this legal language make the sonnet seem at first a se-rious effort at emotional fortification, but the puny phrase "poor me" of the couplet shifts the weight onto fear of loss instead.

This is one of the sonnets that seems not at all like an actual message for the friend's perusal. Rather it is a solitary love plaint, cast in the form of an imagined legal brief, a sort of retreat for comfort to the verbal mode of those very societal sanctions so notably lacking for the poet's love.

The extended syntactic units neatly pegged down with patterned repeti-tions of phrase and of grammatical structure—along with the diction just cited—recreate that formal mode most effectively. The first occurrence of the contractual phrase "Against that time" is followed immediately by a grammatical interruption defining a subjunctively stated first contingency upon which all the ensuing is to depend: "if ever that time come." With "Against that time" the second quatrain also begins, this time proceeding directly to the second contingency, the feared symptoms of cooling love: "when I shall see thee frown" and "when thou shalt strangely pass, / And scarcely greet me" and "when love . . . / Shall reasons find of settled gravity." "Against that time" the poet begins a third time, with judiciary punctiliousness, still not having reached an independent clause; and now with the "ifs" and "whens" duly stacked in rows, he at last arrives at his statement: "I do ensconce me here." The statement cannot be left so stark and unclothed, however: I do ensconce me—where?—"Within the knowledge of my own desert, / And this my hand against myself uprear, / To guard the lawful reasons on thy part." The seemingly positive "desert" or worth of the poet is thus quickly extenuated, with lawyerlike skill, to its reverse meaning: no desert. The heavy couplet rhyme on "strength of laws" and "allege no cause" concludes the rhetorical crushing of the poet's ego.

The road to such mastery in casting extended periods into a miniature lyric form in pentameter lines must have been rockier than we are apt to notice, but a sonnet like #43 shows Shakespeare stumbling a bit on the way, preoccupied with rhetorical figures worthy of Watson or many another "metrician." The oxymoron of bright darkness or dark light dominates the poem from start to finish, and within its arc of reiteration more figures of word play dance and darkly flash before the dreamer: the antimetaboles of "darkly bright—bright in dark" and "days are nights . . . / And nights bright days"; the epizeuxes of "shadow shadows" and "form form"; and the polyptoton of "clear day—clearer light." Thus figures of sense and figures of sound work together in the poet's witty word play.

> When most I wink, then do mine eyes best see,
> For all the day they view things unrespected,
> But when I sleep, in dreams they look on thee,
> And darkly bright, are bright in dark directed.
> Then thou, whose shadow shadows doth make bright,
> How would thy shadow's form form happy show
> To the clear day with thy much clearer light,
> When to unseeing eyes thy shade shines so!
> How would (I say) mine eyes be blessed made
> By looking on thee in the living day,
> When in dead night [thy] fair imperfect shade
> Through heavy sleep on sightless eyes doth stay!
>   All days are nights to see till I see thee,
>   And nights bright days when dreams do show thee me.

Line 4 begins a direct address that we expect to hear completed with a finite verb ("Then thou, whose shadow is bright, *art* brighter still"). Instead we must, after waiting in vain for the verb through a seeming interruption, restart at line 4 and then switch out of its direct address mode at the start of line 5, recognizing that line 4 has been a mere attention gesture to the "thou," now to be subsumed in the possessive "thy." Related acceptable syntax can be adduced: "then you, who shine so brightly, how could you be dark?" But by casting the pronouns in the possessive (whose and thy, not who and thou) to set up his shadowy epizeuxis, Shakespeare has produced a syntactically loose and obscure passage, schematically: "Then thou, whose shadow is so bright, how bright must thy body ('form') be?" The sonnets' uses of sentences extended over eight or more lines are usually crowned with better success, as in the flowing, elegant #12 "When I do count the clock that tells the time," where all fourteen lines comprise one sentence.

Through writing dozens of sonnets, Shakespeare learned not only how to construct smooth and convincing extended periods within the given structure, but also how to contrast them effectively with interspersed staccato statements each taking only a single line, as in #107:

> Not mine own fears, nor the prophetic soul
> Of the wide world, dreaming on things to come,
> Can yet the lease of my true love control,
> Suppos'd as forfeit to a confin'd doom.
> The mortal moon hath her eclipse endur'd,
> And the sad augurs mock their own presage,
> Incertainties now crown themselves assur'd,
> And peace proclaims olives of endless age.
> Now with the drops of this most balmy time
> My love looks fresh, and Death to me subscribes,
> Since spite of him I'll live in this poor rhyme,
> While he insults o'er dull and speechless tribes;
>   And thou in this shalt find thy monument,
>   When tyrants' crests and tombs of brass are spent.

The opening quatrain is one of those elegant, smooth, one-sentence blocks that we remember as especially characteristic of the sonnets. Quatrain 3 is another, but it has been set off and made all the more elegant by the contrasting structure of the intervening quatrain 2, with its series of brief, forceful, one-line statements about the qualities of this time into which the love of poet and friend, against all odds, has survived.[53] After this review of hopeful events, the shapely and serene third quatrain can speak convincingly, in one smooth clause, of "the drops of this most balmy time" when even death succumbs to poetry. Here we can note again the formal diction of Shakespeare's characteristic declamatory mode, which sometimes uses legalese for specific purposes but goes far beyond it, in such phrases as "the prophetic soul / Of the wide world," "forfeit to a confined doom" (limited to a fixed term), "olives of endless age," "this most balmy time," and "dull and speechless tribes."

53. This is the sonnet that has generated the most efforts at dating, the frequent conclusion being 1595.

One more feature of oratorical mode common in the sonnets remains to be illustrated, the use of elaborated metaphor, sometimes so far extended that it takes on a quality of narrative or of pictorial motion. This is of course a favorite technique of preachers and other orators, especially useful for revivifying traditional imagery, as when the *peregrines et hospites* trope is spun out into a tale of a Christian's life journey. Thus Shakespeare takes the conventional Horatian trope of the poet as mariner trimming the sails of his verse and fantasizes a sort of naval foray between the contrasted "barks" of himself and the rival poet (#80 and #86). Passionate love as analogous to uncontrolled, health-threatening appetite, a favorite humanist moral analogy, supplies the meat of #75, where the metaphor has been elaborated into a depiction of the poet's emotional state as comparable to that of an erratic dieter, alternately stuffing and starving himself:

> So are you to my thoughts as food to life,
> Or as sweet-season'd showers are to the ground;
> And for the peace of you I hold [a] strife . . .
> Now counting best to be with you alone,
> Then better'd that the world may see my pleasure;
> Sometime all full with feasting on your sight,
> And by and by clean starved for a look; . . .
>   Thus do I pine and surfeit day by day,
>   Or gluttoning on all, or all away.
>   (lines 1–3, 7–10, 13–14)

Some of the extended metaphors are unconventional productions of the image-maker's individual fancy, as in #143, where the poet depicts himself as a yowling small child in need of the dark lady's maternal comforting, making the poem into a delightful little vignette of a harried woman trying to chase down an escaped bird and at the same time shush up the poet-baby's "loud crying," complete with sexual overtones to the desired comforting and stilling. Some efforts are not so successful. #24 begins by declaring the poet's eye to be a painter doing an image of the beloved friend on a canvas (the poet's heart) surrounded by a frame (his body). All is well until in line 7 the terms shift confusingly: the poet's "breast," no longer part of a picture frame, becomes a painter's "shop," the glazed windows of which are the eyes of the friend, who must peep through them into the poet's breast to see his own image! Having come to so unseeable a result, the poet in the couplet throws up his hands in whimsical self-critique: "Yet eyes this cunning want to grace their art, / They draw but what they see, know not the heart."

The luxuriant metaphorical richness of the sonnets is an enormous topic, and I make no pretense here to exhaustive illustration. My point is that the extending, the conscious elaboration, the spinning out of detail of a metaphor in lyric poetry suggests declamatory mode rather than speech or song. Metaphors in conversational speech are characteristically brief, perhaps effective but quickly touched, then left behind in the flow of conversation. Even Donne's lyrics, where they spin out and elaborate a conceit at length, are to that extent more declamatory than speechlike. When metaphors in song are to be stressed, a composer must do so through repetition, usually patterned reiteration of conventional images and fixed phrases, as in refrains. Conceptually subtle articulation or detailed elaboration of imagery is not characteristic, primarily because it would be lost in most kinds of singing.

Considering, then, the sonnets' distinctive declamatory/oratorical features—their syntactically intricate extended periods pinned to the form's miniature frame, their conceptually complex interweaving of both figures of sense and figures of sound, their often obscure and semantically patterned diction, and their frequent extended, subtly articulated metaphors—considering these characteristic features, we understand why composers of Shakespeare's time could not know how to set the sonnets to music. Nor have they been attractive to composers of later eras. But in the next half-century after their publication, a new form of oratorical lyric would emerge, one suited to a new form of oratorical music, a reconstituted *rapprochement* between the two arts not yet thinkable in Shakespeare's England. We must leave that matter until we come to Crashaw, Milton, and Cowley.

Contrafactum, Quantity, and Song Rhythms in Hume, Dowland, and Campion

So far I have illustrated speech, song, and declamation in Elizabethan poetry in order to convey a concrete impression of these modes and their development in English lyric, at the same time showing how the awareness of them can enrich our reading of poetry. We now concentrate on song-mode verse for the remainder of this opening chapter, specifically on two related developments, already introduced in connection with Sidney and Watson and of continued importance for Jacobean song verse, namely *poesia per musica*, or contrafacta verse, and quantitative meters.

A musical translator (like Watson) and seemingly author of texts for his own music was Captain Tobias Hume, who published *The First Part of Ayres, French, Pollish, and others . . . With Pavines, Galliards and Almaines* (1605) and *Captaine Humes Poeticall Musicke. Principally made for two Basse-Viols* (1607). In his songs we breathe a different air from that of learned Watson's works. They concern the joys of battle, hunting, and tobacco, as well as love or the frightful nightmares of a "leaden" depression. Tillyard cites an elegant stanza from Hume's "Fain would I change that note" to illustrate what good poetry could be written under the direct influence of music.[54] Hume's authorship of his own texts is indicated by the

54. E. M. W. Tillyard, *The English Renaissance*, p. 63.

claim that they derive from French or Polish originals, presumably collected on his travels. At any rate, most display a strangely personal quality and intimate interaction with the music, which suggest that Hume, primarily an instrumental composer, devised them as variant versions of instrumental pieces.

The texts sometimes use odd, nonstandard constructions, as in line 3 of this passage from "Alas, poor men":

> On crutches Virtue halts,
> Whilst men most great in faults
> Suffers best worth distressed,
> With empty pride oppressed.
> Alas, poor men, why strive you to live long
> To have more time and space to suffer wrong?
>
> O Virtue, yet at length
> Rouse thy diviner strength,
> And make no music more.
> Out, sad state that's deplore!
> Then alas, poor men, why strive you to live long
> To have more time and space to suffer wrong?
> (Fellowes, *English Madrigal Verse*, p. 543)

"Men" must be the subject of the singular verb "suffers," an existent usage though crude sounding in verse. But the next line goes beyond crudeness into such sloppiness of structure that one can only conjecture a meaning, perhaps "Suffers [those of] best worth [to be] distressed." By the verb *deplore* Hume seemingly means the participle *deplored*. What "state" is meant, anyway? And what sense does it make that Virtue should rouse herself and stop making music?

"Cease, leaden slumber, dreaming," another piece of Captain Hume's "poetical music" (and by the way a very powerful one, when sung), does not show such feebleness in grammar and sense, but does have an evocative vagueness, ambivalence of phrasing, and idiosyncrasy in word choice:

> Cease, leaden slumber dreaming!
>   My genius presents
> The cause of sweet music's meaning
> Now which breeds my soul's content
> And bids my Muse awake
> To hear sweet music's note,
> That cheerfully glads me, so cheerfully.
>
> Methought, as I lay sleeping,
>   Dreams did enchant me
> With the praise of music and her worth
> And her eternished fame.
> But now I find indeed
> My leaden windows open
> That cheerfully comforts, full cheerfully.

Night gloomy veil to the morn,
 Dreams affright no more.[55]
(lines 1–16 of 21)

A melancholic is taking comfort in the power of music to channel and control his passions. His depressed state is not explained, only darkly imaged in
such terms as "leaden slumber" or "Night, gloomy veil" and in a haunting,
obsessively recurring phrase of the melody for the repeated refrain (last
three lines) of each stanza, interacting with a bass line that starts the phrase
over each time it would end.

Aside from the lines Tillyard liked, Hume's lyrics will not win any prizes
as poetry, but they are useful for us as extreme instances of *poesia per musica*. We imagine someone, after a few mugs of ale perhaps, humming parts
to his consort pieces and putting down whatever concoction of loosely con-
nected rhyming words, in a suitable mood, fall together in his head. The
"meaning" of music does not have a "cause"—this violates accepted usage
of the words. "Eternished" of stanza two seems to be a coinage of Hume's
own. Metrically ambivalent filler words like "now," "still," and "full" occupy the needed slots for smooth musical phrases with notes of equal value.
At one moment dreams are enchanting the speaker with the praise of music,
then suddenly they are frightful dreams, to be dispersed by music and morning. Hardly anything else like this came along in English until poets took to
using opium.

Musical rhythm was the dominant shaping force in other *poesia per musica* too, though other lyricists tidied up their grammar and sense better
than Hume did. Writing contrafacta verse taught them to create musically
imitative rhythms in verse, to produce and in later stanzas reproduce patterns of line and phrase that they would not have thought of otherwise, with
combinations of spondees, trochees, and dactyls alternating with the natural
English iambic rhythm. Lines like "Níght, glóomў véil tŏ thĕ mórn, /
Dréams ăffríght nò móre" are very similar to some of the lyric lines Campion arrived at through the combined influences of music and classical meters. Even though the movement to naturalize classical meters in English
produced little memorable poetry, it often produced lines that, when read
aloud accentually with no effort to impose the classical lengths, proved fascinating for lyricists and composers.

One example is Dowland's setting of a text using the refrain of Sidney's
asclepiadic, "O sweet woods, the delight of solitariness." Ringler rightly
notes that Dowland's melody does not follow the asclepiadic pattern of
longs and shorts,[56] but that does not mean that the verbal rhythms were un-

---

55. Fellowes confuses the third stanza by printing it as if it had a different number of lines
from the others. Actually the three-line conclusion there is merely given a variant text on the
repeat.
56. Ringler, *The Poems*, p. 404. Dowland's text was set again by Henry Lawes.

important to him. The following indicates the accentual scansion of Sidney's lines, not the quantitative, with which it does not correspond:

Ó swéet wóods, thĕ dĕlíght ŏf sòlĭtárĭnĕss,
Ó hŏw múch dŏ I lóve yŏŭr sòlĭtárĭnĕss

Dowland's refrain melody does not exactly reproduce this pattern, but it is clearly the one inspiring the musical rhythm, rather than the asclepiadic pattern of (−− −∪∪− −∪∪− ∪−): the music gives either length or first-beat accent to "O," "woods," "-light," "-ta-" and in the second lines "O," "much," "love," "-ta-"; it gives short (eighth) notes to "de-," "-ri-," "do I," and "-ri-."

from O sweet woods

Philip Sidney/anon.　　　　　　　　　　　　John Dowland

(measures 1–15)

The poetic rhythm of mixed trochees and dactyls has suggested a musical passage that floats between duple and triple time. As the refrain sung to open the song and again after each strophe, it is played off against the smoother, mostly duple meter of the stanzas' iambic pentameter lines.

Pattison credits Dowland with "exceptionally discriminating" literary taste and speculates that he "may have written a number of the [song] texts himself," citing commendatory poems by Dowland in songbooks by Farnaby and Alison.[57] He did at least adapt preexisting texts to suit his musical purposes (someone else could have done this for him, but we have no evidence that composers worked that way). Besides "O sweet woods," another example is "To ask for all thy love," apparently a paraphrase of one stanza of Donne's "Lovers infinitenesse." Dowland's text is a good illustration of song mode, while Donne's conceptually complex poem is in a mode of speech and declamation. Dowland probably read the poem and thought, "Excellent, but this will never do for a song," then put together a paraphrase.[58] Of Donne's stanza in mixed tetrameters and pentameters, each statement of two or three lines is paraphrased into an expanded, conceptually simplified song stanza such as this first one:

> To ask for all thy love and thy whole heart
> Twere madness.
> I do not sue
> Nor can admit,
> Fairest from you
> To have all yet.
> Who giveth all hath nothing to impart
> But sadness.

We shall look at this stanza form later in connection with Herbert.

If composers using texts in neoclassical meters usually scanned the texts

57. Pattison, *Music and Poetry*, pp. 72–73. Diana Poulton repeats the suggestion in *John Dowland*, pp. 254–55.

58. R. W. Ingram, "Words and Music," discusses this rewriting of Donne's stanza for song setting, noting that the text also occurs in a later manuscript that attributes it to Donne himself. Probably the attribution merely recognizes his authorship of the original version.

for their accentual pattern and ignored the arbitrary quantitative pattern (Byrd did the same with English quantitative verse), they did not always find a lack of correspondence between the two scansions. Sidney wrote some verse in accentual forms of classical meters, making stressed syllables coincide with longs, unstressed with shorts. As Derek Attridge observes in *Well-weighed Syllables*, Sidney in many quantitative poems achieved a high degree of this coincidence, and in two poems complete coincidence: "My muse what ails this ardour" from the *Old Arcadia*, in a form of anacreontics, and "When to my deadlie pleasure" from the *Certain Sonnets*, in aristophanics.[59] Sidney's admirer Thomas Campion[60] worked in this vein until it produced his *Observations in the Art of English Poetry* and influenced his song lyrics in ways that have not yet been fully appreciated, even though we have much perceptive analysis of Campion.[61]

I have been noting some of the interacting influences of quantitative experimentation and music as they affected the developing richness of song-mode lyric from Elizabethan to Jacobean times. Campion the poet-composer displays most perfectly the conjunction of these influences. It has been too easily assumed that when his *Observations* treatise was badly received, he saw the error of his argument, forgot about quantitative verse, and went back to writing simply in the native tradition. Pattison, however, read the *Observations* sympathetically and noted some of the interesting perceptions it offers about English prosody, despite the fact that Campion's proposed meters never took root; and more recently, Elise Jorgens has described the influence of French *musique measurée* on Campion's "homorhythmic" musical style.[62] In fact, Campion's ear for stress-adapted classical meters continued to influence his verse, long after he had ceased writing whole lyrics in them. In many songs the characteristic pattern of certain classical meters, heard accentually, becomes a rhythmic figure that receives both verbal and musical elaboration.

To see how this worked for Campion, we must first recall his basic principle for adapting classical meters, namely that the heavy stresses and slowness of spoken English, compared to classical and romance languages, required English verses to have fewer syllables than their classical counterparts:

> I haue obserued, and so may any one that is practis'd in singing, or hath a natu-rall eare able to time a song, that the Latine verses of sixe feete, as the Heroick and Iambick, or of fiue feete, as the Trochaik, are in nature all the same length of sound with our English verses of fiue feete; for either of them being tim'd with the hand, quinque perficiunt tempora, they fill up the quantity (as it were) of fiue sem'briefs . . . . our English monosillables enforce many breathings

59. Attridge, *Well-weighed Syllables*, pp. 175–85.
60. Davis discusses the influence of Sidney on Campion (Introduction, pp. xix–xxi).
61. Pattison (*Music and Poetry*, pp. 128–36), Ing, Davis, Lowbury et al., and other works have already been cited. See notes 3, 5, and 8.
62. See Pattison, ibid., and Elise Jorgens, *The Well-Tun'd Word*, pp. 92–103.

which no doubt greatly lengthen a verse, so that it is no wonder if for these reasons our English verses of fiue feete hold pace with the Latines of sixe.[63]

In each of Campion's proposed meters, whether "licentiate iambics," "English sapphics," or a "kind of Anacreonticks," this principle is at work: using musical rhythm as a sort of metronome, he found that "our English verses of X feet hold pace with the Latins' of X+Y feet." Thus iambic pentameter equals hexameters; his "Sapphic" line is one syllable shorter than even the lesser Sapphic of Greek and Latin; his English dimeters (second and third lyrical meters) have five syllables ($´ˣ´ˣ´$) instead of the eight of classical dimeter (two metra, or four feet: $∪∪−∪ \ −∪−⌣$). Taking into account Elizabethan pronunciation of Latin and schoolboy stress-ictus reading of Latin verse, Attridge has considered to what extent length and stress were distinguished in Campion's thinking, concluding that at certain points they remain distinct, though in any case Campion usually regarded stress as inviolable in English verse.[64] Certainly Campion's examples in the *Observations* make clear that his adapted meters consist of accentual patterns, not quantitative ones.

His later song lyrics give evidence that classical meters, translated into accentual patterns, continued to supply him with rhythmic suggestions, both poetically and musically. A good example is "Come, cheerful day," which contains several lines rhythmically similar to the metrically foreshortened verses of the *Observations*; they might be described as accentual asclepiads with initial truncation. The classical asclepiad was: $−− \ −∪∪− \ −∪∪− \ ∪−$, truncated, $−∪∪− \ −∪∪− \ ∪−$. Campion's opening line, as his music for the song confirms, should be scanned: "Cóme, cheèrfŭl dáy, párt ŏf mў lífe, tŏ mé." He does not continue this pattern through the whole poem—the result would sound strained and unnatural—though it recurs in line 11, "Párt ŏf mў lífe ìn thăt yŏu lífe dĕnў." But the choriambic foot of the asclepiad (accentually $´ˣˣ´$) becomes both musically and verbally a kind of rhythmic leitmotif running through the song.

> Come, cheerful day, part of my life, to me;
>   For while thou view'st me with thy fading light,
> Part of my life doth still depart with thee,
>   And I still onward haste to my last night.
> Time's fatal wings do ever forward fly,
> So every day we live a day we die.
> But, O ye nights, ordained for barren rest,
>   How are my days deprived of life in you;
> When heavy sleep my soul hath dispossessed
>   By feigned death life sweetly to renew.
> Part of my life in that you life deny;
> So every day we live a day we die.[65]

63. Campion's *Works*, ed. P. Vivian, pp. 39–40.
64. Attridge, *Well-weighed Syllables*, p. 222.
65. For the music see Fellowes, *The English School of Lutenist Song Writers*, ser. 2, 1:22–23.

The phrases that the melody treats in choriambic rhythm are "Come, cheerful day" (♩♩ ♪ ♪ ♩ —measures 1–3), "Part of my life" (♩♩ ♪ ♪ ♩. —measures 12–14), "Time's fatal wings" (♩ ♪ ♪ ♩. —measures 21–22), and "So every day" (♩♩ ♪ ♪ ♩—repeated sequentially, measures 25–28). This reverse-stress or choriambic rhythm is the standard opening figure for the sixteenth-century French chanson, and Campion's use of it displays, I believe, the coalescence of musical influence with that of quantitative verse.

Analysis of the poem's rhythms as in part reminiscent of the asclepiad might be thought fanciful. But just as Dowland played off asclepiads (in that case Sidney's) against iambic pentameter, Campion has done so here, though he may not have been conscious of working this way. In any case, traditional scansion of the poem simply as iambic pentameter with a few irregularities would not reveal Campion's distinctive interweaving of the two rhythms in both text and music. And it is exactly this rhythmic interplay that gives the poem its fascination as a lament for human mortality—as if life were a dance of day and night, night and day, with a steady iambic pulse rhythm, but intermittently sent into a choriambic flutter by the thought of coming death. If we ignore the rhythms, the poem will seem drably conventional. "Come, cheerful day" is an excellent example of the kind of significant aural patterning poets learned to create in Jacobean song-mode lyric.

Another case of an echo from classical meter in Campion (again with the line shortened by one syllable) is the anacreontic pattern in "Shall I come, sweet love, to thee?" The first four lines of each stanza are accentual anacreontics catalectic—the anacreontic line is ∪∪−∪ −∪−∪−⏒ and they scan xx′x′x′.

> Shall I come, sweet love to thee
>   When the evening beams are set?
> Shall I not excluded be?
>   Will you find no feigned let?
> Let me not, for pity, more
> Tell the long hours at your door.[66]
>   (stanza 1 of 3)

Line 5 would normally be read as in the trochaic meter mentioned earlier as Sidney's importation, but the music treats it as anacreontic also. Line 6, as the conclusion of stanza and melody, has a special rhythm of heavy stress and in the music is given emphasis by repetition: "Tell the long, long hours, Tell the long hours at your door." In reading we tend to scan it "Téll thĕ lóng hóurs ăt yŏur dóor," a pattern to which the final lines of stanzas 2 and 3 correspond, with their "long love" and "cold nights." The result is an appealing, rhythmically patterned lyric. We enjoy the flow of the meter with the skipping start of each line, and the trochaic beat of lines 5 and 6 in each

---

66. Fellowes, *English Madrigal Verse*, p. 401.

stanza changes the pace, signaling the coming pause between stanzas, just as the final measures do in the music.[67]

Such a lyric, though simple enough, is a long way from the rhythmic blandness of the song verse in the early Elizabethan miscellanies. It is usually noted that Elizabethan song versifiers achieved smooth-flowing lines after the metrical roughness and uncertainty of much of earlier Tudor poetry. But we must not think of song mode as merely regular, flowing verse with end-stopped lines and conventional sentiment. With Campion and other Jacobean poets, its most notable feature is audible rhythmic patterning, often over the scope of the whole stanza, a rhythmic patterning that works to give new depth and fascination to whatever conventional imagery the lyricists treat, whether playfully or passionately. As we saw with versifiers like Watson (in his madrigal contrafacta) and Hume, the dominance of music over an evolving text gave much impetus for this rhythmic patterning. For more able poets like Campion and whoever wrote Dowland's texts, the other impetus working hand in glove with the first was the effort to adapt and use classical meters. The coalescence of these two factors is no surprise when we recall what Sidney's Dicus-Lalus debate reflects, that the whole humanist revival of classical meters was motivated by a wish to recreate the supposed ancient union of music and poetry through correlating verse scansion and musical rhythm.

In "When to her lute Corinna sings," to take one of Campion's most striking songs, we can see again how much of the poem's force derives from the play of choriambic against iambic rhythm. Even without looking at the music we recognize ´ˣˣ ´ in the beginning of several lines, and the pattern, once established, induces us to read other monosyllabic, metrically ambivalent line openings in the same way: Whén tŏ hĕr lúte, Bút ĭf shĕ dóth, E'én frŏm mў́ héart. This pattern is too distinct to be characterized as an occasional trochaic substitution in iambic meter; rather, the whole line might be called a kind of accentual aeolic with initial truncation of two syllables. Whatever we call it, the lines having this structure, ´ˣˣ´ˣ´ˣ´, are played off against the iambic tetrameter lines, which they slightly outnumber.

> When to her lute Corinna sings,
> Her voice revives the leaden strings,
> And doth in highest notes appear
> As any challenged echo clear.
> But when she doth of mourning speak,
> Ev'n with her sighs the strings do break.
>
> And as her lute doth live or die;
> Led by her passion, so must I.

---

67. Pattison discusses the rhythms of "Shall I come, sweet love" and gives the melody (*Music and Poetry*, pp. 132–33).

For when of pleasure she doth sing,
My thoughts enjoy a sudden spring;
But if she doth of sorrow speak,
Ev'n from my heart the strings do break.
(Fellowes, *English Madrigal Verse*, p. 657)

The music, similarly, uses the choriambic figure for the opening of exactly half the lines.

When to her lute Corinna sings

Lyrics beneath the first staff:

But when she doth of   mourn-ing speak,   Ev'n with her sighs, her sighs,
But   if she doth of   sorrow   speak,   Ev'n from my heart,   my heart

Lyrics beneath the second staff:

her sighs   the strings do break,   the   strings   do break.
my heart   the strings do break,   the   strings   do break.

Campion here revivifies a conventional metaphor: the lute equals the expressive self of the poet-lover; his heart strings equal instrumental strings that the lady tunes and plays upon. The poem begins with the literal lute in Corinna's hands. Its strings are in sympathetic vibration with her voice: they become suddenly vivid ("revived") for her bright notes. Then for her sighs (as in madrigals, the sighs are represented by disruptive rests), suddenly, they break. The melody marks the "break" with a drop of a triad, then with a melisma on the repeat of "the strings" (measures 14–16). The text as read also marks this shift of mood for the final two lines of each stanza by returning to choriambic rhythms after the middle two iambic lines (3–4 and 9–10). In stanza 2, which in Campion's frequent fashion closely duplicates the phrasal rhythms of stanza 1, the sympathetically vibrating lute becomes the poet-lover himself, clasped in the lady's arms, humming to her every vibration, then suddenly with his heart strings broken. Donne's playing with conventional conceits is no more witty than this. But the means whereby Campion managed it are those of song mode rather than of speech.

By examining some of the work in song mode of Sidney, Watson, Hume, Campion, and others, as contrasted with lyric verse in speech and declamatory modes, we have considered some ways in which this skill with rhythmic patterns, complying with the natural sounds of English words, became so highly developed by the second decade of the seventeenth century. Campion's modified classical meters and the success he achieved with a few of them have generally been regarded as flukish, a dead end, but in fact their verbal rhythms are related to those of his later songs—he merely gave up systematizing these rhythms and propagandizing for them. He little needed to encourage imitation, for many other song lyricists were also producing excellent lyrics with subtle rhythmic patterning making use of interspersed choriambs, dactyls, and trochees—the new rhythms the Elizabethans had learned to use, largely through contrafacta and neoclassical verse. Thus by the time of Dowland and Campion, song mode accommodated a range of rhythmic definition, from metrically regular, often isometric stanzas to the individually crafted, sometimes-repeated rhythmic stanza shapes of the lutenists. The great "metricians" soon to "flourish"—Herbert and Herrick —would make the most of this varied rhythmic heritage in song mode. Later poets would turn mainly to other modes and their characteristic devices, but would still allude significantly to this English tradition of song-mode lyric.

II.   Herbert's "Divine and Moral Songs"

Herbert's Song-Mode Prosody and Lute Songs

he Herbert of the speaking-voice lyric, star pupil in the school of Donne, is well known to us. A currently less-well-known Herbert is the song-mode lyricist of the lute-song tradition, the poet of "Vertue," "The Call," the "Antiphons," "A Parodie," "Bitter-sweet," "The 23d Psalme," and "Sunday"—which depend more on figures of sound than on figures of sense for their primary effects. This second Herbert has been beloved of hymnologists of the eighteenth and nineteenth centuries and anthem composers of the twentieth. But the seventeenth-century composers who set Herbert to music usually chose his speech-mode lyrics. This seemingly odd fact is readily explained when we consider the stylistic changes in seventeenth-century English lyric and song setting.

As we have just seen in Campion's work, poets of the lute-song era had reached a high level of rhythmic skill in contriving complex metrical patterns. Their lyric song mode produced a verse texture of fluid phrases separated by distinctly audible pauses that together create pseudomusical patterns of alternating motion and rest—more distinct, more regular motions and rests than we hear in the poetic mode of simulated speech. Herbert wrote such song verse with great facility, as in "A Parodie":

> O what a damp and shade
>   Doth me invade!
>   No stormie night
> Can so afflict or so affright,
>   As thy eclipsed light.[1]

---

1. *The Works of George Herbert*, ed. F. E. Hutchinson, p. 183; subsequent citations of Herbert, other than from Wilson's song text, also follow this edition. Rosemond Tuve suggested a psalm tune that might be sung stanzaically with Herbert's "Parodie" ("Sacred 'Parody' of Love Poetry, and Herbert").

Herbert, like Sidney, was so much at ease in both speech and song modes that he could effectively contrast them, as in several two-part poems that begin with complex reflections in a speaking voice, then move into prayerful song.[2] "An Offering," for example, begins in the rough voice of that snappish parson Herbert sometimes projects:

> Come, bring thy gift. If blessings were as slow
> As mens returns, what would become of fools?
> What hast thou there? a heart? but is it pure? (lines 1–3)

The fourth such stanza concludes, "Then bring thy gift, and let thy hymne be this" (line 24). The hymn then begins, in song mode:

> Since my sadnesse
> Into gladnesse
> Lord thou dost convert,
> O accept
> What thou hast kept,
> As thy due desert. (lines 25–30)

Herbert usually wrote each poem primarily in one mode, and composers, we assume, ought to prefer song mode. However, as the dramatic lyric of the speaking voice, evolved in the late sixteenth century and perfected by Donne, became more popular, English composers more often chose speech lyrics and "dialogues" for setting, rather than the earlier flowing, metrically patterned lyrics. As I noted in Chapter I, midcentury composers developed a style especially suited for speech-mode and declamatory-mode lyrics, the highly literary song styles of, for example, Henry Lawes, John Wilson, and Charles Coleman. The midcentury prominence of this declamatory song style[3] probably accounts for the fact that most of the Herbert lyrics chosen by seventeenth-century song composers are primarily in speech mode, though Herbert was a master of song lyric.

The known settings of Herbert texts are as follows: John Jenkins's for three voices, of "Christmas" part 2, "The Dawning," "Grieve not the Holy Spirit" (divided into two songs), and "The Starre" (also divided into two); Henry Lawes's "23rd Psalme"; John Wilson's setting of four stanzas of

2. They are "Christmas," "Easter," "Good Friday," "The H. Communion," "An Offering," "The Church-floore," and "Vanitie" (II). In "Herbert's Double Poems," John Shawcross argues that the combinations of texts in most of these "double poems" were not Herbert's doing, since parts of some of them appear separately in the Williams manuscript. But "An Offering," with its transitional line "Let thy hymne be this," shows that Herbert conceived of and used such double-meter structure, which in any case had been used by earlier song versifiers.

3. On the differences between declamatory songs and tuneful airs see Elise Jorgens's excellent account in chaps. 4–6 of *The Well-Tun'd Word*. Both kinds were popular in the midcentury, but according to Ian Spink, "more or less declamatory" songs prevail over tuneful ones, both in Playford's songbooks and in manuscripts (*English Song, Dowland to Purcell*, pp. 133–34).

"Content"; "The Altar" by John Playford, the music publisher;[4] John Blow's "Grieve not the Holy Spirit"; and Henry Purcell's setting of several stanzas of "Longing."[5] "Vertue" and "Antiphon" (II) seem to have been sung in the seventeenth century to preexisting tunes.[6] According to Vincent Duckles, the Jenkins settings are the earliest, perhaps dating from Herbert's lifetime.[7] The Lawes and Wilson settings are probably of the 1640s, the Playford "Altar" of the 1650s or 1660s. These settings (excluding Blow's and Purcell's) represent the declamatory style praised by Milton in his sonnet to Lawes for being able "to span / Words with just note and accent."[8] In a sort of *aria parlante*, composers imitated the meter, nonmetric rhythms, and accentuation of verse as closely as they could, with variable rhythm; they allowed the rise and fall of melody to be governed by patterns of pitch and stress; they carefully marked syntactic junctures; and they tried to reflect the sense of the words, melodically and harmonically, in as many ways as possible, sometimes using madrigalian pictorialisms in solo song. The settings were heightened renderings of the poems, and some can still be enjoyed as such if well performed. Although such pieces have generally been considered by music historians to have little interest, they are valuable both as data for the history of stylistic change in both arts and as records of contemporary readings of the poems.[9]

In terms of suitability of lyrics for settings in different compositional styles, Herbert is a Janus-faced poet. His lyrics in song mode, looking back to the Elizabethan-Jacobean lute-song era, deserve study in that context. His lyrics in speech mode, appealing to midcentury declamatory composers, look forward and deserve study in that light. Accordingly, we will first examine Herbert as a Jacobean lute-song lyricist, a perspective that reveals

4. See Louise Schleiner, "The Composer as Reader: A Setting of George Herbert's 'Altar.'"

5. The sources of these are as follows: Jenkins—Christ Church MSS. 736–38; Lawes—British Library Additional MS. 53723; Wilson—Bodleian MS. Music b. 1; Playford—*Psalms & Hymns in Solemn Musick* (1671); Blow and Purcell—*Harmonia Sacra*, I (1688). There are modern editions of Wilson's "Content" (*Poèmes de Donne, Herbert et Crashaw*, ed. André Souris [Paris: Editions du Centre National de la Recherche Scientifique, 1961]) and of Purcell's "Longing" (ed. Ina Boyle, Oxford University Press, 1943; also in Purcell's complete works).

6. Rosalie Eggleston ("A Study of Some Relationships between Late Renaissance Music and *The Temple* of George Herbert," Ph.D. diss., University of New Mexico, 1969, p. 163) points out that Herbert's "Antiphon" (II) appears as an anthem text, without music but with "N. S." as the composer, in James Clifford's service book, *The Divine Services and Anthems Usually Sung in His Majesties Chappell*, 2d ed., 1664, pp. 169–70. "N. S." might be Nicholas Strogers, the Elizabethan composer, whose anthems continued to be sung in the seventeenth century. "Vertue" seems to have been sung, in the Restoration and eighteenth century, to a preexistent tune known in various versions as "Cheerily and Merrily," "Cold and Raw," "Stingo," and "Sweet Day." See *The Songs of England*, ed. J. L. Hatton and E. Faning, 2:65.

7. Vincent Duckles, "John Jenkins's Settings of Lyrics by George Herbert."

8. John Milton, *Complete Poems and Major Prose*, ed. Merritt Hughes, p. 144.

9. For example, Pamela Willets in *The Henry Lawes Manuscript*, p. 8, in comparing Lawes's Ariadne lament with Monteverdi's Ariana monody, finds that Lawes's piece "is restless and loses dramatic power" and furthermore produces an effect of "rhythmic poverty" because it follows the text too closely and thus loses musical coherence.

much about his prosody, before considering midcentury musical treatment of some of his lyrics.

Herbert's careful metrics and complex stanza forms have received much analysis. Most book-length studies of him discuss them, at least in passing; W. Coburn Freer has examined them in some detail, pointing out intricate relationships between form and meaning.[10] But Herbert's metrics and stanzas require study in the context of the partsongs and lutenist airs of his youth.[11] We have many indications of his youthful musical interests—Walton and other contemporaries tell us that he set and sang his poems to lute accompaniment.[12] Though commentators have generally assumed that he devised complex stanza forms especially to fit his poems as he wrote them, there are indications that a number of his stanzas were shaped by tunes, either of his own or someone else's composing. Such thematically related metrical pairs as "Peace" and "The Pilgrimage" or "The Invitation" and "The Banquet" were very likely sung to a common tune. And some of his nonisometric stanza forms are identical or close to those of extant songs.

Herbert apparently did not write profane lyrics. Like the sixteenth-century "spiritual song" versifiers, he wanted to redeem passionate love poetry by directing it away from woman toward God.[13] But we need not stick to "divine and morall songs," as Campion called them, in considering what influenced Herbert's metrics. His familiarity with lyrics, both sung and spoken, clearly extended to many of those "light conceits of lovers" disavowed in such poems as "Jordan" (1) and "The Forerunners." Having staked out a broad field for comparisons, I must add two clarifications. In comparing Herbert poems with particular songs, I am not claiming that Herbert was imitating exactly those songs. Neither am I recommending my combinations of Herbert texts with lute-song tunes as musical entities; they do not deserve serious performance. They are merely to suggest how music could relate to and influence the metrics of poems meant to be sung. We do not know what tunes Herbert sang,[14] but there are plenty of similarities between Herbert's song-mode metrics and the song metrics of his time. We shall consider these metrical structures: fourteeners or common meter lines;[15]

10. *Music for a King: George Herbert's Style and the Metrical Psalms.*

11. For mention of this context, see Margaret Bottrall, *George Herbert*, p. 124; Louis L. Martz, *The Poetry of Meditation*, pp. 272–73; A. Alvarez, *The School of Donne*, p. 76; Joseph Summers, *George Herbert: His Religion and Art*, pp. 160–70; and Alicia Ostriker, "Song and Speech in the Metrics of George Herbert."

12. Marchette Chute, *Two Gentle Men: The Lives of George Herbert and Robert Herrick*, p. 118; and Izaak Walton, *Lives of Donne and Herbert*, ed. S. C. Roberts, p. 100.

13. See the two early sonnets preserved in Walton's *Lives*, which appear in Hutchinson, ed., *The Works of George Herbert*, p. 206. Herbert's poems will hereafter be cited by title only.

14. If Herbert did preserve any of his music, it was presumably among the papers destroyed in the fire at Highnam House (ibid., p. 586).

15. Following George Saintsbury's *History of English Prosody from the Twelfth Century to the Present Day*, 2:109–11, one might object to a conflation of fourteeners and common meter. Saintsbury noted that a caesura after the eighth syllable was not inevitable and that

similar structures consisting of a longer and a shorter line (10.6, 8.10); and dimeters.

Fourteeners or common meter and its variant poulter's measure (12.14 or 6.6.8.6) were widely used in late-sixteenth-century England. Scholars have assumed that Thomas Sternhold, wishing to popularize psalm singing, adopted them for their ballad associations. Edward Doughtie has suggested that the "old version" psalter itself may have been the major influence in popularizing common meter, which was then increasingly used by balladeers.[16] In any case, most lyricists at the turn of the century had heard enough of "old Tom Sternhold's meter." As we have seen, Campion was experimenting with his anglicized classical meters.[17] Other song lyricists, following the lead of Sidney's psalms and Arcadian poems and some of the miscellanies, were trying out many line-length combinations, on the principle formulated by George Wither: "The auncient *Iewes* had both such kinde of Verses, as some of ours are, and the same freedome in their Composures that we vse; . . . they varyed the Staffe at their pleasure, making it now longer, now shorter, as they listed, or best fitted the matter."[18] The repetition of one air in stanzaic song forced poets to try, whenever possible, to repeat their complex rhythms. They developed, as Catherine Ing says, "an almost miraculous sense of the shape of phrases, and a capacity for manipulating syllables into shape without doing violence to their natural utterance."[19]

In this time of metrical experiment, the lowly fourteener was not forgotten. It was suited to become a building block in complex stanza forms because of its effect of climax and repose. The longer, eight-syllable unit normally builds up a slight feeling of tension that the shorter unit then resolves, seeming to settle upon a resting point. Each fourteener (however it is printed —see n. 15) is thus a rhythmic whole with a kind of climax just past its midpoint and a pause at the end:

> Yea let me take the mornings winges,
> and let me goe and hide
> Euen there where are the farthest parts,
> where flowing sea doth slide.
>
> (Ps. 139:9, Old Version)

Warner's and Chapman's fourteeners should not be printed as ballad measure. But as Gascoigne had said in *Certeyne Notes of Instruction* (1575), the natural place for a "pause" in a fourteener is "at the end of the first eight sillables." Most sixteenth-century verse supports him on this point. Saintsbury is referring to narrative verse, but for lyricists of the period, the fourteener was a distinct auditory pattern of 8 and 6 in the minds of poet and audience.

16. *Lyrics from English Airs, 1596–1622*, ed. Edward Doughtie, p. 17.

17. Thomas Campion, *Observations in the Art of English Poetry*, especially p. 35.

18. *A Preparation to the Psalter* (1619; rpt., New York: Burt Franklin, 1967), p. 61.

19. *Elizabethan Lyrics*, pp. 135–36.

Fourteeners often suggested a certain musical rhythmic pattern: two beats to accented, one to unaccented syllables (triple time), with a reversal (syncopation) on the penultimate foot of the three-foot line.[20]

from Psalm 1

Archbishop Parker   Thomas Tallis

Man blest no doubt who walkth not out   in   wic - ked men's af - fairs

The syncopation on the penultimate foot has a slowing effect that signals the coming end of the phrase and is thus a musical analogue of the fourteener's verbal rhythmic effect. This musical pattern recurred so commonly that its reinforcement of the fourteener's verbal effect of climax and repose must have been in poets' and composers' minds as they devised more complex rhythmic structures.

Half a century of massive exposure to fourteeners had dulled people's awareness of their characteristic effect. But when an isolated fourteener was inserted into a different metrical context, the effect became audible again:

> I care not for these ladies
> That must be wooed and prayed.
> Give me kind Amaryllis,
> The wanton country maid.
> Nature Art disdaineth,
> Her beauty is her own.
> > Her when we court and kiss,
> > She cries: forsooth, let go!
> > But when we come where comfort is
> > She never will say no.
> > > (*Booke of Ayres*, part 1, song 3, 1601)[21]

Campion here ended his trimeter verse and refrain with a fourteener because a climax on the penultimate line and a sense of repose at the end were just the effects he wanted, for an obvious reason. Campion's use of the fourteener for a rhythmic sense of "full close" was not original, but he certainly knew how to make the most of it. His music reinforces the emphasis on the lengthened penultimate line with a tripping, dancelike phrase in the lute accompaniment ending on each accented beat after the first one.

20. From *The whole Psalter translated into English Metre* (London, 1567) sig. Biiii verso–Ci. Compare William Hunnis's song "A Lamentation touching the follies and vanities of our youth," *Seven Sobs of a Sorrowfull Soule for Sinne* (London, 1583), p. 65; and Richard Allison's redactions of some "old version" tunes (such as Psalm 81) in *The Psalmes of David in Meter* (London, 1599).
21. Song texts are cited from *English Madrigal Verse: 1588–1632*, ed. E. H. Fellowes.

Some Herbert poems that similarly use a fourteener for a sense of repose or full stop are "A Parodie," "Sunday," "The Temper" (I), "The Elixir" (in poulter's measure), "Aaron," and "The H. Communion" from the Williams Manuscript, the first two of which will be examined here. "A Parodie" was written in imitation of the love song "Soules joy," probably by Lord Pembroke,[22] and like its model, it uses fourteeners for a sense of pause or repose at the end of each major clause:

Soules joy, now I am gone,	Souls joy, when thou art gone,
And you alone,	And I alone,
(Which cannot be,	Which cannot be,
Since I must leave my selfe with thee,	Because thou dost abide with me,
And carry thee with me)	And I depend on thee;
Yet when unto our eyes	Yet when thou dost suppresse
Absence denyes	The cheerfulnesse
Each others sight,	Of thy abode,
And makes to us a constant night,	And in my powers not stirre abroad,
When others change to light;	But leave me to my load:
O give no way to griefe,	O what a damp and shade
But let beliefe	Doth me invade!
Of mutuall love,	No stormie night
This wonder to the vulgar	Can so afflict or so affright,
prove	As thy eclipsed light.
Our Bodyes, not wee move.	("A Parodie," stanzas 1–3)
(stanza 1)[23]	

"A Parodie" was, as Rosemond Tuve argues, most probably written to fit a tune for the love lyric, being thus a parody in the musical sense as well as in the sense of sacred use of secular art.[24] The probable musical structure of the song is a fairly common AAB one in the lute songbooks: the opening statement or major clause (here lines 1–5); a second clause repeating the music to the first (thus metrically identical to it); a third section with new melodic material, sometimes a refrain, possibly repeating short phrases of the text in musical phrases of climax or extra intensity.[25] Herbert's stanzas 3 and 6 clearly derive from Pembroke's refrain; despite its layout in the *Temple*, his "Parodie" must have been sung as two long stanzas with variable refrain rather than as six short ones.[26] But the fourteeners mark off the five-

22. It began appearing among Donne's poems with the 1635 edition, but see H. J. C. Grierson's note on the Pembroke attribution, *The Poems of John Donne*, 1:429. The version in *Poems Written by the . . . Earl of Pembroke* (1660) is partial and corrupt.
23. Ibid.
24. Tuve, "Sacred 'Parody' of Love Poetry, and Herbert," pp. 254–55.
25. See, for example, John Dowland's "Now, O now," *First Booke of Songes or Ayres*, 1597; Alfonso Ferrabosco's setting of Ben Jonson's "Come my Celia," *Ayres*, 1609; or Thomas Campion's "Now winter nights enlarge," *Third Book of Ayres*, 1617.
26. A psalm tune repeated with each five lines (Tuve, "Sacred 'Parody,'" pp. 289–90) was probably not what Pembroke and Herbert used. It makes the stanza form 6.8.8.6, merging the two short lines and thus obscuring their rhythmic possibilities, and eliminates the extra intensity implied by the refrain (Herbert's stanzas 3 and 6).

line sections so clearly that we should not be surprised if Herbert's text, intended for readers, shows them as separate stanzas. After each fourteener, readers naturally pause, and in this case the brief interlude gives them time to note the syntactic relationship between the stanza just finished and the one to come. In the song the syntactic structure would have been clarified by the pauses and repeats of the musical structure.

Campion believed that his anglicized classical meters could evoke feelings of pause or close even without the help of rhyme: "Some eares accustomed altogether to the fatnes of rime, may perhaps except against the cadences of these numbers, but let any man iudicially examine them, and he shall finde they close of themselues so perfectly, that the help of rime were not only in them superfluous, but also absurd." [27] In the category of lyric meters "apt to be soong to an instrument," he defined three stanza forms. [28] All three "close" with short lines he calls dimeters. [29] The feeling of "close" that they do in fact create is perhaps not so innovative as Campion supposed.

> Iust beguiler,
> Kindest loue, yet only chastest,
> Royall in thy smooth denyals,
> Frowning or demurely smiling
> Still my pure delight.

The fact that the stanza ends on an accented syllable, suddenly halting the trochaic motion, contributes to the feeling of finality at the end. But its main source is the three-beat line coming after a series of four-beat lines, as in a concluding fourteener. The separations between lines are clearly heard because each line is a distinct syntactic unit, so that even without rhyme the ear recognizes the metric units. After the initial contrast between dimeter and tetrameter and then the succession of tetrameters, the ear expects some further metric shift, to end the stanza or at least to begin the next one, in which the opening dimeter returns. Thus a slight tension is created by the succession of tetrameter lines, then resolved by the concluding trimeter.

The stanza form of "Sunday," from which Walton says Herbert sang stanza 5 to his lute on his deathbed, [30] has a similar rhythmic structure, though the meter is iambic instead of trochaic:

> The Sundaies of mans life,
> Thredded together on times string,
> Make bracelets to adorn the wife
> Of the eternall glorious King.
> On Sunday heavens gate stands ope;

27. Thomas Campion, *Observations*, p. 35.
28. Ibid., pp. 29–31.
29. In adapting classical meters Campion measured English syllable lengths by the ear and looked for equivalents. For his English "dimeters" he sometimes inserted extra, as he called them "common," syllables.
30. Walton, *Lives of Donne and Herbert*, p. 112.

Blessings are plentifull and rife,
    More plentifull then hope.

As in Campion's stanza, Herbert's lengthened isometric lines after the short
opening line create a slight feeling of tension, or expectation of another metric shift, which is continued until the final trimeter line, functioning as the
end of a fourteener, brings us to a full stop. The succeeding trimeter line
beginning each new stanza also forces a pause, though a slighter one. Together the two shortened lines create an interval that distinctly separates the
smoothly flowing middle sections of the stanzas. Thus like the Sundays they
celebrate, the stanzas are separate pearls, "Threaded together on time's
string," both audibly and visually.

So far we have been considering uses of fourteeners for a sense of repose
or full stop, usually at the end of a stanza. Another frequent use of them was
to create a rhythmic contrast within a stanza. Robert Jones's "O thread of
life" (*A Musicall Dreame*, 1609) uses fourteeners for a contrast between emphatic declarations and a succeeding isometric flow.[31]

O thread of life, when thou art spent how are my sorrows
    eased!
O veil of flesh, when thou art rent how shall my soul be
    pleased!
        O earth, why tremblest thou at death,
        That did receive both heat and breath
        By bargain of a second birth,
        That done, again to be cold earth?
        Come, death, dear midwife to my life,
        See Sin and Virtue hold at strife.
            Make haste away.
            Lest thy delay
            Be my decay.
        World of inanity,
        School-house of vanity,
            Minion of hell,
            Farewell, farewell!

Each of the two initial fourteeners states an emphatic acceptance of death
addressed to a guise of the dying self. The meter evokes a feeling of finality
for each statement. The shift to a more fluid tetrameter, giving a feeling of
smooth continuity over six lines, marks a shift to a new perspective: the
dying body as part of a continuing existence (as "earth") that it had before
birth and will continue to have after death. The concluding dimeters provide appropriately breathless rhythms for the dying man's urgency in em-
bracing death. Such ingenuity in relating rhythm and sense, in making the

31. Campion's "Never weather-beaten sail" (*Two Bookes of Ayres*, 1613) uses the same
contrast, going from fourteener to tetrameter and back again.

lines "now longer, now shorter, as . . . best fitted the matter," is what we expect of Herbert, and he learned much of it from the song lyricists.

In "Dialogue" Herbert uses the same contrast between fourteeners and tetrameter, but for different ends.

> Sweetest Saviour, if my soul
>   Were but worth the having,
> Quickly should I then controll
>   Any thought of waving.
> But when all my care and pains
> Cannot give the name of gains
> To thy wretch so full of stains,
> What delight or hope remains? . . .
> *That is all, if that I could*
>   *Get without repining;*
> *And my clay, my creature, would*
>   *Follow my resigning:*
> *That as I did freely part*
> *With my glorie and desert,*
> *Left all joyes to feel all smart—*
> Ah! no more: thou break'st my heart.
>   (stanzas 1 and 4)

As in Jones's song text, the tetrameter rhythm after the fourteeners creates a slight tension. It is never quite resolved until the sharp caesura halts the final line of the poem. The shift back to fourteeners to begin each new stanza serves to mark each switch to the other partner in the dialogue. As in "Sunday," each stanza is a distinct rhythmic unit.

The feeling of slight rhythmic suspense at the end of the first stanza is especially appropriate to its question. The soul has usurped the right of judgment that properly belongs to God, who in stanza 2 asserts his claim. There also the concluding slight rhythmic suspense is appropriate because the soul is still dissatisfied at the end of stanza 2, and in stanza 3 reasserts his unfitness for salvation. In the final stanza the tension of the tetrameter lines is again used effectively: God begins reminding the soul of Christ's passion, and the rhythmic tension contributes to the force of the reminder. The soul ends the dialogue with his rhythmically marked interruptive exclamation of surrender. "Dialogue" would have been a fine text for the kind of semideclamatory dialogue setting that became popular in the late 1620s.

In madrigal and lute-song verse these two uses of the fourteener—as a concluding rhythmic structure to give a feeling of penultimate motion and then repose, and in longer passages meant to contrast rhythmically with other passages—are the most frequent ones. It would be easy to point out, in Herbert and in earlier songs, examples of a device similar to the first of these two: the use of other lengthened penultimate lines (for example, 6.6.10.6), as with concluding fourteeners, to give a sense of climax and repose. But as these rhythmic effects are similar to those just described, we shall move on to another common kind of metrical structure related to four-teeners: various combinations of alternated longer and shorter lines (for example, 10.6.10.6 or 8.10.8.10).

As with fourteeners, the usual result of such metrical structure is that the stanza divides into distinct, two-line rhythmic (usually also syntactic) units. The song section of Herbert's "Christmas," which follows an unbroken 10.6 pattern until the concluding pentameter couplet marks the end, is a good example. "Affliction" (I), which has the same stanza form as John Coperario's funeral song for two voices, "Deceitful Fancy" (*Fvneral Tears,* 1606), adds a rhymed pentameter couplet to 10.6.10.6 lines to make a six-line stanza. Singing Herbert's poem (as well as Coperario's own text) to this tune will illustrate how music could relate to the stanzaic pattern.[32]

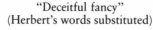

"Deceitful fancy"
(Herbert's words substituted)

Giovanni Coperario

32. For the fuller scores of this and subsequent music in Chapter II (except Wilson's song), see E. H. Fellowes, *The English Lute Songs,* series 1 and 2.

The music follows the contours of the metrical pattern rather closely. Each short line, set off by rests, is a kind of supplement to and musical comment on the preceding longer line: the canto voice for line 2 (measures 4 and 5) echoes a phrase from line 1, and line 2 takes off from and returns to the dominant chord, on which line 1 ended; both voices in line 4 (measures 8 and 9) echo the dotted quarter and eighth note figure of the alto voice in line 3, while the "besides" repeated in parallel thirds tags the line as a supplement to the "joys" just named. The generally upward melodic motion of line 1, echoed in line 2, contrasts with the generally downward motion of line 3, likewise echoed in line 4. And finally, as the concluding pentameter couplet is set apart metrically from the preceding lines, the music makes it a separate (repeated) section, starting afresh after the close in the relative major on "have."

Campion's "Tune thy music to thy heart" (*Two Bookes of Ayres*, 1613) illustrates what happens when the pattern of alternating long-then-short lines is reversed, so that the usual expectation of an equal or shorter line after the first one is crossed:

> Tune thy music to thy heart;
> Sing thy joy with thanks, and so thy sorrow.
> Though devotion needs not art,
> Sometimes of the poor the rich may borrow.

As with fourteeners, or 10.8 or 10.6 patterns, the stanza tends to divide into two-line units. But the lengthening of the second line has a retarding effect, especially apt for moments of reflection or solemnity, which gives weight to the unexpected extra syllables, with the result that the climax or greater emphasis falls at the end of the second rather than of the first line. Campion's music for "Tune thy music" accords with this structure. Instead of drawing out the shorter lines and speeding up the longer ones, as we might expect,[33] he gives the shorter lines two measures and the longer ones three, emphasizing the retard and pause at the end of these longer lines. The melody for line 2 starts out to be a melodic inversion of line 1, but then drops the pattern for the last four syllables (if one were expecting a fourteener, the extra ones) and draws out the final word "sorrow" for a whole measure, ending on an unsettled sonority. "Borrow," on the final cadence, also naturally fits the pattern of slow endings to the longer lines.

The stanza form of Herbert's "Miserie" consists of Campion's 8.10.8.10 pattern plus a refrainlike 4.6 couplet:

> Lord, let the Angels praise thy name.
> Man is a foolish thing, a foolish thing,
>   Folly and Sinne play all his game.
> His house still burns, and yet he still doth sing,
>   *Man is but grasse,*
>   *He knows it, fill the glasse.*

As in Campion's song, most of the 8.10 lines form two-line units, with a retard near the end of the second line, very clear on the repeated phrase in stanza 1. The short final couplet of each stanza may be heard as an extra pentameter line with internal rhyme. In any event, coming after a pentameter line, it breaks the pattern of 8.10 alternation and serves as a signal for the end of each stanza, as do the final pentameter lines in "Affliction" (I) and the concluding fourteener in "Sunday."

Thus we see that Herbert used the fourteener and similar structures to create rhythmic patterns like those in many song texts. But he often discovered even more striking ways of relating them to the sense and momentum of a poem than did the song lyricists, as in the contrast between fourteeners and tetrameter in "Dialogue," which marks the shifts from speaker to speaker and supports the consecutive shades of emotion through which the dialogue moves.

The aesthetician Susanne Langer has discussed the "one- or two-beat" line as an example of a convention for which poets found many uses until it became mere fashion:

> We do not know, for instance, who was the first poet to employ a line of only one or two beats, halting the flow of a stanza which then continues with slowed cadence; . . . Herrick uses it to deepen a feeling or a thought, as in his poem "To Daffodils"; Donne uses it to beget a sense of stiffness and coolness . . . Fletcher lets the short line serve as a response, a formal assent, like a bow:
>
>   Cynthia, to thy power and thee
>   We obey.

---

33. As Willa Evans noted in *Ben Jonson and Elizabethan Music*, p. 26, this was a frequent musical treatment of unequal line lengths.

All the uses of that little instrument, one by one, are exploited . . . It serves as a pause, as an accent, as an echo, as a closing chord, and undoubtedly a little research would reveal various other functions.[34]

Many of Herbert's uses of dimeters are similar to these: the concluding "For thou must die" of "Vertue," for example, is like "a closing chord"; and one result of the short lines in "Easter" is the echo effect ("Sing his praise / Without delayes").[35] Ben Jonson seems to have thought the device was being overworked; he very seldom used it seriously, and parodied it in several poems.[36] But even in Jonson's later years poets were finding new uses, which reflect its longstanding association with lyrical song rhythms.

Herbert's "Dooms-day" takes the conventional love song opening "Come away," doubles it with a rhyming line, and makes them represent Gabriel's trumpet call:

> Come away,
> Make no delay.
> Summon all the dust to rise,
> Till it stirre, and rubbe the eyes;
> While this member jogs the other,
> Each one whispring, *Live you brother?*

The steady tetrameter rhythm after the opening dimeters creates the same feeling of slight tension noted in "Dialogue," "O thread of life," and elsewhere, and thus supports the feeling of growing excitement at the imagined return of flesh and consciousness.

Herbert also used dimeters for emphatic direct address in poems of interior dialogue—a speaker conversing with some aspect of himself—as in "The Method" or in "The Dawning," a setting of which is among the Jenkins pieces mentioned earlier.[37]

> Awake sad heart, whom sorrow ever drowns;
> Take up thine eyes, which feed on earth;
> Unfold thy forehead gather'd into frowns:
> Thy Saviour comes, and with him mirth:
> Awake, awake;
> And with a thankfull heart his comforts take.
> But thou dost still lament, and pine, and crie;
> And feel his death, but not his victorie.

Besides the two-beat line, the stanza is made up of elements we have already discussed. The cumulative effect of these alternating 10.8 lines, with their

34. Susanne K. Langer, *Feeling and Form*, pp. 280–81.

35. On Herbert's antiphonal and echo effects, see Eggleston, "Late Renaissance Music and *The Temple*," chap. 3.

36. For example, "My Picture Left in Scotland" and "A Fit of Rime against Rime," *The Under-wood* 9 and 29.

37. See notes 5 and 7 above, and my "Herbert's 'Divine and Morall' Songs."

measured pauses, is slow solemnity; the insertion of the short line into the stanza brings quickening and excitement. The contrast between man's sadness and Christ's invading quickness is thus reflected in the rhythms.

John Dowland's song "Say Love, if ever thou didst find" (*The Third and Last Booke of Songs or Aires*, 1603) illustrates another way of using the dimeter line, which Herbert was to adopt. It begins:

> Say, Love, if ever thou didst find
> A woman, with a constant mind?
> > None but one.

The dimeter is a kind of forceful response or finishing touch to what has come before it. Many Herbert poems use short lines similarly—"Vertue," "Gratefulnesse," "Peace," "The Pilgrimage," and "The British Church," to mention a few.

> I joy, deare Mother, when I view
> Thy perfect lineaments and hue
> > Both sweet and bright.
> > ("British Church," lines 1–3)

In "Affliction" (IV) Herbert uses the dimeter lines to create a focal point for the image of suffering developed in each stanza. In stanza 1 the sufferer is a broken artifact, useless and cast aside ("A thing forgot"); in stanza 2 he is a flower pained all over by stinging, piercing water drops ("With scattered smart"); in stanza 3 he is a fortress, the defenders of which have deserted their posts ("Quitting their place") to fight with each other. Thomas Morley's song "Absence, hear thou my protestation" (*The First Booke of Ayres*, 1600) has a stanza form almost identical to that of "Affliction" (IV):

> Absence, hear thou my protestation
> > Against thy strength,
> > Distance and length.
> Do what you dare for alteration.
> > For hearts of truest metal
> > Absence doth join and Time
> > > doth settle.

> Broken in pieces all asunder
> > Lord, hunt me not,
> > A thing forgot,
> Once a poore creature, now a wonder,
> > A wonder tortur'd in the space
> > Betwixt this world and that of grace.

Though not all the musical and verbal emphases match well, Herbert's text may be sung to Morley's tune, an exercise which illustrates the musical setting off of the short lines, with pauses before and after them and with plaintive simplicity of phrasing, in contrast to the more heavily declaimed lines surrounding the short ones.

"Absence hear thou"
(Herbert's words substituted)

Thomas Morley

Brok'n in pie - ces all a - sunder, Lord, hunt me not,

A thing for - got, Once a poor creature, once a poor creature, now a

won - der, A won-der tortured in the space Betwixt this world,

Be - twixt this world and that of grace, and that, and that of grace.

Thus in "Absence, hear thou," both verbally and musically the rhyming dimeter lines are used just as Herbert uses them, to emphasize the dominant image of each stanza: absence's "strength, / Distance and length"; a worthy beloved as "Affection's ground"; and so on.

Herbert's "Peace" uses two separated dimeter lines to force distinct pauses after the second and final lines of each stanza:

> Sweet Peace, where dost thou dwell? I humbly crave,
> >Let me once know.
> I sought thee in a secret cave,
> >And ask'd, if Peace were there.
> A hollow winde did seem to answer, No:
> >Go seek elsewhere.

Line 4 also forces a pause, though a less emphatic one than those following lines 2 and 6. Thus the stanza breaks into three audibly distinct rhythmic units.[38] Herbert makes them coincide with the major syntactic units, thereby helping the listener to follow the stages of the speaker's quest and then the answer of the old man, Melchizedek, type of Christ.[39]

Herbert seldom duplicated complex stanza forms, and the reason for his duplication of this one (in "The Pilgrimage"—see n. 38) may well have been a tune that seemed to him especially appropriate for an allegorical journey

38. This description applies to "The Pilgrimage" as well, which differs from "Peace" only in that line 4 of each stanza is a tetrameter rather than a trimeter. They could still be sung to the same tune. See, for example, Campion's two texts for one tune, "Follow thy fair sun" (*Book of Ayres*, 1601) and "Seek the Lord" (*Two Bookes of Ayres*, 1613), which differ just as "Peace" and "The Pilgrimage" do.

39. Melchizedek, king of Salem (Gen. 14:18−20 and Ps. 110:4), was a priest who served Abraham bread and wine and blessed him. Hebrews 6:20−7:28 cites him as the exemplar of a priestly order of which Jesus is high priest.

through failure and deceptive pleasure toward a vision of true good. We do not know what that tune might have been, but John Dowland had written a song for a text with essentially the same stanza form, though the printing layout is different, with the two middle lines each split in half. "To ask for all thy love" (*A Pilgrimes Solace*, 1612) is an amplification and paraphrase of stanza 3 of Donne's "Lovers infinitenesse":

> To ask for all thy love and thy whole heart
> > 'Twere madness.
> > I do not sue
> > Nor can admit,
> > Fairest, from you
> > To have all yet.
> Who giveth all hath nothing to impart
> > But sadness.

The song's melody treats the stanza as the verbal rhythmic structure would suggest. That is, it divides the stanza into three sections, with a major break after line 2, a partial cadence ending line 6 (Herbert's line 4), and natural emphasis on the short phrase, which comprises the final cadence, set off by a rest. Again, these features can be heard if we sing Herbert's words to the suggested tune.

"To ask for all thy love"
(Herbert's words substituted)

John Dowland

We have considered examples in Herbert's lyrics of particular metrical units that create patterns of motion and pause, serving many expressive purposes. When such pauses separate smoothly flowing phrases, the result is a texture that sounds as if music must be behind it[40]:

---

40. Or as Joseph Summers puts it, Herbert's poems can evoke an "imagined music" (*George Herbert*, p. 157).

O what a damp and shade
    Doth me invade!
    No stormie night
Can so afflict or so affright,
    As thy eclipsed light.
                ("A Parodie," lines 11–15)

Unfold thy forehead gathered into frowns:
    Thy Saviour comes, and with him mirth:
          Awake, awake,
And with a thankfull heart his comforts take.
             ("The Dawning," lines 3–6)

I joy, deare Mother, when I view
Thy perfect lineaments and hue
    Both sweet and bright.
             ("British Church," lines 1–3)

The feeling of alternating motion and rest created by varying the frequency of separate sounds is an elemental factor in music. Jacobean song versifiers' uses of various metrical devices to create patterns of significant pauses and fluctuating speeds, in combination with the fluid phrasing characteristic of song-mode verse, resulted in an especially striking texture of verbal song— one hears patterns of alternating motion and rest, more distinctly audible, more regularly occurring patterns than one hears in the poetic modes of simulated speech or declamation. This texture led Bruce Pattison to say of a Robert Jones song that the poet had "gone half-way towards transforming the poem into song."[41] Herbert was a master in the creation and poetic use of this verbal song, and he learned it from the pieces which he "sung to his *Lute* or *Viol.*"

Its influence on his prosody is frequently apparent in the lyrics of *The Temple* and contributes significantly to that often-noted impression of richness in simplicity left by his poems. Simple ideas can be wrought into intricate rhythmic patterns (as in "The Call"); complex ideas can glide by with remarkable ease in song-text fluidity (as in "The Rose"). The discipline of writing for music provided Herbert with a repertoire of rhythmic skills that helped to define his mature poetic idiom, the "sweetnesse redie penn'd" of "Jordan" (II): as he fought against what he considered ostentatious wit and pride, the "curling" and "winding" Donnean lines and metaphors of his youth were often submerged in a rhythmic flow.

Herbert's Speech Mode and Declamatory Song

But Herbert not only could write lyrics and passages of lyrics in practically pure song mode, he could write them equally well and equally often in speech mode. And his tone of voice then was his own, not Donne's nor

---

41. Bruce Pattison, *Music and Poetry of the English Renaissance*, p. 146.

anyone else's. Just how aware he was of new developments in vocal music during his last years we do not know. Being at Cambridge, then retiring to Bemerton, he may have had little knowledge of the work of court composers such as Herrick's friend Robert Ramsey, or of Nicholas Lanier and the new declamatory songs, though perhaps he heard some of them in his sociable weekly "music meetings" with Giles Tompkins and the singing men of Salisbury Cathedral.[42] In any case, several of his speech-mode lyrics would prove especially suitable for declamatory setting in the midcentury decades.

As Vincent Duckles has said, English declamatory composers aimed "to give poetry a reading more penetrating, more profound than the sound of speech alone could convey."[43] Or as their contemporary Roger North expressed it, they "took pleasure in putting music to poems."[44] Whatever our modern views of the text-music relationship in song may be, students of seventeenth-century poetry and vocal music must take seriously this belief of declamatory song composers that they were doing a "reading" of the text, since that belief directly affected their compositions. Such settings as responses to their texts often point up features of the poems that might not be noticed without the musical perspective. Furthermore, analysis of the relation between text and music allows us to clarify the musical features of such song and sometimes to enjoy a piece despite the absence of memorable melody. Ian Spink, after appreciative analysis of several Lawes settings, concludes that while Lawes is vulnerable to criticism, they can be appreciated "in performance rather than on paper," for then "the full subtlety and refinement of his technique can be recognized."[45] As the madrigal is best enjoyed by its singers, conversely the declamatory song is best enjoyed not by someone humming it through but by someone listening carefully to a skilled performance of it. In examining the setting by John Wilson of Herbert's "Content,"[46] we can discover a measure of musical interest as well as a significant relationship to the poem.

Henry Lawes in a commendatory poem spoke of Wilson in terms similar to those Milton used in praising Lawes himself:

> Thou taught'st our Language, first, to speak in Tone.
> Gav'st the right accents and proportion;
> And above all (to shew thy excellence)
> Thou understand'st good words, and do'st set sense.[47]

Wilson is praised for knowing how to select fine and meaningful verse and to "set sense." Whether or not the accolade was just for his whole corpus,

---

42. See Amy Charles, *A Life of George Herbert*, pp. 163–66.
43. Duckles, "John Jenkins's Settings," p. 475.
44. Cited in ibid., p. 474.
45. Ian Spink, *English Song, Dowland to Purcell*, p. 86.
46. See note 5 above.
47. Quoted in Willa Evans, *Henry Lawes: Musician and Friend of Poets*, pp. 219–20.

his stanza selection for the through-composed setting of "Content" suggests that it was so here. Of the poem's nine stanzas only four (1–3 and 9) comprise his text:

> Peace mutt'ring thoughts, and do not grudge to keep
>   Within the walls of your own breast:
> Who cannot on his own bed sweetly sleep,
>   Can on anothers hardly rest.
>
> Gad not abroad at ev'ry quest and call
>   Of an untrained hope or passion.
> To court each place or fortune that doth fall,
>   Is wantonnesse in contemplation.
>
> Mark how the fire in flints doth quiet lie,
>   Content and warm t' it self alone:
> But when it would appeare to others eye,
>   Without a knock it never shone.
>
> Then cease discoursing soul, till thine own ground,
>   Do not thy self or friends importune.
> He that by seeking hath himself once found,
>   Hath ever found a happie fortune.[48]

Thematically Herbert's poem is part of a tradition of moral lyrics on the subject of self-reliance versus fawning ambition. The madrigal and lute-song books of Herbert's youth contain many such songs, often showing the honest, self-reliant man in a pastoral or georgic scene, as opposed to city or court. Herbert treats this "rest with yourselves" theme (to borrow a phrase from such a song by Richard Allison[49]) with a series of carefully spun conceits imaging self-reliance: fire resting quietly in flint, not showing itself except at a "knock" from without; "the pliant mind," able to stretch to a crown or contract to a cloister cell; the sturdy soul for whom the whole world is a "well-furnisht tent"; a scorn of fleshly glory, since the "fumes" that rise from a "private body" are the same as those from a king's corpse; and finally a love of privacy that prefers merely having one's body gnawed by worms to having one's name and reputation in books "chaw'd" and digested by bookworms and by "others pens and tongues." By retaining only one striking conceit and the simpler, injunctive stanzas ("keep within," "gad not abroad," and so on), Wilson places his song, even more clearly than Herbert's poem was, within the tradition of earlier "rest with yourselves" songs, which like Herbert's first, second, and ninth stanzas praise self-knowledge, inner repose, and resourceful independence in a straightforward, didactic manner. But Wilson's primary intention in selecting stanzas was probably to eliminate the conceptual difficulties of Herbert's more intri-

---

48. *Works*, ed. Hutchinson, pp. 68–69.
49. *An Howres Recreation in Musicke*, no. 11 (London, 1606).

cate conceits, which would be hard to understand even in declamatory song. Thus he was able to focus his expressive interest on the vivid fire-in-flints metaphor.

Peace mutt'ring thoughts

George Herbert   John Wilson

Peace, mutt'ring thoughts, and do not grudge to keep within the walls of your own breast:

Who cannot on his own bed sweet - ly sleep, can on a - nother's hardly

rest. Gad not a - broad at ev' - ry quest and call of an un - train - ed

hope or passion. To court each place or for - tune that doth fall is wantonness in

con - templa - tion. Mark how the fire in flint doth quiet lie, content, and

warm   to   it-self alone: But when it would appear   to o-thers' eye,

without a knock it   ne - ver shone.   Then peace, discour - sing soul,

plough thine own   ground,   Do not thy - self or   friends im -

por - tune.   He   that by see —   king

once   him - self hath found,   hath e - ver found a   for - tune.

Retaining as melodic units the long phrases of the text as read, Wilson's setting follows Herbert's syntax meticulously, continuing the musical line where there is enjambment, breaking it where there is not. Though in a few lines we can see musical imitation of the iambic meter for a short stretch, notably in lines 1–2, "doe not grudge to keepe / Within the walls," Wilson did not follow the poetic meter consistently, but instead emphasized the syllables that would get strong stress in reading, as in line 5: *gadd, abroad, quest*, and *call* (measures 10–11). The leap of a minor seventh up to "Gadd" (measure 9) and immediately back down a fourth ("Gadd" would have strong stress and thus a higher pitch in reading) illustrates Pattison's observation about the rise and fall of the melody as governed by the stresses of the words. Again, in measures 28–29 ("Do not thyself or") the initial high pitch and succeeding descent follow the verbal pitch pattern. The melodic repetition on "his own bed sweetly sleep" (measures 5–6) is a pictorialism, imaging the steady breathing of the peaceful sleeper. Likewise, the descending scale to the tonic of the piece's relative major (Ab) on "Then peace discoursing soul" (measures 25–26) reflects musically the peace of the self-knowing soul. Another patterning of music on the verse is Wilson's division of the song into two-line units, following Herbert's two-line units, which in the poem consist of alternating pentameter and tetrameter lines. Thus, following the poem as read, the song emphasizes stressed words, follows the suggested pitch patterns of the voice, reinforces semantic content with pictorialisms, and moves through lengthy, regular melodic phrases suitable to the poem's mood of quiet intensity.

In the fire-in-flints passage, Wilson carefully distributes accents so that the listeners hear the important words, for they must hear them well enough to get something of the power of the image, even if they do not grasp the precise terms of it. They need not think, "Self-reliant soul equals flint-stone with potential spark; as the stone does not give off sparks until struck, so the soul does not reach out until it is struck by a clear occasion, call, or need." But when they hear the stressed words *fire-lie-content-warm-self-alone* and then *appear-eye-knock-never-shone*, they will have a distinct sense of how the fire image relates to "Peace, mutt'ring thoughts" and "Gadd not abroad."

Wilson even provides a harmonic attention signal, a sudden C major chord at the beginning of the line (measure 18—"Mark how the fire . . ."), after ending the previous line in C minor. The power of the fire is suggested by the leading tone on the word *fire*, resolved as the fire is declared quiescent in the succeeding phrase. The musical line lasting through "itself alone" (measure 21) fluctuates between major and minor chords, the unclear tonality imaging the fire's obscurity within the flint, until the uncertainty is resolved in the unambiguous major chords, tonic and dominant of the piece's relative major, on the lines "When it would appear to others' eye . . ." (measures 22–25). Thus the emergence into major tonality reflects the fire's emergence from its concealment. I do not know whether Spink would consider this to be among the "contorted and contrived" harmonic effects he notes as characterizing Wilson's declamatory songs,[50] but to me it seems to work well enough musically in its expressive content.

50. *English Song, Dowland to Purcell*, p. 126.

The fire-in-flint stanza is set off from the others harmonically, and the major chord progression at its end is a climax that the final stanza, at a slower pace and back in the key of F minor, resolves.[51] The variant reading in Wilson's text on the line "Then peace [,] discoursing soule," (instead of "Then cease discoursing, soul"), whether it is deliberate or due to textual corruption or oral transmission, is for Wilson's purposes an improvement. It recalls the song's opening phrase, "Peace, mutt'ring thoughts," and with the addition of the word *then* ("Then peace"—measure 26) signals the conclusion of the argument: "plough [instead of 'till'] thine own ground," find yourself.

So we see that Wilson, with his careful stanza selection, pictorialisms, following of the poem's syntax, effective distribution of accents, and coordination of his harmonic climax with the climax of the text's argument, has read the poem well and structured his text and music in accordance with its prominent features. In one passage the melody and bass lines drag noticeably, with the obvious purpose of allowing the lutenist to supply harmonic elaboration through inner moving parts.[52] I refer to the penultimate line of the text, in Wilson's version "He that by seeking once himself hath found" (measures 32–35), a slow chromatic phrase suggesting modulations for a lute part or keyboard realization. The chromaticism suspends tonality temporarily, and we may be sure that Wilson, a virtuoso lutenist, would have found harmonically expressive ways to elaborate this "seeking" before finally arriving at the concluding F minor cadence.

The value of the song for enriching our reading of Herbert's poem lies in its focus on the fire-in-flints image—not just because Wilson selected it and none of the others, but because he made the passage containing it work well as the climax of his song. His selection reveals a sensitive reading, for this image is the key to what is special about Herbert's treatment of the "rest with yourselves" theme, the sense that the independent, self-reliant man is really a man for other people as well as for himself; his power for good, his "fire," is not hoarded but preserved for the right occasion, the right "knock." The other images of the middle stanzas, though they are more complex than those of earlier "rest with yourselves" songs, do not add anything substantially new to the classical and Renaissance concept of the happy man— adaptable, self-reliant, with integrity "for all seasons," invulnerable to fortune and slander. The fire-in-flints image means that for Herbert *integer vitae* is not simply towering above a lonely countryside, preserving one's purity in isolation, or otherwise withdrawing from social intercourse. Finding

51. "Content" is in the key of F minor, though it is signed with only three flats because of the lingering modal harmonic system of the time.
52. As Duckles points out in "The 'Curious' Art of John Wilson," Wilson left space for the lute score for all the songs in his manuscript, but filled it in (or had it filled in) only for a small group of songs at the end, not including the present example.

oneself is seen as a function of right relations with other people—one should husband personal energy and resources so that one need not "importune" anyone, so that contacts with other people will always be occasions for mutual benefit, will be only those that will call forth personal strength or warmth.

I do not mean that Wilson made such a conscious analysis of Herbert's image. But its power and originality must have been apparent to him, must have suggested a song that would explore a sense of controlled personal intensity or energy. His expressive song goes beyond any surface imitation of the poem.

Of course music and poetry are different arts. The sensory pleasures of poetic imagery—of being sparked to fresh perceptions of significant shapes, colors, or ideational patterns—are not evoked by song. Nor can it evoke the pleasure of seeing images function in a variety of ways in argumentation or subtle evocation of ideas, nor that of hearing abstract rhythmic patterns in simulated language. These are all literary pleasures—music has its own characteristic pleasures: the vitality of simulated movement, melodic patterns that take on a life and desirability of their own, evocation of mood penetrating beyond the reach of words, mathematically elegant proportion articulated in linear fashion, and others. In song, listeners are normally conscious of only a few features of the text: its most heavily stressed words, the tone quality of its vowel sounds, and a surface level of signification extending at best over a relatively brief clause or phrase, as a unit. Often they retain or are conscious of only a single word out of a phrase or clause, even if the performer's diction is perfect—thus part of the usefulness of repetition, parallelisms, and refrains is to help the words come through.

As a compositional mode suited to lyrics of simulated speech and simulated verbal declamation, declamatory song hardly ever uses such helps. Its intended audience was a circle of people who already knew the poems; many of Lawes's songs were composed at the request of the poets themselves. Such listeners were not interested in distinguishing between literary and musical pleasures. Listening to a setting of a poem one already knows well gives an extra dimension to the pleasure of hearing music. Present musical perception is enhanced at certain moments by memory. The poem can be in the back of one's mind as one listens to music that has been inspired by it, noting pictorialisms, imitated emphases, and dramatic effects, and sometimes perceiving a new direction in which the music takes off from whatever in the poem inspired it. Of course one's memory of the poem may be more vivid than the present perception of the music, so that one does not so much listen as reminisce about the poem—if Milton really liked most of Lawes's declamatory settings very much, one might explain his approval in this way. But declamatory songs at their best are capable of providing, for a prepared audience, this double, literary-musical pleasure. It was for this pleasure that Milton, Herrick, and many other poets valued them so highly.

Since Herbert lived his last years in a village and died obscurely, and since his image as royalist/Anglican saint grew slowly, achieving prominence only toward the end of the Commonwealth era and in the Restoration, midcentury composers had little political or other nonmusical motivation to set his texts. But in fact, some of the best of them did so. It seems likely that they took an interest in the "sweet singer of Bemerton," as Walton would later dub him, both because they could recognize the thorough and consistent song-relatedness of his prosody, reminding them of the recent glories of the lute-song era, and because at the same time they could find in his speech-mode verse, with its dominant "affetuoso" tone of intensity, suitable texts for the new style of their small-scale declamatory or monodic songs.

III.   Herrick's Songs and the Character of *Hesperides*

he critical instinct behind Swinburne's praise of Robert Herrick as the greatest English songwriter was good; Herrick was indeed, of the notable poets of his time, the one most at home in song-mode lyric.[1] Awareness of the prominent song features of his verse and of its musical contexts is useful both for responsive reading of the poems and for understanding their reception by Herrick's contemporaries. The large quantity of extant seventeenth-century settings of his poems indicates that they were especially popular for both tuneful and declamatory song: at least forty settings of thirty-one poems are to be found in manuscript and printed songbooks from 1624 to 1683, far more than we have of texts from other important English poets of the first half of the century, excluding Campion, who set his own poems.[2] The settings were done by the best-known composers of the period: Henry and William Lawes, John Wilson, Robert Ramsey, and others. Furthermore, as is indicated in *Hesperides*, Nicholas Lanier, Ramsey, Henry Lawes, and possibly others did set-

1. Algernon C. Swinburne, *Studies in Prose and Poetry*, p. 45.

2. As compared with twelve seventeenth-century settings of Donne texts (see Mary W. Kime, "Lyric and Song: Seventeenth Century Musical Settings of John Donne's Poetry") and eleven of Herbert texts (see Chap. II above and my essay "Seventeenth-Century Settings of Herbert: Purcell's 'Longing'"). C. L. Day and E. B. Murrie (*English Song-Books 1651–1702: A Bibliography*) list twenty-three settings of Carew texts; thus he ranks second to Herrick in number of settings. Of Herrick settings I find: by Henry Lawes 15; William Lawes 7 (6 of these are in William Lawes, *Six Songs*, ed. Edward H. Jones); John Wilson 4; John Gamble 3; Robert Ramsey 3; William Webb 3; John Hilton 2; Walter Porter 1; John Blow 1; and 1 anonymous. Many of these appear in either *English Songs: 1626–1660*, ed. Ian Spink (*Musica Britannica*, vol. 33), the facsimile reprint of John Playford's *The Treasury of Music* (1669); or *Major Poets of the Earlier Seventeenth Century*, ed. Barbara K. Lewalski and Andrew J. Sabol. On an error perpetuated in this last, see note 6 below.

tings of Herrick poems for performance at court that apparently have not survived.[3]

Some of the surviving settings are datable to Herrick's London years (1623–1630), but more to the 1630s and 1640s, to judge from their positions in cumulatively compiled manuscript songbooks. Thus it would seem that Herrick and his poems were not so forgotten in "dull Devonshire" as *Hesperides* sometimes suggests, at least not among his musician readers. Fully one-quarter (eight of thirty-one) of the poems in the group of extant settings are not in *Hesperides*, a figure which indicates that many more of Herrick's poems were in circulation than he included in "his booke" of 1647–1648. For these eight poems are identifiable only by happenstance mentions of his name,[4] and we must suppose that more of the anonymous texts in the songbooks of the period are Herrick's: they contain many beloved Oenones and Julias, emblematic flowers, prankish Cupids, and imaginary neopagan rituals.[5] Of the eighteen songs to Herrick texts known to have appeared in print during the seventeenth century, all but one were almost certainly composed before 1650.[6] The fact that they were not published until the 1650s and 1660s, when after a two-decade gap in music publishing John Playford's enterprises provided the opportunity for secular songs again to appear, should not cause us to treat them as evidence of Herrick's popularity with readers during the 1650s and 1660s. Henry Lawes said in the preface to his *Ayres and Dialogues* of 1653 that he had great store of such songs (as his autograph manuscript confirms) and would publish more if those present met with encouragement. Almost all the Herrick poems contained in twelve printed songbooks of the period were part of such backlogs.[7]

3. A number of poems in *Hesperides* are described as having been "set and sung," and sometimes a composer is given. See, for example, *The Poetical Works of Robert Herrick*, ed. L. C. Martin, pp. 70, 85, 159, 342, 364, 366, 367. Also, in *Lachrymae Musarum . . . Elegies upon the death of Henry, Lord Hastings* (1649) is a Herrick dialogue poem, "The New Charon," subtitled as "being set by Mr. Henry Lawes."

4. In one case the identification is only a likelihood based on the fact that the song occurs between two settings of poems that are in *Hesperides*. See Willa Evans, *Henry Lawes: Musician and Friend of Poets*, p. 157.

5. John Cutts's conclusion to this article ("A Bodleian Song-Book: Don. c. 57") is that "Bodleian manuscript Don. c. 57 . . . bears witness to the great popularity of Herrick and Carew."

6. John Blow's "Go, perjur'd Man, and if thou e're return" must have been later. The setting of "How Lillies came white" that appears in Playford's *Treasury of Music*, book 2 (1669— possibly a reissue of a 1663 songbook) is there erroneously attributed to Nicholas Lanier. In fact it was composed by William Lawes (it appears in his autograph manuscript) and thus dates from before 1645, when the younger Lawes died. The erroneous attribution is noted by Murray Lefkowitz in *William Lawes*, p. 159.

7. Thus it is not quite accurate to say (J. Max Patrick, ed., *The Complete Poetry of Robert Herrick*, p. xii) that "between 1649 and 1674, almost a hundred of [Herrick's poems] were reprinted, usually without credit to him, in 28 different collections." Twelve of these twenty-eight were songbooks, and their Herrick texts are not "reprintings" from *Hesperides* but earlier texts; they attest to Herrick's popularity with composers from about 1624 to 1650, but have little bearing on the popularity of his poems as verse after 1650.

Herrick's skills as a songwriter and his popularity among composers of his day are useful considerations as we learn to enjoy him in our own time. Since the appearance of Max Patrick's appreciative edition and Roger Rollin's book on Herrick of 1966, many commentators have countered the long-standing opinion that Herrick's verse, while elegantly crafted, is minor poetry because it lacks seriousness. We have been shown Herrick's preoccupation with such serious topics as virtue, death, and reverence for life;[8] and Earl Miner's fine chapter on order and disorder in Cavalier poetry has demonstrated Herrick's concern with balancing the claims of these two poles in art and life.[9] Such studies have added much to our appreciation of Herrick. But the impression of lightness or insubstantiality, not to say triviality, that many people still bring away from close reading of him cannot be completely discounted. A partial explanation of this impression lies in the song-text features of many poems, or more precisely in our failure to recognize them as such and to read them with an ear for musical suggestiveness. Herrick compiled *Hesperides* for readers, and some of his revisions reflect this aim, but most of the songs he included remain essentially songs. And to them especially the poet's advice ("When he would have his verses read") applies: not "in sober mornings" two hundred pages at a stretch, but at the sociable fireside, "when men have both well drunk and fed, / Let my Enchantments then be sung, or read"—a few at a time.

Early songbook versions of some poems differ from the *Hesperides* versions, and thus can offer insights into Herrick's "perfecting" process; these revisions need to be considered in the context of the differences between song mode and speech or declamatory modes. One might ask whether the songbook texts are, instead of Herrick's early drafts, versions produced by composer revision. Presumably they do contain a few such changes, but besides the fact that composers of this period in the main respected the integrity of their texts, there are consistent patterns of revision, as we will see, suggesting that these poems were first stanzaic song lyrics, which acquired a somewhat different character as Herrick condensed and prepared them for *Hesperides*.

We begin with "To Musick. A Song." Its anonymous setting,[10] probably composed in 1624 or earlier,[11] has a text two lines longer than that of *Hesperides* (where lines 3 and 4 are omitted):

8. See the extensive bibliography in *"Trust to Good Verses": Herrick Tercentenary Essays*, ed. Roger B. Rollin and J. Max Patrick, especially pp. 249–78.

9. *The Cavalier Mode from Jonson to Cotton*, pp. 156–63.

10. In one of the manuscripts (Bod. Don. c. 57) where this setting appears, it falls between a song by William Lawes and one by William Webb (it appears under his name in a later printed songbook). Thus one might speculate that either Webb or William Lawes composed it.

11. John P. Cutts ("'Mris. Elizabeth Davenant 1624' Christ Church MS. Mus. 87," p. 29) says of this manuscript, including "To Musick," that he can date no item later than 1624.

Musick thou Soul of Heaven care charming spell
    That strik'st a stillnesse into Hell:
Thou whose soft accents & alluring tones
    Give life & motion unto stones
Thou that calm'st Tygers & fierce stormes that rise
    With thy soule melting Lullabies
Fall downe [fall downe][12] from those thy chyming Spheares
    & charme our soules as thou inchant'st our Eares.
          (Bod. MS. Don. c. 57, p. 101)[13]

In his descriptive article on Bod. MS. Don. c. 57, John Cutts states that the two lines Herrick later omitted "give better balance to the poem," and he repeats the observation in his article on the other songbook containing "To Musick."[14] Cutts's reaction to the shortened version is perhaps visual: a lyric poem ("To Musick" does not read like an epigram) with such long lines stretching out across the page ought not to be so short; it looks like an extract, perhaps one stanza of a longer poem. In fact it is an extract. The version of the poem discovered by Margaret Crum in a midcentury commonplace book,[15] taken together with the other texts we have, reveals that what Herrick originally wrote was a stanzaic song text. The first stanza of this commonplace-book version is approximately the same as that above; the metrically identical second is as follows:

If the Sweete Thracian could with his soft numbers
Lull the madd Furies into Slumbers
If that Arion could allure to Swimme
The Blew backd Dolphin after him
Or if Amphion Stones to kisse could bringe
with his delicious singinge
Thy circumfused rapture much more then
must move to love us softer moulded Men.

The two stanzas of Crum's text are probably a reproduction from memory of Herrick's original song text: music is still the "Soul of heaven" rather than Herrick's later "Queen of Heaven"; the "soft accents and alluring tones" of line 3 have not proved memorable enough and have been replaced by "accents and conspiring tones"; music is now made to "raise" rather than to calm the storms of line 5 by a substitution of "doth raise" for "that rise" (a reversal of meaning that could easily go unnoticed in song); and the inflectional final *t* of "enchant'st" is omitted—such a consonant cluster is

12. The copyist of this text has not written out the repetition, and thus the line as it stands is metrically defective, having only eight syllables where the stanzaic pattern calls for ten. In Chr. Church MS. Mus. 87 the line is complete.

13. Printed in Cutts's article on Bod. Don. c. 57, p. 206.

14. For the two Cutts articles, see the Bibliography.

15. See her "An Unpublished Fragment of Verse by Herrick."

too much trouble for the ordinary singer. What similar changes may have occurred in stanza 2 we cannot know since we have only this version of it.

Herrick's original poem was a good song text, using standard song-text devices of repetition of sounds (for example, word repetition: fall down, fall down; and alliteration: strik'st—stilnesse, charm—inchant'st, Arion—allure), a conclusion rhythm of final pentameter couplet after alternating 10.8 line pairs, and the piling up of conventional images to illustrate one point. These devices provide regular musical phrase lengths, help make words comprehensible in song, and produce a strong cumulative impression. In revising for *Hesperides* Herrick was thinking of readers speaking the poems to themselves rather than singing them, and accordingly felt a pull toward speech or declamation. Probably, too, he was thinking of the now-fashionable through-composed declamatory settings, which had no use for stanzas nor for extensive thematic repetition.

To Musick. A Song.

MUSICK, thou *Queen of Heaven*, Care-charming-spel,
    That strik'st a stilnesse into hell:
Thou that tam'st *Tygers*, and fierce storms (that rise)
    With thy soule-melting Lullabies:
Fall down, down, down, from those thy chiming spheres,
To charme our soules, as thou enchant'st our eares.[16]

The repetition of "soul" ("Soul of Heaven," "soule melting Lullabies," "our soules"), potentially valuable in song, is of no particular value for a reader, and Herrick replaces "Soul of Heaven" with the visually sharper "*Queen of Heaven*." The word repetition "fall down, fall down" (or in the Christ Church manuscript "come down, come down") is revised to produce, in a spoken version, an onomatopoeic simulation of the chiming spheres ("down, down, down")—an effect that would be especially stressed in a through-composed declamatory setting of the words.[17] Seven traditional examples of music's lulling power may not be too many for a stanzaic song, but they might lull someone to death in a poem to be read; three will do there. Herrick keeps enough of stanza 1 to state the conventional argument of the poem and to preserve the most elegant phrases: the "chiming spheres" make a fine image, and the phrase "soule-melting" pleased him so much that he used it in another song as well, "Amarillis, by a Springes (softe and soule Meltinge) Murmeringes" ("Upon Mrs. Eliz: Wheeler," set by Henry Lawes). The notable phrases of the second stanza, "delicious singinge" and "circumfused rapture," are excellent sounds for music but cannot be kept with-

---

16. *Poetical Works*, p. 103.
17. The composer could give it fitting treatment since the phrase would not have to suit other words in subsequent stanzas.

out the redundant "lulling" examples that contain them, and Herrick lets them go.

We cannot know how many of Herrick's poems underwent such a cutting process, but this excerpting may well have contributed to the often-noted effect of lightness or insubstantiality in *Hesperides* as a collection. In many sections of the book we seem to move too rapidly from one miniature to the next, even if we skip the epigrams (or actually omit them, as one editor did). We come across elegant, original turns of phrase, but often they seem to stand unsupported and undeveloped; before we can take them in thoroughly, we are already beginning still another poem on one of Herrick's few favorite themes.

Another cause for this effect of lightness in *Hesperides* is the fact that song-mode texts as poems characteristically have a certain conceptual bareness or suggestiveness calculated to leave a composer room to work. The little piece immediately following "To Musick" in *Hesperides* is just such a song text:

> To the Western wind.
>
> 1. Sweet Western Wind, whose luck it is,
>   (Made rivall with the aire)
>   To give Perenn'as [*sic*] lip a kisse,
>   And fan her wanton haire.
> 2. Bring me but one, Ile promise thee,
>   Instead of common showers,
>   Thy wings shall be embalm'd by me,
>   And all beset with flowers.

The idea of the wind touching a lady's lips and playing with her hair, a fine theme for musical exposition, is simply suggested and not developed. The poem derives more force from the concluding vow to toss flowers to the wind for joy if the wind will bring the poet one of Perenna's hairs. If we could read this little piece somewhat as John Hilton or William Lawes might have—slowly, attempting to imagine musical interplay with the lady's blowing hair and the flowers drifting downwind—we would probably be close to Herrick's sense of the poem. In a tuneful air, the blowing hair of stanza 1 and blowing flowers of stanza 2 could fit the same music well, though the composer would need more stanzas, or perhaps a refrain, to work with.

"Not to love," the poem immediately preceding "To Musick," has a more thoroughly developed argument, but comparison of it with the earlier stanzaic song-text version in William Lawes's autograph manuscript shows that it, like "To Musick," has been condensed. The final poem is not a miniature because the two original stanzas were long, and Herrick has retained all of stanza 1 and added six new lines (7–8 and 13–16), making a nonstanzaic lyric of it. Again like "To Musick," it thus becomes more suitable for through-composed declamatory setting.

On the Vicissitudes of Love

1. He that will not love, must be
   my Scholar, and learn this of me,
   there be in love as many fears
   as the Summer corn hath ears;
   sighs, and sobs, and troubles more
   than the sand that makes the shoar:
   Now an Ague, Then a Feaver,
   both tormenting Lovers ever.
   Wouldst thou know besides all these,
   how hard a Woman 'tis to please?
   how high she's priz'd whose worth's
      but small?
   little thou'lt loue, or nought at all.

2. He that will not loue must be
   More colder then that he or thee
   Tis a cryme I would not name
   Sure the able haue a flame.
   Sleapy man forbeare to say
   Thou hast a soull thour't nought but
      clay
   Else a fyer growing higher
   Soone would burne thee with desire
   Prithy know tis but disease
   Take this Cure it giues all ease
   Gaze on those eyes and there must
      proue
   If not lasciuious strong in loue.
   (William Lawes's text)[18]

Not to love

He that will not love, must be
My Scholar, and learn this of me:
There be in Love as many feares,
As the Summers Corne has eares:
Sighs, and sobs, and sorrowes more
Then the sand, that makes the shore:
Freezing cold, and firie heats,
Fainting swoones, and deadly sweats;
Now an Ague, then a Fever,
Both tormenting Lovers ever.
Wod'st thou know, besides all these,
How hard a woman 'tis to please?
How crosse, how sullen, and how
   soone
She shifts and changes like the
   Moone.
How false, how hollow she's in heart;
And how she is her owne least part:
How high she's priz'd, and worth but
   small;
Little thou't love, or not at all.
   (*Hesperides* text)

Stanza 2 is hard to follow, the text being apparently corrupt, but the argument is somewhat as follows: the man disinclined to love is told that he is not cold enough after all to escape love, or if he is, he lacks normal human warmth, is a soulless lump of clay, and should take a "Cure," namely a look into the eyes of some beauty who will make him "lasciuious strong in loue." This seemingly ironic reversal of the first stanza's argument derives part of its wit from being sung to the tune of stanza 1 while contradicting it. For a readers' version Herrick rejects the self-contradiction. The notion of a lover's fire with which stanza 2 had played is briefly incorporated (line 7) into the enlarged list of conventional sufferings. The new lines 13–16 expand on the notion of woman's untrustworthiness with the conventional image of lunar changeability and lead well to the conclusion, "Little thou't love, or not at all." The *Hesperides* version is a more fully and carefully developed poem than the original, and its argument builds more coherently to

18. Stanza 1 from *Select Ayres and Dialogues* (1659), stanza 2 from B. M. Add. MS. 31432, William Lawes's autograph manuscript. See John P. Cutts, "British Museum Additional MS. 31432: William Lawes' Writing for Theatre and Court," p. 233.

a conclusion. But the original stanza alone, cheeky and succinct, is a better song text, made all the more fun by the tongue-in-cheek reversal or submission to love the second time through.

William Lawes's setting (*Select Ayres and Dialogues*, 1659, p. 8) shows what a composer could do with Herrick's original stanzas. He treats the lovers' woes (measures 5–16) with devices inherited from the madrigal tradition: sequential figures for parallel phrases, rests setting off the "sighs" and "sobs," and half-cadences for poignancy.

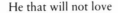

He that will not love

both tor-men-ting Lo - vers e - ver.   Wouldst   thou

know be - sides all these,   how hard   a Wo - man 'tis   to please?

how high she's priz'd whose worth's but small?   little thou'lt love or nought at all.

The list of woes comprising lines 5–7 (expanded to lines 5–9 in *Hesperides*), brief as it is when read, is quite long enough for song; a longer list would tempt a composer to continue too long with conventional expressive devices. After the lovers' woes, Lawes effectively changes to triple time for the misogynist antilove arguments: the difficulty of pleasing a woman and her small value as compared to a lover's inflated estimate of her. This section, set in the contrasting frame of common time before and after it, reflects the poem's mock-scornful jocularity—as if the man is dancing to the lady's tune in spite of himself, a suggestion repeated by the "cure" passage for the triple-time section in stanza 2. Even the less readable second stanza, when sung, contributes to this ironic mood. Herrick's first stanza is perfectly apt for the kind of treatment Lawes gave it: just long enough to complete a readily understandable, lightly posed argument, just short enough to fit a stanzaic, semideclamatory song structure (as opposed to dialogue or other longer forms).[19]

This ability to say just enough to make a punchy argument but not too much for the musical scope of brief solo song was one of Herrick's assets as a songwriter. Another was his genius as a phrasemaker. His smoothly flowing lines were inset with little gems of suggestive phrases. Henry Lawes was especially taken with such phrases as the "Spring's / Soft and soule-melting murmurings" mentioned above, or "The sweets of love are wash'd with tears," from "The Primrose," or "Time has spilt snow upon your hair," from the song version of "To a Gentlewoman, objecting to him his gray haires"

19. Herrick wrote quite a few longer poems for such treatment and some of the settings are extant. But I am here concerned primarily with his short, usually stanzaic songs.

(*Ayres and Dialogues*, 1653, p. 19).[20] In this song, Lawes's opening measures build up to the phrase, which becomes an emphatic cadence.

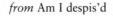

from Am I despis'd

Robert Herrick   Henry Lawes

(measures 1–12)

The last two phrases mentioned above have both been altered in *Hesperides*, where the first reads, "The sweets of love are mixt with tears." Perhaps the idea of "sweets" being "washed" struck Herrick as too loose a metaphor for reflective readers. But such a consideration would not trouble anyone hearing it sung, and the original version, with its suggestions of purification and of great quantities of flowing watery tears, seems superior as potential music. The phrase about Time spilling snow from "To a Gentlewoman" is likewise more suggestive musically than the longer phrase that replaces it (see below). Herrick made numerous changes in this song:

To his Mistress objecting his Age.	To a Gentlewoman, objecting to him his gray haires.
Am I dispis'd because you say,	Am I despis'd, because you say,
and I believe, that I am gray?	And I dare sweare, that I am gray?
know, Lady, you have but your day,	Know, Lady, you have but your day:

20. Willa Evans gives two more examples (*Henry Lawes*, p. 157): "weeping superabundantly" from "Leanders Obsequies" and "it frisks, it flyes, now here, now there" from "The Kisse."

and night will come, when men will swear	And time will come when you shall weare
Time has spilt snow upon your hair;	Such frost and snow upon your haire:
Then when in your glass you seek,	And when (though long it comes to passe)
but find no Rose-bud in your cheek,	You question with your Looking-glasse;
no, nor the bed to give the shew,	And in that sincere *Christall* seek,
where such a rare Carnation grew;	But find no Rose-bud in your cheek:
and such a smiling Tulip too.	Nor any bed to give the shew
Ah, then, too late, close in your chamber keeping,	Where such a rare Carnation grew.
it will be told	Ah! then too late, close in your chamber keeping,
that you are old,	It will be told
by those true tears y'are weeping.	That you are old;
(Henry Lawes's text)	By those true teares y'are weeping.
	(from *Hesperides*)

The first change, from "I believe" to "I dare sweare," makes the poem right away more a reader's or declaimer's and less an arioso singer's text. The rougher, slower phrase suggests a speaking voice, replacing a light, smooth phrase that had attracted no attention. For the day-night contrast of lines 3–4, one of those elemental sensory contrasts so effective in song, Herrick substitutes a metaphorically more consistent phrase, one which does not conflate the day-night and summer-winter images for transitoriness but instead concentrates only on winter. The new passage begins by alluding to the speaker's gray hairs mentioned in the new title, introducing the lady's grayness somewhat more gently or subtly than the first version had. The change is proper, for tactical subtlety can be valuable in lyrics to be read; here it creates a tone of gentleness that adds to the thrust of the argument. In song, on the other hand, such subtlety is usually lost; sharp contrasts and emphatic direct statements are more common. Thus in the revision, "Time has spilt snow upon your hair" is replaced by the longer, less blunt sentence with parallel subordinate clauses ("when . . . and when"). The imagined looking-glass scene is thus introduced a little more slowly and, as it seems, more gently: the new concessive insertions "(though long it comes to passe)" and "when . . . / You question with your Looking-glasse" bring out the bad news gradually. The last hint before actual statement of it is the new telling phrase for the mirror, "that sincere *Christall*." The "smiling Tulips" of line 10, which Henry Lawes found useful for intensifying the sense of loss over the lady's vanished floral beauty, are discarded as extra padding in the argument, after the roses and carnations. After the ten isometric lines, the mixed rhythms of the final four lines, with the pauses set up by their concluding fourteener and its internal rhymes,[21] clearly suggest song more than speech,

---

21. A fourteener after isometric lines became a common device of song-text conclusion during the madrigal and lute-song era, and many variants of it were used, as I noted in Chap. II.

as if the gentle, aging lover would conclude his answering reproach with a sympathetic moment of musical lyricism, a suggested refrain structure after an isometric stanza. This ending Herrick keeps intact in the new version.

There is no need to find fault with most of Herrick's alterations. Some are improvements unrelated to the differences between song mode and other lyric modes. Certain others, as I have shown, are changes calculated to transform Amphion into Hermes, to remake some of Herrick's fluid song texts into something closer to the wittily reasoned mode of the speaking voice that had become so prominent in English lyric by midcentury, even in many of the lyrics for song setting. Herrick's transformations were never complete, and his songs remain essentially in song mode. Indeed the evidence of the songbooks indicates that he made only minor revisions in most of the song texts he incorporated. The three I have discussed in some detail were more thoroughly revised and are important because they demonstrate that he recognized some differences between songs and lyrics for reading.[22] Since songs constitute such a large proportion of the poems in *Hesperides*, we should keep in mind in reading it that many important features of the poems—their length, their relative density or bareness of imagery, their smoothly flowing rhythms, and their more or less fully developed argumentation—were influenced by the conventions of traditional song mode.

Though Herrick knew some ways to make lyrics more apt for speaking or declaiming, it is not surprising that he wanted to keep most of his songs essentially as they were. Few poets have ever been more enamored of musicality in the sense of smoothly flowing yet subtly varied rhythms, and few have felt a fonder attachment to their "smoothly musicall"[23] literary offspring, the "poor Orphans"[24] the poet would leave behind.

Some of his song texts may be very brief because they were written for rounds or canons, a form which required a miniature text. Three such rounds to Herrick texts, by William Webb, appear in John Hilton's *Catch that Catch Can* (1652): a drinking song, a song of grief, and a little evening prayer.[25] Others may be brief because, as we have seen, Herrick sometimes did considerable cutting. Still others may strike us as light and spare, may seem to glide by too smoothly and easily, for all their elegant, original turns of phrase, simply because they are good song texts, designed to let a composer shape them—quicken or retard the pace, stretch or foreshorten sounds, and create expressive intensity with purely musical means. The talented song composer Charles Coleman,[26] in a commendatory poem for the second

---

22. Another such extensively revised lyric is "Upon *Mistresse* Elizabeth Wheeler" ("Sweet *Amarillis*, by a Spring's"). For Henry Lawes's text see John Cutts, "A Bodleian Song-Book: Don. c. 57," p. 210.

23. From "To *Apollo*. A Short Hymne."

24. See "To his Verses" (Martin, *Herrick's Poetical Works*, p. 218) and "Upon his Verses" (p. 236), among many other fond poems addressed to his "book."

25. "Let me sleep this night away," a "canon," since its text is sacred.

26. On Coleman's merits see Ian Spink, *English Song, Dowland to Purcell*, pp. 115–18.

book of *Select Ayres and Dialogues*, said of Henry Lawes, "Musick does owe Thee much, the Poet more; / Thou lift'st him up, and dost new Nature bring, / Thou giv'st his noblest Verse both *Feet* and *Wing*." Herrick's song texts came already endowed with feet and wings; composers had only to set them in motion and direct their course. The songs they composed can help us to analyze Herrick's lyrics and to read them with alert ears for their proper pleasures.

That song-mode lyric was Herrick's great strength has long been recognized, for example in the phrase "the last Elizabethan."[27] But as we saw with Sidney, Campion, Herbert, and other song poets, smooth simplicity and a sense of conceptual spareness in lyrics are deliberate effects especially characteristic of song mode, an apparent artlessness achieved only with great skill. Modern commentary on Herrick has done well to explore some of the riches in the depths beneath his liquid surface. But even that surface, with its calm places, ripples, or flowing waves, is no mean creation. The gentle, poised sorrow and hurt of that middle-aged suitor, for example, and the plausible mixture of recrimination and sympathy that he serves up to his lady—these would not be what they are nor leave with us such a distinct impression without the patterned, song-mode rhythms that are part of their poetic definition.

27. Leon Mandel, *Robert Herrick: The Last Elizabethan*.

IV. Song Mode in Crashaw

ichard Crashaw's verse has been called "mellifluously musical . . . the song of the nightingale 'bathing in streams of liquid melody' . . . the passage work, the cadenzas, the glissandi of a virtuoso."[1] Ruth Wallerstein saw the "lyric sweep" of his verse as influenced by anthems and instrumental music, with effects akin to polyphony and staccato, and thought that the "Hymn to the Name," read aloud, "displays a symphonic design."[2] While such metaphorical and sometimes anachronistic uses of musical terms can suggest Crashaw's special qualities, I will take a more concrete approach to his musicality, examining his song-mode prosody and rhetoric and studying the manner in which composers have set his texts.[3] Crashaw, we will find, learned to incorporate song-mode passages for special effects into his own version of grand lyric, his mature ode. If Herbert alternated or contrasted song and speech modes and Herrick made subtle adjustments from the one toward the other, Crashaw took still another stylistic approach: he learned to intermingle song-mode passages with primarily declamatory verse.

He wrote practically pure song mode in some of his early verse, as in the poem on the Virgin's assumption, translating a passage from the Song of Songs set by composers in many languages:

Rise up my faire, my spotlesse one,
The Winter's past, the raine is gone:
The Spring is come, the Flowers appeare,

---

1. Austin Warren, *Richard Crashaw: A Study in Baroque Sensibility*, pp. 178–79. On Crashaw's musical allusions see Lee A. Jacobus, "The Musical Duel in 'Musicks Duell.'"
2. *Richard Crashaw: A Study in Style and Poetic Development*, pp. 37–49.
3. Louis Martz, in "The Action of the Self," takes this approach in parts of his analysis of Crashaw's poem on the Virgin's assumption.

No sweets since thou art wanting here.
>Come away my Love,
>Come away my Dove
>>cast off delay:
>The Court of Heav'n is come,
>To wait upon thee home;
>>Come away, come away.[4]

His youthful translations, some preserved in *The Delights of the Muses* and *Steps to the Temple*, gave him practice in such verse. In the vein of earlier "Italian madrigals English'd after the affection of the note," three texts of the late sixteenth century are closely imitated in rhythm and stanza form (the third had been set by Luca Marenzio). Catullus's *Carmen* V, of which Campion, among others, had done an elegant translation and setting, is creditably rendered in tetrameters. Psalm 137 ("By the rivers of Babylon"), a favorite of lyrical translators (for instance, Campion and Carew),[5] is done in a stanza form of mixed line lengths reminiscent of many lute songs. A Latin epigram of Crashaw's is translated into a song in tetrameter quatrains, "Jesu, no more, it is full tide." The song "Lord, when the sense of thy sweet grace," which Crashaw later published with the Theresa poems, also seems to be a relatively early work; an anonymous setting of it appears in a manuscript of songs from the 1630s and 1640s.[6]

Praz has called Crashaw's version of Ceba's song, which duplicates the original meter, a "masterly" rendering.[7]

>To thy Lover
>Deere, discover
That sweet blush of thine that shameth
>>(When those Roses
>>It discloses)
All the flowers that Nature nameth.
. . . .
>>When my dying
>>Life is flying;
Those sweet Aires that often slew mee;
>>Shall revive mee,
>>Or reprive mee,
And to many Deaths renew mee.
>>>(stanzas 1, 9)

As in many such texts, a sense of flowing motion is created by the lengthened line after the crisp dimeters. The many feminine rhymes, such as the

---

4. Crashaw poems are cited from L. C. Martin, ed., *The Poems in English Latin and Greek of Richard Crashaw*, 2d ed.

5. Mario Praz, in *The Flaming Heart*, pp. 242–43, compares Crashaw's version with Campion's.

6. On this manuscript see John Cutts, "A Bodleian Song-Book: Don. c. 57."

7. Cited in George W. Williams, ed., *The Complete Poetry of Richard Crashaw*, p. 545.

conventional madrigalian roses-discloses, arrows-sparrows, borrow-sorrow, and dying-flying, give the song the lilting quality of extended trochaic meter in English. For Crashaw in his mature verse these meters and rhymes would provide a lilting or chiming suggestion of music in appropriate passages.

The song deriving from Marino, using the conceit of love's fire as divisible into the lady's light and the lover's heat, also shows Crashaw's rhythmic skill in creating a song meter and patterned stanza worthy of the original.

> Love now no fire hath left him,
> We two betwixt us have divided it.
> Your Eyes the Light have reft him.
> The heat commanding in my *Heart* doth sit,
> O! that poore Love be not for ever spoyled,
> Let my *Heat* to your *Light* be reconciled.
> So shall these flames, whose worth
> Now all obscured lyes
> (Drest in those Beames) start forth
> And dance before your eyes.
>
> Or else partake my flames
> (I care not whither)
> And so in mutuall Names
> Of Love, burne both together.[8]

The meter is primarily iambic, but as in many madrigal and song texts (especially in French chansons), the initial lines of the sections (lines 1 and 7—here also 5, 6, and 9) begin with a trochee or spondee, which can be variously handled by composers, but commonly with a firm half-note or at least a dotted quarter as the opening note in a section or line. In the verse this makes for a recurrent pattern of ´ˣˣ´ or ^ˣ´ (a choriambic rhythm, as we noted earlier) playing against the iambic meter. This variation being a common feature of song verse, Crashaw's meter here is highly regular.

Having established a pattern of alternating trimeter/pentameter lines, the song's opening section breaks that pattern with a rhymed pentameter couplet, resulting in what I have called a conclusion rhythm (see Chapter II) for this portion of the poem. The two following four-line trimeter sections imply an ABB structure sometimes found in lute songs, whereby the melody for section 2 (lines 7–10) would be repeated or closely imitated in section 3 (lines 11–14). John Wilson, Crashaw's contemporary, did a setting of "Love now no fire," which, while it is through-composed in a declamatory style and not in that of the lute-song era, retains these sections as the verbal rhythms define them.[9]

8. Williams and Martin both print the Italian originals of the songs.

9. For an edition with keyboard realization, see *Poèmes de Donne, Herbert et Crashaw mis en musique par leurs contemporains*, ed. André Souris. The song is from Wilson's manuscript given to the Bodleian in 1656, Bod. Mus. b 1, ff. 138v–139.

from Love now no fire hath left him

Richard Crashaw   John Wilson
(Trans. from Marino)

Love now no fire hath left him, we two be-

twixt us have di - vi - ded it. Your eyes the light have reft him,

— the heat com - man - ding in my heart doth sit.

O that poor Love be not for - e - ver spoil - ed

let my heat to your light be re - con - ci - led.

(measures 1–18)

As in Chapter II we see Wilson, like other midcentury declamatory composers, closely imitating verse rhythms and the pitch patterns of the reading voice, attempting thus to preserve in song and even to intensify the poem's meaning. He reflects the ´ˣˣ´ or ˆˣ´ pattern in various rhythms: slow notes followed by sixteenth notes in measure 1, and syncopation in measure 3 (used again in "Drést ĭn thŏˣse béams"). He takes "Ó! thăˣt pŏˣor Lóve bĕˣ nŏˣt" in line 5 as a hint for dactylic meter, switching to triple time for lines 5 and 6, as he does again for the final quatrain with its "mútŭăl Námes ŏf Lòve búrn." The interpretive harmony of the song also deserves notice. It images the poem's central conceit, love's fire as the lover's heat and the light in the lady's eyes. For example, at the start of measure 8, a cross relation between G and the G♯ of the lute part marks the division between the light and the heat. After this harmonic divergence, the C major chord ending "Let my heat to your light be reconciled" provides a contrasting harmonic reconciliation in the relative major key of the initial A minor.

Besides the feminine rhymes and metric and stanza patterns common in song texts, such as those observed in "To my lover" and "Love now no fire," we find in parts of Crashaw's poems another distinctive feature of song verse: its frequent use of rhetorical "figures of sound," such as anaphora, epiphora, anadiplosis, epanalepsis, ploce, antimetabole, and alliteration.[10] These are especially useful in song, aiding auditors' word comprehension. For the same reason they are frequent in oratory or declamation also, as we noted in Chapter I. But they stand out more prominently in song verse, since in declamation they usually compete for notice with other foregrounded artifices of rhetoric and syntax. Thus smooth, grammatically simple verse making frequent, prominent use of them is apt to sound songlike, to evoke musical associations. They abound in E. H. Fellowes's *English Madrigal Verse: 1588–1632*: for anaphora, John Bartlet's "All my wits hath will enwrapped; / All my sense desire entrapped; / All my faith to fancy fixed"; for anadiplosis, Dowland's "Now, O now, I needs must part, / Parting though I absent mourn. / Absence can no joy impart"; for antimetabole, Dowland's "Gone are all my joys at once. / I loved thee and thee alone, / In whose love I joyed once" (joys, loved—love, joyed); for ploce, Robert Jones's "She hath an eye, ah me! ah me! / She hath an eye, an eye to see; / Ah me, that an eye / Should make her live" (the repeated word *eye*).

Crashaw's "Hymn of the Nativity" is a dialogue song of a type that, as we have noted, was popular at court in the late 1620s and the 1630s in declamatory settings by Italianate composers such as Nicholas Lanier and

10. For further illustration of such devices in song and declamatory mode see Chap. I above. Eugene R. Cunnar, in "Richard Crashaw and the Hymn Tradition," notes that anaphora and epistrophe (epiphora) are characteristic of classical hymns, and he sees Crashaw's use of them as part of the hymnic nature of his mature poems.

Robert Ramsey. It affords many examples of the favorite rhetorical devices of song.

> Tell him [the sun] hee rises now too late,
> To shew us ought worth looking at. ·   10
>
> Tell him wee now can shew him more
>   Then hee e're shewd to mortall sight,
> Then hee himselfe e're saw before,
>   Which to be seene needs not his light:
> Tell him *Tityrus* where th'hast been,   15
> Tell him *Thyrsis* what th'hast seen.
> . . . . : . . . .
>
> The Babe lookt up, and shew'd his face,
>   In spight of Darknesse it was Day.   20
> It was thy Day, Sweet, and did rise,
> Not from the East, but from thy eyes.
> . . . .
>
> Welcome to our wondring sight . . .   53
> Great litle one, whose glorious Birth,
> Lifts Earth to Heaven, stoops heaven to earth.
>   (from stanzas 2–4, 10)

Anaphora is especially prominent here (lines 9, 11, 15, 16 and 12, 13). Lines 15 and 16 combine anaphora and epiphora, thus forming an example of symploce. Anadiplosis (lines 20–21), ploce (the *shew*s of lines 10–12), and antimetabole (lines 56–58) are also used. These devices work nicely to help keep Crashaw's word play on the Christmas paradoxes clear and to give a sense of smooth symmetry despite the intellectual effort embodied in the argument.

The smoothness, metrical patterning, and rhetorical devices of song mode, used skillfully, could aid a poet in spinning out a conventional, perhaps even paradoxical, conceit without losing the auditors. The singer or auditor might not follow the precise variations on the conceit, but would at least be aware, through the word repetitions, of which one was being played with. Crashaw's "Song of Divine Love" (1648 title) following the Theresa poems is a good illustration.

> Lord, when the sense of thy sweet grace
> Sends vp my soul to seek thy face.
> Thy blessed eyes breed such desire,
> I dy in loue's delicious Fire.
>   O loue, I am thy SACRIFICE.
> Be still triumphant, blessed eyes.
> Still shine on me, fair suns! that I
> Still may behold, though still I dy.
>
>   Second part.
>   Though still I dy, I liue again;
> Still longing so to be still slain,

So gainfull is such losse of breath,
I dy euen in desire of death.
   Still liue in me this louing strife
Of liuing DEATH & dying LIFE.
For while thou sweetly slayest me
Dead to my selfe, I liue in Thee.

The smooth meter and correlation of lines with syntactic units, in conjunction with couplet rhymes and frequent alliteration, make the verse flow and glide. The middle section of the poem uses the devices of ploce (the many repetitions of "still" for the undying divine love) and anadiplosis (linking the two stanzas through the repeated "though still I dy"). Alliteration becomes dense in the final quatrain (live, loving, living, Life), adding intensity to this formulation of the Pauline paradox of reborn living as dying. And finally, lines 12–14 display an intricate double antimetabole: the AB–BA word-form pattern of die, death–Death, dying is interlocked with that of live, loving–living, Life. "Lord, when the sense" is probably Crashaw's purest example of song mode. Warren notes some of its song features and calls it "incantatory." [11]

In placing this song after the last Theresa poem, Crashaw follows the same format as do some of Herbert's two-part poems (such as "An Offering" or "Christmas"—see Chapter II, n. 2): a meditation in speech rhythms is followed by a song-mode lyric as an act of prayer. An anonymous setting of the late 1630s or 1640s had used an earlier version of the poem; [12] the difference between it and the 1648 version confirms this view of Crashaw's revision. Its text reads, instead of lines 13–14 above ("Still live in me . . ."), "O welcome high and Heavenly art / Of life and death in one poore heart." But in the 1648 *Steps to the Temple* Crashaw made the song a fourth and final poem of the Theresa sequence and therefore introduced the new "living death" and "dying life" antimetabole to link it closely with the end of the third Theresa poem: "Let me so read thy life, that I / Vnto all life of mine may dy."

Heightening the effect of emphatic words and phrases in declamatory fashion, the composer of the song has closely followed Crashaw's text. Through elongation of certain words—just before or during which a singer would have improvised ornaments or "graces"—the composer stresses the key terms of the poem's conceit, a sacred parody of the one in the love song discussed earlier: while the soul's love takes the form of "delicious" heat, God's grace or love (line 1) is the light of favor beaming from those "faire sunns," the "blessed eyes" of God's face. The composer elongates exactly these words, "grace" and "eyes."

11. *Richard Crashaw*, pp. 173–74.
12. The song is from Bod. MS. Don. c. 57, f. 68; see note 9 for a modern edition of this song also.

Lord, when the sense of thy sweet grace

Richard Crashaw   anon.

Lord, when the sense of thy sweet grace sends up my soul to see thy face, thy blessed eyes breed such de-sire, I die in Love's de-li-cious fire. O Love I am thy sac-ri-fice. Be still tri-um-phant bles-sed eyes. Still shine on me, fair suns, that I still may be-hold though still I die. Though still I die, I live a-gain, still longing so to be still slain. So gainful is such loss of breath, I die ev'n in de-sire of death.

Besides the emphasis on "grace" and "eyes," another reflection of the text is the melody for the first two lines of stanza 2. Except for those, the setting is strophic—the second stanza repeats the melody for the first. But there the composer changed the music to imitate the anadiplosis on "though still I die," which bridges the pause between stanzas: the melody is repeated when the phrase occurs the second time (measures 12–14), with the result that the music does not match that of the corresponding passage in stanza 1. Also, by revising the melody of these two lines, he could reflect the longing "to be slayne" in jerky, dotted-note rhythms.

The song does indeed reflect the dying and dying again of the text, though musically it seems rather heavy-handed. Here we see the declamatory composer devoted to his text in a way in which the lutenist composer would not have been. Such were the new settings Crashaw would have heard at Cambridge and perhaps at Oxford in the early 1640s,[13] and they must have reinforced for him the song-related poetic devices he already knew and used, even though their expressive treatment of texts was different from that of the lute-song era. "Lord, when the sense" could be considered a "pathetic air" in Elise Jorgens's terms, a strophic song, in style midway between the declamatory and the tuneful.

In Crashaw's early poems he generally based poetic structure on the stanza unit. Praz notes of "The Weeper," "The unit is not the poem, but the stanza, the madrigal," as in Marino's "collection of madrigals on Maddalena a i piedi di Cristo," so that the poem is a "rosary" of self-sufficient stanzas.[14] Such structure recurs even in some presumably late poems, like

13. Martin (*Poems of Crashaw*, pp. xxii–xxxii) describes Crashaw's stays and travels of these years.
14. *The Flaming Heart*, pp. 218–19.

"Sancta Maria Dolorum." But as Warren observes, Crashaw's development was away from small-unit structure toward the large intellectual scope and discursive ordering of his last odes or hymns, as we see in "Prayer. An Ode"; in its 1648 text Crashaw eliminated the stanza divisions of 1646, using only indentations of shorter lines, as in the mature odes.[15] Eugene Cunnar says that the mature Crashaw was influenced by Scaliger to think that irregular verses are apt for expressing the inspiration of the Holy Spirit, as in classical hymns they showed Dionysiac fervor.[16] This was not only Scaliger's view but, as we will note in connection with Milton, a widespread humanist idea; it probably did influence Crashaw. In terms of meter, word repetitions, and other aural features, the idea of intermingled declamatory and song modes will help explain his characteristic effects and will clarify their functions in the poems. The apparent absence of stanzas in the mature verse does not mean that Crashaw forgot about stanzas or about song, though his verse divisions are not marked with spacing. Declamatory mode is there interspersed with passages displaying features of song mode: smoothly flowing meter, sometimes isometric verse and sometimes variable lines creating patterned rhythms leading to a pause or conclusion, rhyme syncopation,[17] feminine rhymes, tripping anapestic or dactylic substitutions, and the favorite rhetorical devices of song poets.

To illustrate, I want to discuss the much praised—but sometimes dispraised—"symphonic" hymn "To the Name," where the song-related effects need careful explication. First, in examining its metric structures and their correlation with syntax and thematic development, we find that Crashaw's habitual loose stanzas of nine to eighteen lines are present, as in earlier works, though they are marked not by spacing but by conclusion rhythms, syntactic full stops, and subsequent emphatic opening phrases for each new "stanza." Most of these "stanzas" are in declamatory or oratorical mode and are similar in rhythm and pace to the stanzas of Cowley's odes, but certain of them are in song mode or are close to it, comprising, as it were, brief inset songs or chants at appropriate points in the argument.

The predominant declamatory mode is well illustrated in the following passage near the beginning of the poem, with its free-swinging meter, heavy accentuation, and lengthy periods, wherein the poet makes figurative preparations for Holy Name Sunday.

> Goe, SOVL, out of thy Self, & seek for More.
> 　　　Goe & request
> Great NATVRE for the KEY of her huge Chest

---

15. *Richard Crashaw*, pp. 164–66.
16. "Richard Crashaw and the Hymn Tradition," pp. 143–44.
17. The rhyming of unequal lines is named "rhyme syncopation" in Joseph Summers's *George Herbert*, pp. 228–29, nn. 4–5.

Of Heauns, the self inuoluing Sett of Sphears
(Which dull mortality more Feeles then heares)
. . . .
And beat a summons in the Same
      All-soueraign Name
To warn each seuerall kind
And shape of sweetnes, Be they such
      As sigh with supple wind
      Or answer Artfull Touch,
That they conuene & come away
To wait at the loue-crowned Doores of
      This Illustrious DAY.
Shall we dare This, my Soul? we'l doe't and bring
No Other note for't, but the Name we sing.
          (lines 27–31, 35–45)

Using imagery from "speculative" and "practical" music, the speaker invokes both music's natural powers (of the spheres, which our souls as harmonic beings sense) and its human or artificial powers. The "shapes of sweetness" are wind and string instruments called to assemble at the church door for this "work of Love," celebrating the feast day. The percussionist beats a summons in the Name (perhaps a dactylic *in nomine domini*), and even the "note" or mode of the music ("No Other note for't, but the Name") will be, not Dorian or Phrygian, but the "Name of Jesus" mode, as if the letters *Iesu* could define a set of tones, as Bach later would compose variations on the theme defined by his own name. Such musical metaphors dominate what I would call stanzas 3–7 of "To the Name," down to "And in the wealth of one Rich *Word* proclaim / New similes to Nature." Together they portray a scene of all creation as a grand chorus and orchestra singing the Name.

The speaker has begun the poem by doing some of that singing, part of the divine entertainment of the day.

I sing the NAME which None can say
But touch't with An interiour RAY:
The Name of our NEW PEACE; our Good:
Our Blisse: & Supernaturall Blood:
The name of All our Liues & Loues.
Hearken, And Help, ye holy Doues!
The high-born Brood of Day; you bright
Candidates of blissefull Light,
The HEIRS Elect of Loue; whose Names belong
Vnto The euerlasting life of Song;
All ye wise SOVLES, who in the wealthy Brest
Of This vnbounded NAME build your warm Nest.

The opening lines, paraphrasing First Corinthians 12:3, which says that no one can confess Jesus except in the Spirit, are regular iambic tetrameters down to "Hearken and Help," a choriambic substitution, as I have noted, so common in song verse that it can be considered regular. Creating a conclusion rhythm such as we found in Campion and Herbert, the truncated line 8 after iambic tetrameters, along with the pentameter couplet following it ("The Heirs . . ."), signals the approaching end of the first rhythmic unit or "stanza" on the couplet with its choriambic opening, "All ye wise Soules" (lines 11–12). Only the last line has heavy, irregular accentuation, as if the invocation to the saints should end on whole notes. This lengthening of the lines to pentameter, hexameter, or even heptameter is Crashaw's usual way, in the hymn to the Name, of providing a conclusion rhythm for each section or "stanza." He often then adds another long line, to end a section with an isometric rhymed couplet. Besides the choriambic substitutions ("Hearken and Help," "All ye wise Soules") and the metrical smoothness, other features evocative of song here are the use of ploce (the Name in lines 1, 3, 5, 9, and 12) and dense alliteration (Hearken, Help, holy, high-born). The saints in their redeemed state within the "everlasting life of Song" are here well invoked.

The second "stanza" continues in song mode:

> Awake, My glory. SOVL, (if such thou be,
> And That fair WORD at all referr to Thee)
>   Awake & sing
>   And be All Wing;
> Bring hither thy whole SELF; & let me see
> What of Thy parent HEAVN yet speakes in thee.
>   O thou art Poore
>   Of noble POWRES, I see,
> And full of nothing else but empty ME,
> Narrow, & low, & infinitely lesse
> Then this GREAT mornings mighty Busynes.
>   (lines 13–23)

A rhythmic shift signals the end of the question and the beginning of the answer. After the speaker has asked how much of heaven is in him, the short lines "O thou art Poore / Of noble POWRES, I see" create an appropriate pause, signaling that we are now beginning the answer to the question. Then, as in most of the poem's other "stanzas," the lines lengthen for the conclusion, on the pentameter couplet. Besides the smoothness and this metrical patterning, another feature suggesting song here is the repeated injunction to "Awake . . . Awake and sing," with its use of the short-lined couplet reminiscent of many songs, for example Byrd's madrigal "Awake, mine eyes, see Phoebus bright arising."

After this opening in song mode comes the lengthy declamatory invocation to all creatures to join in musical praise, described above. Then the speaker demonstrates his claim to a place in the throng singing the Name with a tender song of apology to the angels and saints, "stanza" 8.

> May it be no wrong
> Blest Heauns, to you, & your Superiour song,
> That we, dark Sons of Dust & Sorrow,
>   A while Dare borrow   100
> The Name of Your Delights & our Desires,
> And fitt it to so farr inferior LYRES.
> Our Murmurs haue their Musick too,
> Ye mighty ORBES, as well as you,
>   Nor yeilds the noblest Nest   105
> Of warbling SERAPHIM to the eares of Loue,
> A choicer Lesson then the ioyfull BREST
>   Of a poor panting Turtle-Doue.
> And we, low Wormes haue leaue to doe
> The Same bright Busynes (ye Third HEAVENS) with you.   110
> Gentle SPIRITS, doe not complain.
>   We will haue care
>   To keep it fair,
> And send it back to you again.

This "stanza" or section is itself a song in three six-line stanzas. The first of these (lines 97–102) follows a common lute-song stanza pattern (short, long, long, short, long, long), using rhyme syncopation (see note 16) except for the concluding couplet. The second follows an equally common pattern (long, long, short, long, long, short), again with four syncopated rhymes. The third ("And we . . .") uses a favorite Herbertian conclusion pattern (4, 2, 2, 4), which Crashaw also uses to end some other "stanzas" of the poem, such as the song section ending on line 196. Along with these rhythms, the smooth meter from lines 101–14, the dense alliteration, and the stock madrigalian rhymes *sorrow-borrow*, *desires-lyres*, and *complain-again* suggest song, as do the frequent short syntactic units neatly corresponding with verse lines, especially from "Our Murmurs" onward. The poor mortal singing a "choice lesson" of love among immortal angels is a striking figure who makes a still stronger impression when we notice the verbal music of his song.

Following this apology comes the climactic midsection of the poem, the invocation to the Name itself and its subsequent appearance. The triune invocation falls into three roughly equal "stanzas" beginning respectively "Come, lovely Name," "Come, Lovely Name," and "Come *Royal* Name." The first "stanza" (in contrast to the "dove" song relatively emphatic and declamatory in mode, with plosive consonants and a few clustered accents) ends, like the "dove" song, with the 4, 2, 2, 4 rhythm. The second and third "stanzas" are songlike, metrically smoother, and reminiscent of many love songs, perhaps especially of Dowland's famous "Cóme awǎy, cóme, swěet lóve, / Thě gólděn mórnǐng bréaks," cited in Chapter I. The several repetitions of "Come" and "Come away" and the use of anaphora (Lo, lo how, lo how; O see, O see) are among the song-related features of these last two sections of invocation to the Name:

Come, louely Name; life of our hope!
Lo we hold our HEARTS wide ope!
Vnlock thy Cabinet of DAY
Dearest Sweet, & come away.
          Lo how the thirsty Lands
Gasp for thy Golden Showres! with long stretch't Hands
          Lo how the laboring EARTH
          That hopes to be
          All Heauen by THEE,
          Leapes at thy Birth.
The'attending WORLD, to wait thy Rise,
          First turn'd to eyes;
And then, not knowing what to doe;
Turn'd Them to TEARES, & spent Them too.
Come ROYALL Name, & pay the expence
Of All this Pretious Patience.
          O come away
And kill the DEATH of This Delay.
O see, so many WORLDS of barren yeares
Melted & measur'd out in Seas of TEARES.
O see, The WEARY liddes of wakefull Hope
(LOVE'S Eastern windowes) All wide ope
          With Curtains drawn,
To catch The Day-break of Thy DAWN.
O dawn, at last, long look't for Day!
Take thine own wings, & come away.
          (lines 125–50)

The traditions of the aubade (lovers' dawn song) provide special intensity here.[18] First the speaker poses as a lover outside the window calling "Unlock thy Cabinet" and "come away," as if the name were a lady being serenaded at dawn. Later, the soul is cast as the lady, waiting indoors with eastern windows thrown wide, longing for the first glimpse of daylight to signal the expected approach of the divine lover, King of names. Thus the speaker's love for the Name is imaged from both male and female perspectives on love.

This passage of two song-mode "stanzas," minus the lines on the world as eyes and the final couplet ("O dawn at last . . ."), was chosen by the modern composer Edward Bairstow as text of an anthem for baritone with optional chorus. Bairstow prints the text as a "lyric of the spirit" in two ten-line stanzas, which he considered so self-sufficient that he gave no hint of its context. As Bairstow's setting reflects, the choriambic substitution is so frequent in this passage as to become the most audible rhythm: "Cóme, lòvelў Náme, lífe ŏf oùr hópe"; "Ló hŏw thĕ thírstў"; "Gásp fŏr thў Góldĕn"; "Ló hŏw thĕ lábŏrĭng Eárth"; "Léaps ăt thў Bírth." Just as we saw in Campion's "Come, cheerful day" (see Chapter I), the choriambic rhythm is

18. Louis Martz, *The Wit of Love*, pp. 142–43, notes the importance of lovers' dawn songs for Crashaw's "An Hymne of the Nativity."

played off against the iambic. Its frequency within primarily iambic lines gives Crashaw's passage something of the feel of a courant, a dance in moderate tempo, noted for its frequent hemiola, or shifts between triple and duple time (6/4 with accents every second beat).

After this passionate song of appeal and desire, Crashaw returns to declamation to describe the Name's descent in a vividly imagined emblem. The white dove of the Spirit, immortal counterpart of the mortal dove who sang earlier, descends,[19] bearing the Name on his back in the form of a honey-laden, hive-shaped crown surrounded by angels as "diligent bees"—all common elements of emblem literature. A "*Synod* of All sweets" (perhaps imagined as a border of white-robed figures of saints holding fragrant "golden bowls of incense"—Rev. 5 : 8) surrounds and frames the dove, the hive, and its encircling bee spirits. This described emblem of the poem somewhat resembles the actual emblem printed with it by Thomas Carr.[20] The "synod" is proclaiming the imagined motto or superscript of the emblem: "That no Perfume / Forever shall presume / To passe for odoriferous / But such alone whose sacred Pedigree / Can prove Itself some kin (sweet name) to Thee," a scented version of the teaching from Acts that there is no other name whereby we must be saved.

Crashaw then turns once more to song, this time primarily isometric, to celebrate his emblem, in a passage some modern readers have found unpalatable.[21]

```
SWEET NAME, in Thy each Syllable
A Thousand Blest ARABIAS dwell;
A Thousand Hills of Frankincense;           185
Mountains of myrrh, & Beds of spices,
And ten Thousand PARADISES
The soul that tasts thee takes from thence.
How many vnknown WORLDS there are
Of Comforts, which Thou hast in keeping!     190
How many Thousand Mercyes there
In Pitty's soft lap ly a sleeping!
Happy he who has the art
        To awake them,
        And to take them                      195
Home, & lodge them in his HEART.
```

Anadiplosis links the song to the emblem depiction ("sweet name," "SWEET NAME"). The metrical pattern produces a sort of tetrameter sonnet, isometric down to line 193, so that the 4, 2, 2, 4 conclusion rhythm is espe-

---

19. A dove, in the usual Annunciation scene, announces the name Jesus.

20. See L. C. Martin's edition. George Williams, in *Image and Symbol in the Sacred Poetry of Richard Crashaw*, p. 108, denies this.

21. Livio Dobrez, in "The Crashaw-Teresa Relationship," calls "To the Name" a failure because this climactic passage covers the reader with "an avalanche of lollies."

cially prominent by contrast. The ploce of exorbitant numbers of sweets for the soul's delectation ("a Thousand," "a Thousand," "ten Thousand," "many Thousand") echoes the many kisses of Catullus's famous love song— in Crashaw's own translation:

A Thousand, and a Hundred, score
An Hundred, and a Thousand more,
Till another Thousand smother
That, and that wipe of another.
Thus at last when we have numbred
Many a Thousand, many a Hundred;
Wee'l confound the reckoning quite,
And lose our selves in wild delight.
(lines 11–18)

Images of taste and smell are especially favored by song poets because, lacking the articulation and detail of visual images, they can be forceful and easily apprehended in song. Nor is the song auditor apt to find repetitions of them cloying.[22] We should not read this passage as a piece of arithmetic and total the sweets; it is evoking a delirium of pleasure.

In remembering the three syllables of *Iesu* Crashaw may be thinking of Herbert's punning epigram ("Jesu") on the comforting name of Jesus as "I ease you." With the idea of the "Comforts" of the name, he turns from his mountains of spices to the image of a suckling baby in the lap, tasting divine pity and hearing a lullaby. The lilting rhythm of "Ĭn Píttў's sòft láp lỳ ă sléepĭng" makes us sense as well as conceive of a lullaby. We may be reminded of songs such as John Attey's "Sweet was the song the Virgin sung," with its many "lulla, lullabies." Having appealed supremely to the sense of sight with his dove emblem, Crashaw in his succeeding song fills out his appeal to the senses for perception of heavenly joy by turning to images of smell, taste, touch, hearing. The result suggests a kind of baroque *Gesamtkunstwerk*: the Name has brought us as much of the goodness of heaven as all our senses can perceive. The poem can return to Crashaw's forceful mode of declamation, this time with an epigrammatic quality, for the somber conclusion, the praise of the ancient martyrs and the warning of Judgment Day.

If portions of the poem are primarily in song mode while other passages are not (or only slightly so), we may wonder why Crashaw designated the whole poem a "hymn." Would not all of it, by implication, be singable? It would. But a setting of it following seventeenth-century conceptions would cast the bulk of the text as recitative, while the song-mode portions I have discussed would be sung to more lyrical or arioso melody. To this matter of Italian-style monodic setting, we turn our attention in the coming chapters on Milton and Cowley.

22. See John Bennet's madrigal, "O sweet grief, O sweet sighs, O sweet disdaining."

In our excursion through Crashaw's song verse and his ode or hymn "To the Name," I have noted many features of his style that relate to song verse, both as a mode of lyric and as words within settings. His characteristic mature idiom was strongly influenced by the conventions of songs. The same is true of other poets, but Crashaw was influenced in two special ways: in the frequency with which he created song-related effects for appropriate moments within the capacious scope of his mature "hymns," and in his ability to integrate these moments of song into vivid pictorial images. St. Theresa with the flaming arrow in her heart must not only "taste and see that the Lord is good" but also hear ravishing music, and we hear it too; the assembled majesty of heaven around the Name of Jesus must not only inhale, taste, and touch, it must also listen courteously to the mortal poet-dove warbling his songs, and we hear them too.

With this examination of Crashaw's hymnic odes, we have begun to follow the line of "grand lyric" development in seventeenth-century English poetry. Tracing the nexus of musical influence and major lyric poetry takes us in this direction. For while brief song lyrics continued to be written and set in the second half of the century, and while some of these are fine pieces, poets and composers in that vein did not continue to learn from each other as they had earlier. They did keep learning in this way in the ode and in the dramatic music of extended vocal pieces for public performance. In the first half of the book we have studied sonnets, madrigals, stanzaic lyrics both isometric and in stanza patterns of variable lines, dialogues and other lyrics apt for through-composed declamatory song, and, finally, a poet who began with these lyric forms but went on to use their effects in extensive odes. Now we turn to Milton and Cowley, to the "monody" of "Lycidas," the odes and monodies of *Samson Agonistes*, the inset lyrics of *Paradise Lost*, and then to Cowley's "Pindarics." It is cantata and chamber settings of such forms that point ahead to the achievements of eighteenth-century English vocal music.

V. Milton, G. B. Doni, and Italian Dramatic Song

aking as our guide the philologist and musical humanist Giovanni Battista Doni (1594–1647), we begin by tracing Milton's experiences of the theory and practice of Italian dramatic song. In that context we can appreciate his achievement with his own musically influenced, mainly declamatory/oratorical mode of lyric, his monody "Lycidas," the monodies and odes of *Samson Agonistes*, and the inset lyrics of *Paradise Lost*. For while this lyric verse is far from traditional English song mode in many respects (syntax, periodicity, absence of regular rhyme, complexity of imagery, and so on), it nevertheless has important connections with song—especially with the dramatic song forms of Italian music drama and chamber music. In such monodic song, with its interspersing of recitative and arioso passages, Milton experienced a musical milieu suited to his own developing mode of lyrical-dramatic verse: recitative, with its great flexibility of rhythm and tempo, had been developed especially to accommodate the sweeping arcs and grand rhythms of oratorical lyric as practiced by Tasso, Guarini, della Casa, and their imitators. So much has long been known to Miltonists familiar with the music of the period,[1] but we must consider its application to Milton's mature lyric verse. He has left us ample clues for the task.

---

1. Gretchen L. Finney, in *Musical Backgrounds for English Literature, 1580–1650*, p. 237, writes, "The oratorical quality of 'Lycidas' and its freedom of verse line may have been influenced by an imagined *stilo recitativo*." Angus Fletcher, in *The Transcendental Masque*, pp. 166–67, finds in *Comus* "an infusion of something like the impassioned feeling-tone of operatic recitative into Milton's prosody." MacDonald Emslie, in "Milton on Lawes," discusses Milton, Lawes, and the influence of recitative.

From *Comus* to *Paradise Lost* and *Samson Agonistes*, Italian theory and practice of musical-dramatic song were ingredients in his thinking about poetic genres. Even before he visited Italy he was reading *dramma per musica*, in part modeling *Comus* on "La Catena d'Adone" (1626, Ottavio Tronsarelli, music by Domenico Mazzocchi).[2] In calling "Lycidas" a monody he indicated what could be surmised anyway, that his pastoral *lamento* in modified canzone verse was related to contemporary monodies, dramatic monologues usually of lament, sung *in camera*, largely in recitative—for which mode of performance "Lycidas" is well suited. In Rome he witnessed a music drama at the Barberini Palace in February 1639, which must have been "Chi soffre, speri" (Giulio Rospigliosi, music by Mario Marazzoli and Virgilio Mazzocchi).[3] The academies and noblemen's chambers that he frequented offered performances of monodies, dialogues, and other musical-dramatic pieces;[4] on some such occasion he heard Leonora Baroni, the famous soprano (see the Leonora poems). Voltaire relates a tradition that he saw a performance of Giambattista Andreini's "L'Adamo" (1613), a partly spoken, partly sung *sacra rappresentazione*, and was thereby inspired to begin a tragedy of the Fall (such plans are indeed extant in the Trinity Manuscript).[5] True or not, Voltaire's story reflects the strong likelihood that Milton witnessed public, religious music dramas as well as private, usually secular ones such as "Chi soffre, speri." A fresh recollection of the *sacre rappresentazioni* and perhaps of oratorios was behind his recommendation in "The Reason of Church Government" (1642) that the populace should be inspired and instructed by "solemn paneguries" (moral entertainments of drama and music) rather than by "the interludes of libidinous and ignorant poetasters."[6] In the 1650s Milton aided in the release from prison of the Royalist William Davenant, who with Milton's former musical collaborator

2. Clay Hunt, in "*Lycidas" and the Italian Critics*, p. 191, is not convinced that "La Catena d'Adone" influenced *Comus*. But I find the parallels cited by Finney (*Musical Backgrounds*, pp. 175–94) quite convincing, implying a closer relationship than could be explained by common derivation of the two works from Marino. On "Lycidas," Hunt says that Milton had presumably subtitled the poem "A Monody" because "he had encountered the theory of monody as a modern musical form created by the Italian humanists, [and] formed the idea of a new art-form that would encompass almost everything he put into the writing of *Lycidas*" (p. 168).

3. Finney, *Musical Backgrounds*, pp. 175–95. For a brief account of the libretti of Rospigliosi (later Pope Clement IX) see Robert Haas, *Musik des Barocks*, p. 70.

4. G. B. Doni, lecturing in Florence in the early 1640s, said, "Here we daily hear comedy sung with such great diligence and grace that to many it seems that it could not be better" ("Qui sentiamo giornalmente Comedie con tanta grazia, e diligenza cantate, che non pare a molti, che si possa immaginar meglio") (*Lyra Barberina Amphichordos*, 2:167). This refers to frequent performances in Florentine chambers and academies.

5. See William R. Parker, *Milton: A Biography*, 2:830. On Milton and "L'Adamo," F. T. Prince, in *The Italian Element in Milton's Verse*, p. 153, says, "There is no doubt that Milton knew it." For a description and sampling of Andreini's text see John Arthos, "Milton, Andreini, and Galileo." On "L'Adamo" see also John Demaray, *Milton's Theatrical Epic*.

6. John Milton, *Complete Prose Works* (Yale edition), 1:819–20.

Henry Lawes then staged a musical entertainment and some music dramas.[7]
In the preface to *Samson Agonistes* Milton refers to certain humanist con-
cepts about Italian music drama as a revival of ancient theater, to suggest
what readers of this avowed closet drama should set up in their imagina-
tions for a mode of performance:

> *Chorus* is here introduc'd after the Greek manner, not antient only but modern,
> and still in use among the *Italians*. In the modelling therefore of this Poem,
> with good reason, the Antients and *Italians* are rather followed . . . . The mea-
> sure of Verse us'd in the Chorus is of all sorts, call'd by the Greeks *Mono-
> strophic*, or rather *Apolelymenon*, without regard had to *Strophe, Antistrophe*
> or *Epod*, which were a kind of Stanza's fram'd only for the Music, then us'd
> with the Chorus that sung, . . . or being divided into Stanzas or Pauses, they
> may be called *Allaeostropha* [stanzas of various length].[8]

What did Milton mean by chorus in "the Greek manner . . . still in use
among the Italians"? Gretchen Finney observed general parallels between
uses of chorus in *Samson* and in two early music dramas before turning to
oratorio as a background for *Samson*.[9] This work was a beginning, but
much remains to be explained. As Finney says, "still in use" must refer to
more recent practices than those of Tasso and other sixteenth-century writers, deserving as these are of study by Miltonists.[10] Considering what we
know of Milton's reading and travels, the period that can explain this telling
reference is the 1620s and 1630s, climaxing with his extended tour of Italy
in 1638–1639, when his impressions of Italian practice were fixed.

What did he believe about *antico-moderno* drama? Why did he distinguish a "chorus that sung" from some other kind of chorus? How could he
write choral odes in a "measure of verse" that is a mixture "of all sorts" of
lines? Oratorio seems to offer little help in these matters, but music drama
offers much, especially if one considers its theory as well as its practice. For
Milton was influenced not only by what he saw and heard performed in
Italy but also by humanist theoreticians of ancient and modern poetics and
music drama, some of whom in the 1620s and 1630s were still seriously
attempting (as earlier humanists such as Vincenzo Galilei had attempted)
to make musical-dramatic practice a revival of the legendary powers of ancient song.

The most notable such theorist was Doni, a classical philologist and
scholar of ancient and modern music, poetry, and theater. Although a native

7. See Parker, *Milton*, 1:419, and Martha W. England, "John Milton and the Performing
Arts," p. 29. In "Commonplace Book" entries tentatively dated 1637–1638 and 1639–1641,
Milton defended the theater against sour fathers such as Lactantius, who it seems would have
liked to eradicate theater and music altogether (*Complete Prose*, 1:489–91).
8. *The Works of John Milton*, ed. Frank Patterson et al., 1:332.
9. Finney, *Musical Backgrounds*, pp. 222–23.
10. Prince studies their influence at length in *The Italian Element*, and Clay Hunt further
shows their importance for "Lycidas" in *"Lycidas" and the Italian Critics*.

of Florence who later returned there, Doni worked for the college of cardinals and lived in the Barberini villa where Milton attended a music drama. Milton was in Rome for four months, may have heard him lecture, and may have met him[11]: he mentions Doni in his letter from Florence to Lukas Holste, Vatican librarian, in March 1639, advising Holste to request Doni, then supposedly about to leave Rome for Florence, to do a bibliographical task in Florence.[12] Thus we know that Milton knew who Doni was (he mentions Doni's appointment to the chair of Greek letters in Florence).

Looking through the glasses of nostalgic theorists like Doni, Milton would have considered what he saw and heard as in large measure a revival of ancient musical-dramatic practice, even though for composers this concept was by 1639 little more than a pretty commonplace for a dedicatory epistle.[13] We know now that Doni's views on music drama, rooted in the works of Peri, Caccini, and Monteverdi of three decades earlier (from which he usually draws examples), and especially his constant plea for a return to partly spoken performance were outmoded. But in 1638–1639 this fact would have been clear only to musicians and to a few astute observers. The term *opera* for music drama had not yet come into general use: sung dramas were still called *dramma per musica, favola musicale,* and so on. Rome and Florence had no public opera houses; Venice had just opened its first ones, San Cassiano (1637) and SS. Giovanni e Paolo (1639), where the later-famous Francesco Cavalli was producing his first work, "Le Nozze di Teti e Peleo" (1639), in the style of earlier Florentine *aria parlante* (and that would soon change).[14] The bourgeoisie and peasantry as yet knew music drama only through the *sacre rappresentazioni* of the Jesuits and friars, which in accord with their didactic purpose were often still performed partly spoken. In the late 1640s, opera would begin to spread abroad, but as yet, except for occasional performances by traveling companies, it was still an Italian affair. Libretti (more rarely the scores) of music dramas from noblemen's theaters were read in many parts of Europe (as Milton had read "La Catena d'Adone"). For readers and audiences, opera was not a separate genre but a sung form of drama, a revival of ancient theater; classicists could still argue that composers and librettists were following, and ought more closely to follow, ancient example. Thus what Milton experienced was not opera as the later seventeenth century would know it, but aristocratic, privately performed music drama on the one hand, and public, didactic *sacre rappresentazioni* on the other, in both forms regarded as a revival of ancient theater.

11. On Doni's works and the likely Milton-Doni connection, see my article "Milton, G. B. Doni, and the Dating of Doni's Works."
12. *Complete Prose*, 1:335.
13. See for example "La Regina Sant' Orsula," by Andrea Salvadori, composer Marco da Gagliano, Florence, 1625.
14. See Haas, *Musik des Barocks*, pp. 133–35.

Doni was no recluse but a favorite and companion of the Barberini, staging performances in their theater along the lines of his theories and also lecturing and directing performances in Roman academies and chambers, such as a sung performance of a scene from Seneca's *Troades* in the Eruditi academy, which may have occurred while Milton was in Rome.[15] In the spirit of ancient drama as religious spectacle, Doni advocated public performances of partly spoken music drama to inspire the people to good morals,[16] though he had little praise for the monkish efforts in that line, as he called them.

Milton's commendation of "solemn paneguries," his plans for a partly sung drama of the Fall, his aid in making possible the Lawes/Davenant productions, and his concept of verse forms and chorus in *Samson*—all are in the vein of such efforts to revive ancient drama. Milton after the Restoration was lucky to be alive and in no position to imagine staging *Samson*; he published it as a closet drama. But if he conceived or began it during Cromwell's time or earlier, as has been argued,[17] he might then have had other plans. Whenever he planned and wrote it, Italian theory and practice of music drama of the 1620s and 1630s were influencing his thinking and can provide clues for good reading—for inner performance—of *Samson*.

Furthermore, Doni's theories are helpful not only for study of *Samson* but for that of other Miltonic works as well, for Doni wrote much about monody, defining the *stile monodico* or *stile recitativo* (equivalent terms in their broad senses) of sung dramatic poetry and arguing that epics also should be performed in recitative and airs, to harp accompaniment. Whether Milton ever wished for such performance of portions of his epics we do not know, but many passages in them are highly suitable for it, as eighteenth-century oratorios and cantatas would demonstrate.[18] Since the monodic style of mixed recitative and airs was the basic component of the conception and practice of music drama, we begin with Doni's treatise on monody and will return later to consideration of *Samson*, with its monodic and choral lyric verse.

Doni, Musical-Dramatic Monody, and "Lycidas"

Doni's first published work was the *Compendio del Trattato de' Generi e de' Modi della Musica. Con un Discorso sopra la Perfettione de' Concenti* (Rome, 1635). His correspondence of 1636 shows him receiving notes

15. Doni, "Lezione V, Sopra la Musica Scenica," *Lyra Barberina Amphichordos*, 2:204, misnum. 202. See note 50 for this passage.

16. Doni, "Lezione I, Del modo tenuto dagli Antichi nel Rappresentare le Tragedie, e Commedie," *Lyra Barberina Amphichordos*, 2:169.

17. On the dating of *Samson* see Parker, *Milton*, 2:903–17, and Merritt Y. Hughes, ed., *John Milton: Complete Poems and Major Prose*, pp. 539–42. Subsequent citations of Milton's poetry will be from Hughes.

18. See England, "John Milton and the Performing Arts," and Brian Morris, "'Not without Song': Milton and the Composers."

thanking him for copies sent to scholars in various parts of Europe,[19] and the book could have reached London booksellers with equal speed. Milton at this time was busy with private reading at Horton, where he could thus have known Doni's work even before he left for Italy in 1638, though it does not matter exactly when he became acquainted with such ideas.[20]

The *Compendio* is two treatises, the second of which, "sopra la Perfettione delle Melodie, o de' Concenti," is about poetics as well as music, defining *stile monodico* and advocating the revival of "Recitationi col Canto de' Poemi Heroci." Monody, Doni says, is solo song, usually with, but possibly without, accompaniment; later he expands the definition to include song in unison or with a single leading melodic voice, by an ensemble thought of as one speaker; he several times praises, for example, a canzone of Andrea Gabrieli's, "Poiche à Damon fù pur dal Ciel Concesso."[21] Monody is older than and superior to polyphonic singing, which he claims derived from polyphonic organ music (pp. 98–99). While some pieces in *stile madrigalesco* have worth and harmonic richness, this style alters syllable lengths and distorts and confuses words (p. 100). He praises Giulio Caccini and other Florentine poets, singers, and composers of the 1590s for reviving monody with their songs and dialogues for dramatic scenes and with appropriate new vocal ornamentation ("gl'accenti, passaggi, trilli, gorghiggiamenti, e simile"— p. 101). The perfection of monody, he says, consists in "making the sentiments of the poet understandable, without losing the word, and not in the fullness and sweetness of harmony, which can be produced more sonorously by instruments."[22]

So far, Doni admits, he has been repeating earlier humanist ideas (p. 112), but he has more specific recommendations. Poetry *col canto* like other poetry, he says following Plato and Aristotle, is of three sorts: narrative, representative or imitative, and mixed. Poets and composers must find appropriate styles for each sort. In the narrative poem the poet speaks in his own voice ("sempre in persona sua"), in the representative (drama as well as dialogue and other short dramatic forms) others talk from beginning to end, while in the mixed sort the poet sometimes speaks and sometimes represents

19. Angelo M. Bandini, *Commentariorum de vita et scriptis Ioannis Bapt. Doni libri quinque* (Florence, 1755). Some of the letters were from Michelangelo Buonarroti, Benedetto Fioretti (one of Milton's later Florentine acquaintances), Iacopo Soldani, the bishop of Würzburg, and Ferdinand II, Duke of Florence.

20. Parker (*Milton,* 1:124) cites Milton's statement in the "Second Defense" that, in his years of private study, he sometimes went to London to buy books and to learn something new in mathematics and music.

21. Doni, *Compendio del Trattato de' Generi . . . Con un Discorso* (1635), pp. 96–98, 114. Most subsequent page references to this work are given parenthetically in the text.

22. "Ma quelli che sostengono la parte delle Monodie dicono che la perfettione della Musica consiste . . . nel fare intendere tutti i sentimenti del poeta; senza che le parole si perdino; e non nella pienezza, e soavità del Concento: il quale più sonoro senza fallo si può fare con instrumenti artificiali" (*Compendio,* p. 103).

others speaking (pp. 113–14). Doni illustrates each sort with poems of Guarini, Tasso, and Marino (p. 114). In sung performance of a "representative" or dramatic poem we may at times have several voices together representing one speaker, so that the audience "ought to imagine that one [of them] is the one who is speaking *col canto*."[23] Then the arrangement of voice parts must not hinder the audience from perceiving the ensemble as one speaker, as for example if two singers should simultaneously sing different portions of the text, which, however, is permissible in fugal, sequential, echo, or similar reiterative passages.[24]

He notes that the parts of a long poem that are suitable for polyphonic setting are brief passages serving some special function, such as "breve epiloghetti," "breve inviti," "acclamationi," "giubbili," "applausi," "vinate," or "serenade" (pp. 116–18). *Stile madrigalesco* is also suitable for remarkable and exciting scenes involving numerous characters, such as games, battles, or hunts (p. 117). An entire hymn, *laude*, or *canzone* should be set as monody—for solo voice or for an ensemble in unison or homophony. Sonnets, which he says "correspond to the hymns and paeans of Greek poetry, ought commonly to be set to one voice alone," though sometimes they may with more difficulty be set in *stile madrigalesco* (p. 118).

Doni believed that in ancient theater, besides choruses and the prologue (*pura favola*), only those passages were sung that were devoted to some "particolare expressione d'affetto,"[25] lyrical-dramatic expression of a particular mood or emotion to be inspired in the audience at that point (the passages that would be arias in opera). The rest of the play was spoken. These lyrical (*affetuosi*) passages were sung solo to instrumental accompaniment, often by a trained singer substituting for the actor's voice at that point and "singing behind the hand" (*ad manum cantare*).[26] It was these sung solo passages that originally defined the Greek word *monody*.

23. "Ne' primi [narrative sort] non pare che si possa con molto decoro introdurre diuerse Voci che cantino più clausole insieme: . . . Et in vero mala gratia hauerebbe se mentre vn Messo mi racconta per essempio il principio d'vna zuffa, sopragiugnendo vn'altro mi narrasse l'esito di essa. . . . perche debbiamo imaginarci che vno sia quello che fauelli col canto" (*Compendio*, p. 114).

24. ". . . almeno acconciamente gli può ammettere; come, per darne alcun saggio in quei del Guarino, doue s'esprime qualche mistura, o vnione di varie cose; verbigratia in quello *Anime pellegrine*, *&c.* o doue vna gradate amplificatione par che ricerchi queste Fughe, e Imitationi; ponghiamo caso *Felice chi vi mira*, *&c.* ò doue s'accozzano insieme molti Atributi, e si ripetono l'istesse parole di sentimento perfetto, come *Vdite amanti*, *Vdite*, &c." (*Compendio*, pp. 114–15).

25. G. B. Doni, "Lezione V: Sopra la Musica Scenica," *Lyra Barberina Amphichordos*, 2:198: "Siccome non ogni sorte di Soliloquio è adattabile, e proporzionato alla Musica . . . verbigrazia dove qualsisia personaggio discorre seco medesimo pianamente, e senza commozione d'affetto, massime a di lungo, ovvero con gli spettatori stessi (sebbene ciò non è lodato) così tengo per fermo, che non tutti i Soliloquj siano veramente Cantici; ma solo quelli, che contengono qualche particolare espressione d'affetto; e per dirlo in una parola, i Patetici senza più."

26. Doni, "Lezione I," *Lyra Barberina Amphichordos*, 2:174.

Thus with Doni as with other musical writers of the time, *monody* is used in both a broader (see the opening definition above) and a narrower sense, in this latter to mean solo song within a dramatic production, lyrically expressing an appropriate emotion or mood.[27] Within this narrower sense, one must further distinguish between long monodies, suitable to comprise a whole scene and usually divided into sections (such as Monteverdi's "Arianna"), and short monodies, depicting a lyric moment within a scene and similar in length and musical style to most of the independent songs or *arie* of the monodic songbooks (see note 90).

In ancient theater the accompaniment for monody, Doni claims elsewhere,[28] was occasionally played by a lyre but more commonly by a *tibia* (flute), since wind instruments blend best with the human voice, as he says Aristotle observes (*Compendio*, p. 125). For the modern accompaniment of monody Doni recommends (following earlier writers such as Zacconi[29]) contrapuntal music, to produce vivacity of rhythm and harmonic *affetti*, so long as the pauses are opportunely placed to preserve intelligibility of the words (p. 123). Viols are ideal for such accompaniment in a chamber performance: as bowed instruments they have the same "held" quality (prolongation of tone) as winds. For "heroic music in some spacious temple," an organ will be best (p. 124).

Stile monodico is especially suitable for grave and heroic matter, though now it is generally applied to effeminate or amorous subjects; a praiseworthy exception is Pongasi's setting of Petrarch's noble canzone, "Italia mia" (p. 122). While some composers scorn monody as too simple and easy, others say it is more challenging than polyphony, Doni concludes, just as it is harder to paint a nude figure perfectly than to do a clothed one, or harder to do one figure in perfect detail than to do several only intimated (p. 124).

Milton may have read this 1635 treatise on monody (lyrical-dramatic verse sung in recitative and arioso style) shortly before writing his famous "monody" in 1637. In any case Doni's treatise provides the useful contemporary, musical-poetic definition of the term Milton chose for his poem. He intended the word not only in its classical sense of a solo lament but also in its modern, related musical-dramatic meaning. "Lycidas" is a dramatic monody of the third or "mixed" type, in Doni's terms. The poet's voice speaks only at the end, a *breve epiloghetto*: "Thus sang the uncouth Swain to th'Oaks and rills, / While the still morn went out with sandals gray . . . ." Five other characters have spoken: the uncouth swain, whose warbled monody proper, to an oaten flute, comprises the bulk of the poem and de-

---

27. On monody in the broader and narrower senses ("eigentliche Monodie") see Girolamo Frescobaldi, *Arie Musicali*, ed. Helga Spohr, p. 8, a very helpful account.

28. Doni, "Trattato della Musica Scenica," *Lyra Barberina Amphichordos*, 2:104.

29. Lodovico Zacconi, *Pratica di Musica*, 1592 (II, vol. I, chap. 64) recommends solo song with polyphonic accompaniment as giving all musical satisfactions (see Haas, *Musik des Barocks*, p. 7). Doni was obviously no purist among musical humanists.

fines it; Apollo, who declaims a brief piece on heavenly fame (lines 79–85); Hippotades, herald of the sea, who acquits the winds of Lycidas's death in a little *Acclamatione* that, according to Doni, might be set polyphonically (it would image sleek Panope with her sisters playing on the sea—lines 97– 99); the river Cam, a Cambridge don in academic garb, who declaims one line, which doubtless would be set with several repetitions: "Ah! Who hath reft my dearest pledge?"; and St. Peter, who thunders the lines on the corruption of the clergy (lines 113–31), which have sometimes been considered a distracting flaw, despite Minturno's view of such digression as appropriate to "high lyric." Milton probably supposed that he had well avoided disunity by writing a "mixed sort" of monody, by creating different voices, each introduced by the singer of the monody and fitting as an apparition of his grieving fantasy; thus declamations that might have been digressive are put into the mouths of speakers appropriate to them.

The uncouth swain as a youthful, lamenting pastor should probably be thought of as a tenor, singing alternating airs and recitative. St. Peter, by contrast, would be a powerful bass voice, loudly singing a judgment in declamatory recitative, the least tuneful form, closest to the speaking voice of a reader or orator. This contrast of voices is suggested not only by the poem's dramatic situation but also by the swain's reaction to St. Peter's declamation: this "dread voice," he says, has dried up the lyric streams of Alpheus (the lover turned river in pursuit of his nymph), which must return before the swain can sing the lyrical flower passage depicting a fancied funeral for Lycidas's missing body. Further confirmation of this suggestion is the frequent contrast Ian Spink observes in English dialogue settings of the 1620s and 1630s featuring a "horrific" otherworldly bass Charon and a quieter tenor suppliant begging passage to the afterlife, or similarly a bass Abraham and tenor Dives, or Samuel's ghost versus Saul.[30]

By calling "Lycidas" a monody Milton suggests that an imagined musical-dramatic performance was part of his concept of it.[31] In Doni's terms, the poem is a long (scene-length) monody divided into sections, a kind of work that was either an excerpted *lamento* scene from a music drama or an independent piece of like scope and style.[32] It could include brief passages by

---

30. *English Song, Dowland to Purcell*, pp. 52–53.

31. Gretchen Finney gives specific suggestions for musical treatment (*Musical Backgrounds*, pp. 198–208), but I see little basis for them in the poem.

32. Ibid., pp. 213–18, sees "Lycidas" as corresponding to a whole oratorio or music drama, but the poem has the smaller scope of a scene-length monody. As Hunt ("*Lycidas*" *and the Italian Critics*, p. 191) says, Finney's claim that "Lycidas" was modeled on an oratorio including choruses and on the Striggio/Monteverdi *Orfeo* is disproved by Milton's calling the poem a monody, by definition a solo form. Hunt concludes that "Milton conceived 'Lycidas' as essentially a musical structure" (p. 128). Hunt's account of "Lycidas" with the "grand lyric" as Milton's model is excellent, but it lacks the distinction between the long (scene-length) and the short monody, which explains how other voices can briefly interrupt the swain's lament though his solo still defines the whole as a "monody."

other singers responding to the soloist's "monody" proper, which comprised the bulk of the piece. Thus for "Lycidas" one should imagine an accompanied soloist (to a flute if one takes the pastoral pipe literally, or to a viol ensemble if one imagines a usual contemporary accompaniment for monody), in whose grief-stricken fantasy other figures briefly appear and sing (possibly as an ensemble for Hippotades's lines on the sisters at play), plus a narrator, voice of the poet, who steps forward at the end to do the epilogue or *commiato*.[33] Or an alternative treatment of the *breve epiloghetto*, according to Doni, would be as a part-song, again sung by the combined soloists other than the swain. This would follow most suitably the lines just before it, which depict Lycidas in heaven "entertained" by the "solemn troops, and sweet Societies / That sing, and singing in their glory move, / And wipe the tears for ever from his eyes" (lines 179–81).

Famous monodies were so performed *in camera* in Milton's time, as today we have unacted concert performances of operatic scenes.[34] Secular monodies were sometimes reissued later with sacred texts, thus becoming even more widely known, as Monteverdi in 1641 republished the "Arianna" in solo form as sorrows of the Madonna. Probably Milton's experience of such Italian works before he wrote "Lycidas" had been limited. He could have heard Nicholas Lanier's Italian-style recitative monody, "Hero and Leander" (circa 1630).[35] In his composer-father's household there were Italian music books and sometimes Italian musicians. The "Arianna" was famous in England as elsewhere, later inspiring among other imitations an Ariadne monody, which Milton praised, by his friend Henry Lawes.[36] But for Milton in 1637—enjoying his warm friendship with Charles Diodati, enamored of things Italian and well read about them, soon to embark for Italy—sung performance of scene-length monodies was probably more a fascinating imagined dimension for his poem than a concrete musical projection.

Strict or modified canzone verse forms such as that of "Lycidas" (see note 33) were common in monodies—as we saw, Doni included the *canzone* among forms proper to be set as monody. The meter was part of Milton's initial conception of a songlike texture for the verse of "Lycidas," which begins in a mixed mode of declamation and song (see Chapter I). But we can observe a shift in the poem from this mixed mode of the opening to almost pure declamatory mode, which takes over in the section on heavenly fame

33. Prince, *The Italian Element*, pp. 72–73, describes the verse form of "Lycidas" and speaks of the epilogue as a *commiato*.

34. Haas, *Musik des Barocks*, p. 60, gives some examples of such excerpts done as concert pieces: besides Monteverdi's "Arianna," the *lamento* of Jason ("Giasone," 1633, composer Sigismundo d'India).

35. For the score of this see *Words to Music*, ed. Vincent Duckles and Franklin Zimmerman, pp. 28–42.

36. Milton praised Lawes, in a dedicatory sonnet for a book of his airs (Milton's Sonnet 13), for "tuning" the poets' "happiest lines in hymn or story." A marginal note in Lawes's songbook explains that the "story" is Cartwright's Ariadne poem, set by Lawes.

(lines 64–84) introducing the first envisioned figure, Apollo, and continues to the end. It is as if these declaiming voices of the swain's reverie set the high tone for the rest of the poem—indeed, for Milton's later uses of declamatory mode for lyric passages in *Paradise Lost*. In the early sections we note several prominent features of song mode that are later left behind: frequent rhymed couplets (in contrast to more irregular rhyme later); fairly frequent shorter lines of canzone form (very rare later); rhyme syncopation (see Chapter IV, note 17); smooth meter; frequent "figures of sound" such as anaphora in "Begin then—Begin, and," antimetabole in "Together both—and both together," and anadiplosis in "now thou art gone, / Now thou art gone."

> Begin then, Sisters of the sacred well,
> That from beneath the seat of *Jove* doth spring,
> Begin, and somewhat loudly sweep the string.
> Hence with denial vain, and coy excuse,
> So may some gentle Muse
> With lucky words favor my destin'd Urn,
> And as he passes turn,
> And bid fair peace be to my sable shroud.
> ·
>
> Together both, ere the high Lawns appear'd
> Under the opening eyelids of the morn,
> We drove afield, and both together heard
> What time the Gray-fly winds her sultry horn,
> ·
>
> Meanwhile the Rural ditties were not mute,
> Temper'd to th'Oaten Flute;
> Rough *Satyrs* danc'd, and *Fauns* with clov'n heel
> From the glad sound would not be absent long,
> And old *Damaetas* lov'd to hear our song.
> But O the heavy change, now thou art gone,
> Now thou art gone, and never must return!
>   ("Lycidas," lines 15–22, 25–28, 32–44)

Thus the elegist begins in a mixed mode of declamation and song, later to shift into almost pure declamatory mode.

To read "Lycidas" in the context of seventeenth-century monody is not to contest the importance for the poem of pastoral elegy and other backgrounds that have been studied but to see that Milton drew inspiration from current musical-poetic theory and practice as well. Pastoral themes predominated in music drama, giving its *lamenti* scenes a natural relationship to pastoral elegy.

The Monodies and Choral Odes
of Samson Agonistes

Gretchen Finney demonstrated parallels in plot and treatment between *Comus* and "La Catena d'Adone." It was a most helpful discovery: picture Milton reading a *favola in musica* (perhaps an edition of only the *libretto*[37]), then writing a text of a mostly spoken "musical entertainment" for child actors and their music teacher, for the limited facilities of Ludlow Castle, and you understand how he produced a piece that has often seemed neither drama nor masque nor music drama, yet is both dramatic and musical. For *Samson Agonistes*, however, we have no particular Italian source, but must work with the statements in Milton's preface, cited above.

Having considered the meaning of musical-dramatic monody, we return to the broader questions of Milton's neoclassical drama, to the nature of both monody and chorus—the lyrical portions, as opposed to the dialogue—in *Samson*. Besides its preface one must also consider Milton's other remarks on "those dramatic constitutions, wherein Sophocles and Euripides reign," namely the passage from "The Reason of Church Government" cited above for its recommendation of "solemn paneguries." Along with the Greeks, the declared model for tragedy is "the Apocalypse of St. John . . . the majestic image of a high and stately tragedy, shutting up and intermingling her solemn scenes and acts with a sevenfold chorus of hallelujahs and harping symphonies."[38] As Barbara Lewalski has observed, Milton thus regarded the Apocalypse structurally as composed of acts marked off by intervening choruses that we should imagine sung, with accompaniment.[39] Like *Samson* it was for him a closet drama, the "image" of a tragedy, not a stage piece.

Choral ensemble with dance, "shutting up and intermingling" the acts, provided the most notable use of chorus in early Italian music drama. Ways of handling it varied considerably. Spoken drama in the sixteenth century had frequently used interludes of pageant, song, and instrumental music between acts. After the turn of the century, the set of *Intermedii* for a given play might be published as a musical entertainment in its own right,[40] and this practice added impetus to the movement toward entirely sung drama. Once the main drama or most of it came to be sung, interludes sometimes

---

37. Or Milton could have seen an edition of "La Catena d'Adone" with the scores of the arias printed together at the end—see Haas, *Musik des Barocks*, p. 72.

38. *Complete Prose*, 1:815.

39. See her "*Samson Agonistes* and the 'Tragedy' of the Apocalypse." In *Paradise Lost*, similarly, Milton makes us imagine the Creation as a play in six acts, with a chorus of angels entertaining "the evening and the morning" of each day.

40. See for example "La Finta Fiammetta" (2d ed., 1611, Francesco Contarini, composer unknown), "Con gl'Intermedii aggiunti in questa seconde impressione."

consisted of miming or might be omitted.[41] When there were no inter-ludes, their function of marking off acts was fulfilled entirely by choruses ending each act, sometimes with dance. These were, at first, often separate *Schlußchöre* (called simply *coro*), singing rhymed stanzaic verses, distinct from the dramatic action and from any other choruses within the acts, which were called *cori in scena* (for example, of nymphs or of devils). These latter took part in the action as attendants upon the characters, sometimes singing, sometimes speaking their parts. "Tirsi" (1618, anonymous), for example, distinguishes a "coro che parlano" from the "coro che suona e canta," indicating the modern practice behind Milton's reference to a "chorus that sung." The speaking chorus there is a *coro in scena*, responding to events with exclamations of amazement, sadness, or joy. The singing chorus, divided into two semichoruses, concludes the final act, singing in rhymed verse. Thus in such works with a separate *Schlußchor*, the two functions of classical chorus were neatly divided, namely to take part in the action and to finish the acts with chanted or sung commentary.

As music dramas came to be completely sung—by the mid-1620s there were apparently no new partly spoken private productions for Doni to cite[42]—the separate *Schlußchor* was rarely used, and its function was filled instead by *cori in scena*, combining in various mixtures to end the acts. Rarely did an act not end with some sort of ensemble, and if it did not, a chorus or ensemble would probably begin the succeeding act, thus producing the same effect of "shutting up and intermingling." Also, some entirely sung works, such as "Chi soffre, speri," which Milton witnessed, continued to be performed with elaborate interludes between acts. Robert Haas's summary of choral practice in Roman music drama from the 1620s up to and specifically including "Chi soffre, speri" will suggest what Milton experienced:

> In the Roman operas the chief emphasis is upon choral and ensemble technique. Duets and trios are common, the choral scenes pack in the most varied kinds of performers and types of singing for constellations of rich diversity. A range is used, from unison choral song (e.g. Vittori's "Galatea") to two- and three-part chorus to scorings in multiple parts; semi-choruses step apart; high- and low-pitched choral groups are set against each other; women's and men's choruses are separated; *a capella* performance continues to exist (e.g. Mazzocchi's "Adone") alongside the full harmony of string accompaniment otherwise used; in the mostly contrapuntal harmonic work, homophonic effects also appear. . . . This trend toward splendor and pomp, which tends to pile up choral

---

41. Haas, *Musik des Barocks*, p. 35.
42. See his lecture of 1624 on partly spoken productions. Doni says that they were common in Mantua in the time of Duke Ferdinand (after 1612) and in Bracciano, where the gods in certain scenes would sing in recitative, while the other actors would speak; he further cites Roman productions of works by a certain Jesuit, "Stefonio" ("Lezione V, Sopra la Musica Scenica," *Lyra Barberina Amphichordos*, 2:203, misnum. 201). On another partly spoken production see Haas, *Musik des Barocks*, p. 34.

masses especially in the act-ending scenes, runs parallel to the development of the scenic arts and of ballet.[43]

In "La catena d'Adone" (1626—cited here by Haas), part of Milton's inspiration for *Comus*, we find a typical mix for the 1620s and 1630s of choruses serving both the functions mentioned above. Choruses of nymphs and shepherds finish each act, sometimes along with dancers, while for the end of the fifth and final act, we have, instead, a backstage chorus ("coro di dentro"); it sings first as two semichoruses, presumably from opposite sides of the stage, which then join for the finale. This splitting up and later reuniting of a chorus in the grand finale is parallel to Milton's use of semichorus and succeeding reunited chorus at the end, and only at the end, of *Samson*, to contribute to the sense of resolution and finality. As Haas indicates, the practice was common in music drama throughout this period—see for example "Il Pastor Vedovo" (1628, Dionisio Rondinelli, composer unknown), or to take examples of works performed during Milton's stay in Italy, "La Delia" (1639, Giulio Strozzi, composer Francesco Sacrati) and "L'Armida" (1639, Benedetto Ferrari, text and music). Doni recommended the use of *dikorian* as in line with the best ancient example.[44]

Merritt Hughes, citing Milton's sketches of the early 1640s for a drama of the Fall, notes that "they fuse or confuse the features of the sacred dramas of the Counter-reformation in Italy with Greek and medieval elements."[45] The medieval elements (such as allegorical characters) were already present in the *sacre rappresentazioni*, so that we can simply say Milton's sketches "fuse" such features with Greek elements. It was a deliberate fusion exactly in the sense of humanist efforts such as Doni's to revive ancient partly sung drama. Milton stipulates sung chorus at the end of each act, with the fourth act ending in an expanded masque ensemble. The chorus (of angels) is to function both as *coro in scena* (it offers resistance to Lucifer and "admonisheth Adam") and as *Schlußchor*: the five acts are to end, respectively, with "a

---

43. Ibid., p. 75: "Das Hauptgewicht liegt in den römischen Opern auf der Chor- und Ensembletechnik. Duett- und Terzettgesänge sind häufig, die Chorszenen mengen die verschiedensten Besetzungsarten und Satzweisen zu Gebilden von reicher Mannigfaltigkeit. Vom einstimmigen Chorgesang (Galatea) wird über zwei- und dreistimmige Gruppierungen bis zu hoher Vielstimmigkeit gegangen, Doppelchöre treten auseinander, hohe und tiefe Chormassen sind gegeneinander gelagert, Frauen- und Männerchöre werden geschieden, a-cappella-Vortrag (Adone) schiebt sich neben die sonst mit Streichorchester begleitende Klangfülle, aus der meist kontrapunktischen Arbeit heben sich homophone Wirkungen ab. . . . Dieser Zug zu Glanz und Üppigkeit, der insbesondere an den Aktschlüssen Chormassen zusammenballen läßt, läuft gleich mit der Ausbreitung der szenischen Künste und mit dem Balletaufwand."

44. Doni, "Discorso della Ritmopeia de' Versi Latini e della Melodia de' Cori Tragichi," *Lyra Barberina Amphichordos*, 2:222. (This treatise appeared in Doni's *Annotazioni sopra il Compendio* [Rome, 1640].) "Ne dico, che sempre tutti i Corici debbano cantare insieme; perchè possono anco ad imitazione degli Antichi dividersi in due squadre, ch'essi dicevano *dikorian*, e cantare una per volta."

45. Hughes, *John Milton*, p. 173.

hymn of Creation," a "song of the battle and victory in heaven" against Lucifer, a bewailing of Adam's fall, "a masque of all the evils of this life," and a brief choral conclusion (see note 91).

In describing the poetic nature of dramatic chorus, as with monody, Doni was both praising those features of modern music drama that he thought consistent with ancient practice and encouraging more such revival. Some of his ideas about chorus were published in "della Ritmopeia de Versi Latini e della Melodia de' Cori Tragichi," included in his *Annotazioni sopra il Compendio* (1640), but they are more fully presented in the "Trattato della Musica Scenica" (1635), which represents his favorite lecture material of the late 1630s and early 1640s (see note 11). In both these works Doni says that modern directors are trying to imitate ancient choral practice and offers advice on how to do this.[46] Several of his statements about ancient and modern choral practice, such as that on semichorus already mentioned, describe the workings of chorus in *Samson*.

Choral dance, he says, is important not only for comedy but for grave dramas such as tragedies as well. The tragic choral dance of the ancients was not quick and "labyrinthine" like that of comedy or festive celebration (Milton also refers to such festive choral dance[47]) but grave and solemn, a sort of stately promenade with practiced motions of feet and arms in time to the music, either around circles (*kyklioi*) or along rectangular figures (*tetragoenoi*).[48] This latter form facilitated the choreography of division into semichoruses: Doni explains that the rectangle would be composed of two files facing the audience, the forward one reciting first, then the two files in promenade reversing their positions for the other semichorus to recite, all then reuniting their song in the continuation of the promenade along the

46. Doni, "Della Musica Scenica," *Lyra Barberina Amphichordos*, 2:95: "Ma se oggi alcuno vorrà praticare a imitazione degli Antichi questi Cori; per quanto comporta il sito delle nostre sale, e la disposizione di quelli; si potrà . . . ridurre la cosa a segno tale, che farà comportabile, e recherà non mediocre diletto, con ordine molto migliore di quello, che si è tenuto sinora; e ciò si potrà conseguire in questo modo." And in the "della Ritmopeia" (see n. 44): ". . . in questo stile [of choral dance] la forza del Ritmo vi si confonde tanto da quei contrarj, e diversissimi movimenti, che appena ve ne resta vestigio alcuno [of the ancient way]. Nè mi si dica, che i Cori si son veduti ballare pure in questo stile, ed in Firenze, ed in Roma, ed altrove; perchè non ballavano se non in quelle parti, dove si cantavano l'istesse note, cioè in una minima parte del Coretto, con clausole brevi, e spezzate, a guisa di canzonette" (*Lyra Barberina Amphichordos*, 2:222).

47. Milton in *PL* 5:618–27 compares the motions of planets and stars to such a labyrinthine choral dance of the angels.

48. "Trattato della Musica Scenica," *Lyra Barberina Amphichordos*, 2:95–96: "Quanto al passeggio, lasciando da parte quegl' inviluppati intrecciamenti, che non fanno a proposito, se non dove si volesse rappresentare qualche laberinto, sarà più espediente farli procedere in semplice giro, come facevano i Cori rotondi degli Antichi, detti *kyklioi*, o in schiera con figure quadre, che si chiamavano *koroi tetragonoi* . . . ; nel che si deve avere principalmente la mira di osservare bene il Ritmo, e ritrovarsi tutti insieme nelle cadenze; e di usare passetti, e figure tali, che abbiano buona connessione, e siano proporzionate alla materia della Poesìa, e alle persone rappresentate."

rectangle. Milton apparently had such a choral promenade in mind, perhaps as part of the celestial scene in the "tragedy" of the Apocalypse, when he wrote of heavenly "solemn troops and sweet societies / That sing, and singing in their glory move" ("Lycidas," lines 179–80). The tragic chorus would not always be in motion, Doni explains, but for some passages would be a *coro stabilo* ("Trattato della Musica Scenica," pp. 95, 102).

Milton imagined such a choral promenade for the first entrance of his chorus of Danites. Samson brings them on, at the finish of his "O dark, dark, dark" monody with the words:

But who are these? for with joint pace I hear
The tread of many feet steering this way.
(*Samson Agonistes*, lines 110–11)

Probably we should picture them continuing their soothing promenade to a slow beat in "joint pace" all through the first chorus, beginning "This, this is he; softly a while," through "By how much from the top of wondrous glory, / Strongest of mortal men, / To lowest pitch of abject fortune thou art fall'n" (lines 115–75). Samson, seemingly musing or abstracted while they recite, rouses himself at the end of this chorus, saying:

I hear the sound of words, thir sense the air
Dissolves unjointed ere it reach my ear,

an appropriate response of a troubled man to a promenading, chanting group. The dance movements of the chorus should fit their role, Doni advises—for example, soldiers would use motions different from those of nymphs—and should fit the theme of each recitation: thus Aeschylus directs a "chorus of Persians" to "flap their wings," suggesting a sympathetic motion of chest and arms, in concord with a weeping lady's lament ("Trattato della Musica Scenica," II, p. 96). What motions would suit *Samson*'s consoling chorus of relatively young Danites (Samson's own age) must be left to each reader's imagination.

For modern adaptations of ancient choral song, Doni recommends three-part song above an instrumental bass. But for *Samson*, Milton perhaps imagined something closer to ancient practice in tragedy, where, Doni and other theorists believed, choral song was mostly in unison or octaves,[49] though sometimes in *ottava divisa* of fourths or fifths (see note 51), accompanied by *choraulicis* (choral flutes), which Doni says resembled the dulcian, a double-reed instrument. In lyrical passages where a character and the chorus together or in alternation celebrate or lament something, Doni says, they sang as an ensemble, and these pieces were *veri cantici*, for example the

49. "Trattato della Musica Scenica," p. 99. Loreto Vittori, the famous castrato and composer, seems to have been the Roman practitioner most interested in continuing to follow humanist advice: as Haas notes (*Musik des Barocks*, pp. 34, 75), he suggested partially spoken performance for his "La Santa Irena" (1644) and used unison chorus in "Galatea."

lament of Hecuba with the Trojan women in the *Troades*, a scene Doni staged for an academy, as we noted above (see note 11).[50] One such lyrical ensemble piece in *Samson* is lines 540–57, with its three-part structure: the chorus first sings of wine, "the dancing Ruby / Sparkling, outpour'd, the flavor, or the smell, / Or taste that cheers the hearts of Gods and men," to which Samson replies, likewise in six fairly regular pentameter lines, with praises of "fountain or fresh current . . . / Against the Eastern ray, translucent, pure, / . . . the clear milky juice allaying / Thirst." The chorus then responds with agreement that Samson's Nazarite beverage "from the liquid brook" is superior. Here, according to Doni's view of ancient practice, the chorus would depart from its usual solemn unison song into brighter melody and multivoiced harmony.[51] It is one of the few bright moments in the play, presenting Samson's lost glory.

Milton's choral prosody in *Samson* has been studied, with respect to sixteenth-century Italian models, by F. T. Prince, who places it within the Spenserian tradition of adapted canzone verse in English, with mixed lines usually of six and ten syllables (in Italian seven and eleven) and occasional rhyme.[52] By contrasting this canzone verse with blank verse, Prince shows, Milton makes us "feel the passage from speech to chant" in Samson's opening monologue, where he begins the monody "O dark, dark, dark," and conversely "from chanted verse to spoken" when the chorus, having ended each act with a lyrical ode, shifts to speech to introduce the new character approaching for the succeeding act (p. 156). These shifts from declamatory dialogue blank verse to a lyric mode of mixed declamation and song are indeed perfectly clear, as are the reverse transitions back to mixed declamation and speech (lines 326, 710, 1061, and 1297, introducing respectively Manoa, Dalila, Harapha, and the Philistine officer). Thus the chorus does its job as *Schlußchor*, "shutting up and intermingling" the acts.

Prince notes that such approximate canzone verse (monostrophic and unrhymed or partly rhymed) is found in certain choruses and other lyrical passages of Tasso's *Aminta* and Guarini's *Il Pastor Fido* (pp. 73–74). Fur-

---

50. *Lyra Barberina Amphichordos*, 2:204, misnum. 202: "Debbiamo anco tener per fermo, che quelle lamentazioni, che si fanno da qualche Personaggio insieme col Coro in molte Tragedie, massime verso la fine (Aristotile nella sua Poetica le addimanda) non altro siano, che veri Cantici; benché se guardiamo all' intervento di più persone, in qualche modo possano apparire Diverbii. . . . [e.g.] dove nelle Troadi il primo coro composto di Donne Troiane con la loro Regina Hecuba vicendevolmente deplora le disavventure loro, e della Patria; senza alcun dubbio può, e deve tra i Cantici annoverarsi: come anco due anni sono in Roma a mia persuasione si rappresentò con gran sodisfazione degli Eruditi, benchè con apparato assai semplice, e quasi all'improvviso." V. Mazzocchi is named as composer for this production (in the "della Ritmopeia de Versi Latini," *Lyra Barberina Amphichordos*, 2:205, misnum. 203).

51. Unlike modern scholars, Doni believed that the ancients practiced part song (ibid., 2:97).

52. Prince, *The Italian Element*, pp. 60–66, says that "Lycidas" shows Milton's early way of using canzone verse, the choruses of *Samson* his later version; see also pp. 145–67. Parenthetical citations in the following discussion are to *The Italian Element*.

thermore, the choruses of Tasso's tragedy *Torismondo* were in loose canzone form, ending with a few rhymed lines, and Prince later adds that the
tragedies of Federigo della Valle (1626–1627) and Andreini's "L'Adamo"
(1613) also use these "metrical liberties introduced by Tasso and Guarini"
(pp. 148–49, 153–55).

Looking further into music drama of the early seventeenth century, we
find more monostrophic, unrhymed or only partly rhymed canzone verse.
For Milton the example of Tasso and Guarini, as well as of Sannazaro's *Arcadia* with its canzone eclogues versus *terza rima* dialogue, was reinforced
by the early music dramas these sixteenth-century works had influenced.[53]
Thus we can account for Milton's avowal of dramatic practices "still in use
among the Italians." As examples of music dramas that use irregular choral
verse, mostly of seven- and eleven-syllable lines, with no rhyme or occasional rhyme, we note "Orsilla" (1615, Giovanni Capponi, composer unknown), "Tirsi" (1618), "Il Pastor Vedovo" (1628, Dionisio Rondinelli—in
the final semichorus/chorus ensemble), and "La Delia" by Strozzi/Sacrati
(1639—choral verse mostly rhymed, but not entirely). Some music dramas
use rhymed but otherwise loose, monostrophic canzone verse in chorus (for
example "Dorillo," 1619). Many do use regular, rhymed stanzaic verse, especially in act-ending choruses, a practice necessitated by the frequent musical use of *Refrainchöre* (such as in "La Catena d'Adone").[54] Such choruses
often contrast with unrhymed, less regular dialogue verse, as Prince noted of
"L'Adamo." In short, many mixtures of verse forms were possible, the over-
riding principle being that the choral verse should somehow contrast in
meter with the dialogue. Doni recommends that the dialogue be in long
verses (pentameter, *undici*, or hexameter), the choruses by contrast in verses
mostly of medium length ("Trattato della Musica Scenica," p. 18).

Milton's play follows the same principle and is close to Doni's version of
it. *Samson* displays a clear contrast between the blank verse of its dialogue
passages and the usually nonstrophic—or as Milton calls them, "allaeostrophic"—partly rhymed choruses in irregular line lengths. Monodies in
Samson, what Doni would call the *affettuosi* solo passages suitable for recitative and *arioso* singing (see p. 108), are usually, like the choral odes, in
this lyric verse form—for example, besides the "O dark, dark, dark" already cited, Samson's "O that torment should not be confin'd" (lines 605–
51)—though a few are in blank verse.

In this contrast between dialogue blank verse and lyrical monodic and
choral verse, in the loose canzone form of that lyrical verse (a modern approximation of ancient irregular verse), in his uses of chorus and semichorus, and in the suggestion of choral promenade or dance—in these four

---

53. Doni speaks of performance of the *Aminta* partly sung and partly spoken ("Trattato
della Musica Scenica," *Lyra Barberina Amphichordos*, 2:15–16).

54. See Haas, *Musik des Barocks*, pp. 32, 36, and 71.

ways Milton was following usual practices of Italian music drama that he regarded as deriving from the ancients. As in the opening of "Lycidas," a mode of mixed declamation and song was his lyrical verse form for monody and chorus.

The matter of rhyme in contrasting verse forms must now receive closer examination, and again Doni can clarify some ways in which Milton saw himself following *antico-moderno* usage. As many earlier humanists had, Doni (citing Minturno) argues that rhyme should generally be rejected in dramatic poetry, though it may be tolerated in comic drama and in brief *canzonetti* sung within the scenes of a serious drama.[55] But he says the dialogue (*ragionamenti*) and choruses in tragedy should not be regularly rhymed: *rime determinate* hinder the poet's precise word choice; their constant repetitions of sound, suitable for hymn or romance, are tedious in serious drama; and they bring about too frequent and too similar cadences in the music. Doni does not here mention occasional rhyme, which Milton uses, but presumably considered it an acceptable rhetorical device. Not regular rhyme and fixed stanzas, he says, but variety, liberty, and looseness are needed to express the powerful *affetti*: the verses should be pronounced "da certo furore divino all' improvviso," as in the best Greek tragedy, where the choral odes were not regular, as the earlier dithyrambs of strophe, antistrophe, and epode had been. Those had been in regular verses so that multiple strophes could be memorized easily and sung to the same tune, but later tragic choruses sung by professionals used "molte varie sorti di versi" to provide the needed variety and free movement of verse and through-composed melody ("Trattato della Musica Scenica," p. 20; see Chapter VI, note 11). In tragic choruses and other *lamentevoli* (*lamento* monodies), Doni says, the verse should not be in stanzas, but "confusamente, e sensa

---

55. "Trattato della Musica Scenica," *Lyra Barberina Amphichordos*, 2:19–21: "in materia della Scena . . . , le rime a giudizio mio si devono rifiutare. . . . Espressione non è altro, che la spiegatura de' concetti mediante la favella; dove io dico, che l'obbligo delle rime non permette al Poeta di scorere liberamente per tutto, e di usare di quelle frasi, e parole che vorrebbe, e che talvolta il concetto richiederebbe. Dà anco fastidio notabile agli uditori quella similitudine di suono, che cosi spesso fanno i versi rimati, e quella corrispondenza, che ha una parola con l'altra; . . . le Rime . . . suggeriscano al Musico una perpetua simiglianza di cadenze; anzi lo sforzano quasi a farle sempre simili: la qual cosa, come diremo più sotto, è viziosa e stucchevole; perocchè l' aria del canto non vuol essere cosi uniforme, e legata; ma varia, libera, e sciolta, per esprimere meglio le varie passioni, e concetti de' personaggi. Nè vale l' esempio delle canzonette; perciocchè quelle si recitano, e cantano, come cose premeditate, e non contengono se non un concetto solo; ma i Ragionamenti scenici, debbono più che si può nascondere l'artifizio, e lo studio che vi si è fatto . . . Ma ne' Cori dirà alcuno, che si ha da fare? hannosi da usare le Rime, o nò? quanto a me io direi che fosse meglio non usarvele; perchè sebbene il Coro non deve celare tanto l'artifizio, e la premeditazione; tuttavia mi pare molto meglio, che mostri ancora esso, che il canto non sia imparato a mente; ma piuttosto formato, e proferito da certo furore divino all' improvviso. A ciò m'induco anco dall' esempio degli Antichi Greci, i Cori de' quali sogliono essere di molte varie sorti di versi, con le strofe, e ritornelli, quando le hanno molto lunghe."

ordine"[56]—that is, monostrophic loose canzone verse. In these last two points we recognize exactly Milton's explanation in the preface to *Samson* of his "allaeostrophic" choral verse in "all sorts of lines."

As other commentators have noted, *Samson*'s occasional rhymes can function expressively; for example, in the ode on women's fickleness they contribute to the effect of "sardonic animation," and in the last ode of the play to the "note of exalted finality."[57] But besides achieving specific emotive effects, *Samson*'s occasional rhymes in loose canzone verse serve to evoke the singing of rhymed verse common in act-ending dramatic choruses and thus are part of the differentiation of the chorus's two functions, as character and as *Schlußchor*.

Highly remarkable rhythms, subsuming and requiring the occasional rhymes, are Milton's primary means of creating the sonority of the odes. These rhythms have often seemed to defy analysis since they conform to no fixed metrical patterns. To achieve just such a *furore divino all' improvviso* in tragic *lamentevoli*, Doni says, modern poets might follow the ancients, who in their music, verse, and dance used three kinds of rhythm—binary, ternary, and quinary (the last meaning mixed 3's and 2's or 2's and 3's)— while musicians today know only the first two. This quinary rhythm, corresponding to the mixed feet of certain of their meters, was reputed most fit for magnificent, majestic subjects.[58]

Milton does not create any such consistent stress-transposed metrical patterns in *Samson*, but the concept is helpful because mixtures of three- and two-syllable units are prominent in the unusual rhythms of the choruses. Prince finds in the ode "O how comely it is and how reviving" (lines 1267– 95) an "exultant rocking movement" (p. 162), an effect which is reinforced

---

56. Ibid., p. 21: "E quando pure si volessero usare in tutti i Cori, io loderei, che si facesse con questa differenza, che i lamentevoli non si disponessero in Stanze, nè avessero le Rime determinate; ma confusamente, e senza ordine, come in quella sorte di poesìe, che dicono oggi Idillj."

57. Louis Martz, in "Chorus and Character in *Samson Agonistes*," quotes Milton's rejection of rhyme for epic (preface to 2d edition of *Paradise Lost*) and assumes that the main use of it in *Samson Agonistes* was to produce effects of deliberate "flatness" or conventionality. But I believe most readers do not find these odes at all flat, particularly the one on women's fickleness. Conventional it is, but not flat, rather too sharp. On the expressive function of these rhymes see Prince, *The Italian Element*, pp. 156–58.

58. "Trattato della Musica Scenica," *Lyra Barberina Amphichordos*, 2:96: ". . . di tre generi di Ritmo, o battuta, che avevano gli Antichi, noi ne abbiamo solo due; la binaria, e la ternaria: essendosi tralasciata la quinaria, e Peonica, cioè quella, che metteva tre tempi nel passare, e due nel levare, o al contrario, la quale era molto stimata, e reputata attissima a soggetti, e molodìe [sic] magnifiche, e maestose, e ragionevolmente per essere mezzana tal sorte di proporzione (che è la vera sesquialtera) tra l'equale, o binaria, e tra la doppia, o ternaria; onde partecipa della vivacità di questa, e della gravità, o placidità di quella; . . . E usandosi tal Ritmo, e battuta in qualche Coro, come gli Antichi facevano in quelle Poesie, che si componevano di piedi Peoni, Cretici, e Bacchei, doverà l'accorto Maestro di danza accomodarvi tempi, e moti tali, che vi calzino bene, e si possano concordemente osservare."

if we picture the chorus promenading in slow rhythm, such as Doni described and Milton alluded to in "Lycidas." Here such stately motion might be produced if the line of choristers took a long step together on each alternate strong stress (pauses at line ends are calculated as stress equivalents):

step   step   step
Ó hŏw cómelў ĭt ís ănd hów rĕvívĭng
       step   step
Tŏ thĕ Spírĭts ŏf júst mèn lóng ŏppŕest!
    step   step
Whĕn Gód ĭntò thĕ hánds ŏf thĭr dĕlíverèr
step   step
Púts ĭnvíncĭblĕ míght
    step   step
Tŏ quéll thĕ míghtў ŏf thĕ Eárth, th'oppŕessŏr,
    step   step   step
Thĕ bŕute ănd bóist'rŏus fórce ŏf vĭolent mén

No regular metric pattern—of 3's and 2's or any other meter—would achieve this effect, none would express so well this *furore divino* of God's deliverer quelling the wicked in violent battle. But there are in each line at least one, and more often two, clusters of unaccented or lightly accented syllables interspersed among the binary feet, which give some approximation to the quinary rhythm Doni refers to in ancient tragic chorus. In the third line, for example, there are only three strong stresses, in the fifth only four, being distributed in each case among ten to twelve syllables. In a promenading recitation of the chorus to a rhythmic beat, such clusters would become triplets or quadruplets, interspersed with the slower binary units, giving the rhythmic effect of a dance with frequent hemiola (shifts between duple and triple time), similar to that we noted in Crashaw's ode "To the Name."

At line 1277, the midpoint of the verse paragraph, the meter changes to firm, regular, hymnlike iambics, creating a little island of metrical simplicity (reinforced by the rhetorical device of polyptoton) in the midst of the paragraph, suitable for the sense of the words:

Heĕ áll thĭr Ámmŭnítiŏn
Ănd féats ŏf Wár dĕféats
Wĭth pláin Hĕróĭc mágnĭtùde ŏf mínd.

We then return to a mixture of binary with longer units that continues until the end of this first paragraph at line 1285:

       hĕ éxĕcútes
Hĭs érrănd ŏn thĕ wíckĕd, whò sŭrprís'd
Lóse thĭr dĕfénce, dĭstŕactĕd ănd ămáz'd.

The second verse paragraph of the ode, on the patience and fortitude of saints, contrasts with this variable, widely swinging, rhythmic action of divine deliverance in battle: the vigorous motion is replaced by a much calmer, more regular iambic rhythm:

> But pátience ĭs móre óft thĕ éxercìse
> Ŏf Sáints, thĕ tríal òf thĭr fórtĭtùde,
> . . . . síght bĕréav'd
> Mă̆y chánce tŏ númbĕr thée with thóse
> Whŏm Pátiĕnce fínallỳ mŭst crówn.

The ode just discussed is the one ending act 4, which has portrayed Harapha's would-be challenge of Samson to combat and Samson's stirring reply. It ends, like the first three such odes, with a clear shift to mixed declamation and speech for a short passage introducing the leading character for the next act. Milton uses considerable variety in these choral passages marking off the acts of his drama. Acts 1 and 3, like act 5, end not with a *Schlußchor* ode alone but with an extended ensemble, akin in form to the act-ending ensembles of music drama.

For the ending of act 1, the dialogue finishes with Samson's speech—the first in which his spirits begin to rise—criticizing his people's leaders for refusing to join him in fighting their Philistine overlords. The act-ending choral ensemble then begins with a battle song of the chorus comparing Samson as deserted or betrayed war leader to Gideon and Jephtha. The song is in alternating tetrameters and pentameters, more regular in meter and steadier in rhythm than the act-ending odes, and concluding with two rhymed couplets of alternating tetrameter/pentameter lines.

> Thy words to my remembrance bring
> How *Succoth* and the Fort of *Penuel*
> Thir great Deliverer contemn'd,
> . . . .
>
> And how ingrateful *Ephraim*
> Had dealt with *Jephtha*, who by argument,
> Not worse than by his shield and spear
> Defended *Israel* from the *Ammonite*,
> Had not his prowess quell'd thir pride
> In that sore battle when so many died
> Without Reprieve adjudg'd to death,
> For want of well pronouncing *Shibboleth*.
>   (lines 276–89)

Prince admires the "tramping rhythm" here, illustrating the "varying musical patterns" of *Samson*'s lyrical verse (p. 162). With its quality of song suggestion, the passage opens the three-part act-ending ensemble. Samson replies to it with three lines of blank verse, which, preceded and followed by choral song or chant, should probably be imagined sung in mixed forms of recitative, with repetitions of the phrases:

> Of such examples add mee to the roll,
> Mee easily indeed mine may neglect,
> But God's proposed deliverance not so.

The succeeding, act-ending ode affirming God's power and righteousness departs from Milton's principle of "allaeostroph" for the other choral odes and just misses (by one extra line in stanza three) being a four-stanza, partly rhymed canzone with a *commiato* (lines 322–25). Each of the stanzas, marked by indentation of its first line, has seven lines mostly of six and ten syllables.

> Just are the ways of God,
> And justifiable to Men;
> Unless there be who think not God at all:
> If any be, they walk obscure;
> For of such Doctrine never was there School,
> But the heart of the Fool,
> And no man therein Doctor but himself.
>   Yet more there be who doubt his ways not just,
> As to his own edicts, found contradicting,
> Then give the reins to wand'ring thought,
> Regardless of his glory's diminution;
> Till by thir own perplexities involv'd
> They ravel more, still less resolv'd,
> But never find self-satisfying solution.
>   (lines 293–306, stanzas 1, 2)

In this meditation on God's righteousness, inspired by the Psalm verse about the fool who said in his heart, "There is no God," such people are deflated and derided by the sudden skipping ternary motion (emphasized by the *school-fool* rhyme) in line 298 after the solid binary tread of the preceding lines, a mixture of 2's and 3's that produces one of the most striking rhythmic effects in all Milton's verse.

It seems in the last two stanzas that the chorus, carried away by its devotion, goes farther into fideism than Milton himself would, with his belief in the rationality of God's justice.[59] Nevertheless the ode is an emotionally charged affirmation of traditional faith (the chorus after all represents tradition), and Milton himself would have sung along happily with the first two stanzas, at least. I see no reason to believe that he deliberately made the ode "flat" (see note 57). The rhymes on scholarly words (*diminution-solution* and so on) are part of a satiric effect: the doubters and "curious" theologians who ramble in "wand'ring thought" are like the theologically talented devils satirized in *Paradise Lost*, who whiled away the time in hell with reasoning "Of Providence, Foreknowledge, Will, and Fate, / Fixt Fate,

59. See Joan Bennett, "Liberty under the Law: The Chorus and Meaning of *Samson Agonistes*."

free will, Foreknowledge absolute, / And found no end, in wand'ring mazes lost" (2.559–61). Milton would not have distanced himself from this satire.

The chorus is here proposing to Samson a total resignation to God's will and a giving up of his effort to rationalize that will—an inadequate choice, but one which must be presented with force and dignity at this stage of his process of regeneration as a possible attitude for him to adopt. The extra eighth line of stanza 3 was probably added deliberately: rejecting the idea that God could be confined, the chorus bursts through the now-established seven-line stanza form:

> As if they would confine th'interminable,
> And tie him to his own prescript,
> Who made our Laws to bind us, not himself,
> And hath full right to exempt
> Whom so it pleases him by choice
> From National obstriction, without taint
> Of sin, or legal debt;
> For with his own Laws he can best dispense.
>   (lines 307–14, stanza 3)

As the stanza pattern is broken by the extra eighth line, so the rhyming of the first two stanzas is likewise cast away in scorn of those who would "confine the interminable." Stanza 4 returns to the established, partly rhymed, seven-line canzone stanza, as the chorus tries to accept God's inspiring Samson to the unlawful act of taking a Philistine bride, then concludes with the *commiato*, "Down Reason then, at least vain reasonings down," and so on. The chorus may be theologically inadequate here, but they are reinforcing—celebrating with the force of communal song—Samson's own initial effort not to blame God for his miseries and to have faith in God's ultimate victory: "Mee easily indeed mine may neglect, / But God's proposed deliverance not so." Samson's solo is the key note to this three-part ensemble.

To review, the ensemble ending act 1 has a distinct rhythmic and musically suggestive structure. It opens with a martial *canzonette*, partly rhymed and suitable for homophonic song, that makes the Danite comforters for the moment a soldier chorus, singing of the God of battles. Samson, inspired by their song, sings a solo in praise of God's victories, which transcend his own failures. Then the chorus responds, probably returning to unison song for clear enunciation of the words, with the concluding stanzaic ode to God's power and righteousness. This communal musical celebration of God's power to conquer, whatever notable leader may sin and fail, is necessary to help Samson take the first step in his regeneration, namely to accept his sin and to start looking beyond it.

In act 2, which has presented Manoa's fatherly sorrow and Samson's shame and misery, the dialogue ends upon Samson's low point of the play, his despairing death wish. The act then concludes, appropriately, with a single, quiet choral ode rather than with a stirring ensemble: a prayer for consolation and a questioning of God's dealings with Samson. Here the Danite chorus, in contrast to the harsh, ideologically fixated "comforters" of Job, proves capable of feeling Samson's misery. Aeschylus's wing motions for the comforter chorus with Hecuba may not do, but some imagined choreography of sympathetic promenade will be in order.

> Many are the sayings of the wise
> In ancient and in modern books enroll'd,
> Extolling Patience as the truest fortitude,
> . . . .
> But with th'afflicted in his pangs thir sound
> Little prevails, or rather seems a tune,
> Harsh, and of dissonant mood from his complaint,
> Unless he feel within
> Some source of consolation from above.
>   (lines 652–54, 660–64)

The next verse paragraph shifts to more urgent prayer, with a moving, partly rhymed passage in mixed binary and ternary rhythms, taking its inspiration from a verse in Psalm 8: "What is man that thou art mindful of him."

> God of our Fathers, what is man!
> That thou towards him with hand so various,
> Or might I say contrarious,
> Temper'st thy providence through his short course,
> . . . .
> Nor do I name of men the common rout,
> That wand'ring loose about
> Grow up and perish, as the summer fly,
> Heads without name no more remember'd,
> But such as thou hast solemnly elected,
> With gifts and graces eminently adorn'd
> To some great work, thy glory,
> . . . .
> Nor only dost degrade them, or remit
> To life obscur'd, which were a fair dismission,
> But throw'st them lower than thou didst exalt them high,
> Unseemly falls in human eye,
> Too grievous for the trespass or omission.
>   (lines 667–70, 674–80, 687–91)

The rhyme of "various"-"contrarious" calls attention to the interplay of ternary with binary rhythms that has already begun on the phrase "God of our Fathers" and continues especially in such words as "inferior," "irrational," "solemnly," and "eminently." The frequent rhymes mark off enough line endings for the ear so that these faster rhythms seem to fall at measured intervals. The most striking rhythm of the clustered light syllables here is the retard effect of "lówer thăn thŏu dìdst" in "But throw'st them lower than thou didst exalt them high," which rhythmically reflects the calamitous halting and dropping into the depths of those who have been exalted by divine favor, then have fallen.

The theological inadequacy of the chorus's sung statements should not cause us to demean them or to regard them as a mere dramatic foil giving wrong answers against which Samson's right answers can appear glorious.[60] Their traditional responses represent necessary stages of Samson's self-examination, and their poetry is not of a lower order than his, though of a different kind, as it presents conventional wisdom. In their utterances Milton is following his biblical models of "elegance": "Yea the Bible it selfe . . . oftimes relates blasphemy not nicely, it describes the carnall sense of wicked men not unelegantly, it brings in holiest men passionately murmuring against providence through all the arguments of Epicurus." The choristers, chanting "not unelegantly," fall between these illustrative categories: they are neither "holiest" men nor especially wicked, but they speak out of a "carnal sense" of Hebrew law-based religion;[61] faced with divine acts that do not accord with received law, they are perplexed, swayed now to celebrate God's right to do as He will, now to "murmur against divine providence." Samson's search for understanding and renewal draws upon and responds to this elegant communal song of the chorus. Their odes have power to sway us to their sense of the moment, unless we are reading the play as a treatise, determined only to get the right answer.

The "shutting up" of act 3, Dalila's last trial of Samson, is accomplished in a different fashion, beginning with the chorus's satiric tirade against women, designed to suggest, among other things, the playful intellectual superiority of Samson in his riddling days:

> It is not virtue, wisdom, valor, wit,
> Strength, comeliness of shape, or amplest merit
> That woman's love can win or long inherit;
> But what it is, hard is to say,
> Harder to hit,
> (Which way soever men refer it)
> Much like thy riddle, *Samson*, in one day
> Or seven, though one should musing sit.

Again the choristers, this time in the momentum of satiric invective, tend to an extreme in singing their conventional wisdom: while they reflect some of Milton's own patriarchal attitudes, he would not have gone so far as to award the male "despotic power over his female in due awe"—alone the word *despotic* would have been anathema to him. The ode is a pithy, con-

---

60. Ibid., p. 151, says that the chorus "defends God's power at the expense of his goodness," thereby showing blind obedience to law and a lack of Milton's concept of a rational Deity, and further that this is "a moral rather than an intellectual failing" in the chorus.

61. *PL* 12.300–306, reflecting St. Paul, speaks of the law as fleshly, the new covenant as spiritual. The passage just cited is from Milton, *Complete Prose*, 2:517.

ventional misogynist response to Dalila's potent final effort to possess and control Samson, which has just occurred—cannon shot for cannon shot. Furthermore, we should recall that an inclination to strong statement or simplification is a frequently noted feature of song verse: bright colors, sharp contrasts, emotive assertions, familiar sentiments are most readily communicable and thus most suitable in sung words—by extension then in words that will suggest choral singing and draw from a pool of conventional wisdom.[62] Fine conceptual distinctions are apt to be lost: the subtleties must be of rhythm and tonal color, the very beauties so notable in these odes of *Samson Agonistes*.

Act 5 ends in the most extensive choral ensemble of all, built around Manoa's solo recitation "Come, come, no time for lamentation now" (lines 1708–44). As soon as the messenger has told of Samson's great death, the chorus begins its lament and celebration with a rhymed verse paragraph to which again they may be promenading, in preparation for the division into semichoruses just ahead.

> O dearly bought revenge, yet glorious!
> Living or dying thou hast fulfill'd
> The work for which thou wast foretold
> To *Israel*, and now li'st victorious
> Among thy slain self-kill'd
> Not willingly, but tangl'd in the fold
> Of dire necessity, whose law in death conjoin'd
> Thee with thy slaughter'd foes in number more
> Than all thy life had slain before.
>   (lines 1660–68)

The rhymed pentameter-tetrameter couplet ending this passage makes a conclusion rhythm, a forceful pause. On the last word the choristers would stop their march, with the forward file in place ready to chant what Milton designates the first "Semichorus" (lines 1669–86). The rhythm here changes, from the binary tread of the previous lines to a mixture of 3's and 2's to express the inebriated state of the Philistines:

> Semichorus: While thir hearts were jocund and sublime,
>   Drunk with Idolatry, drunk with Wine,
>   And fat regorg'd of Bulls and Goats,
>   Chanting thir Idol, and preferring
>   Before our living Dread who dwells
>   In *Silo* his bright Sanctuary:
>   Among them hee a spirit of frenzy sent,
>   Who hurt thir minds.
>   (lines 1669–76)

---

62. See for example Auden's remarks in this vein in *An Elizabethan Song Book*, ed. Noah Greenberg, W. H. Auden, and Chester Kallman, pp. xvi–xvii.

Six tetrameter lines in a row, beginning with the near rhyme of *sublime-wine*, evoke a *vinate* or drinking song of the revelers at their festival, the song then being broken suddenly by the pentameter and dimeter lines "Among them hee a spirit of frenzy sent, / Who hurt thir minds." The first semichorus concludes by pointing to the "blindness internal" of the drunken worshippers of Dagon. The other file then sings as the second semichorus, likewise beginning with a rhymed couplet. As the ode proceeds, the frequency of rhyme words increases until the last eleven lines, with the single exception of line 1704, are rhymed:

Semichorus: But he though blind of sight
        Despis'd and thought extinguish't quite,
        With inward eyes illuminated
        His fiery virtue rous'd
        From under ashes into sudden flame,
        . . . .

        . . . . as an Eagle
        His cloudless thunder bolted on thir heads.
        So virtue giv'n for lost,
        Deprest, and overthrown, as seem'd,
        Like that sélf-begótt'n bírd
        In the *Arábian* wóods embóst,
        That no sécond kńows nór thírd,
        And lay erewhile a Holocaust,
        From out her ashy womb now teem'd,
        Revives, reflourishes, then vigorous most
        When most unactive deem'd,
        And though her body die, her fame survives,
        A sécular bírd áges óf líves.
               (lines 1687–91, 1695–1707)

Here Milton uses frequent rhymes to mark off for the ear a variety of line lengths played against the frame of iambic rhythm, thus producing a sense of rhythmic variety even with mostly steady meter. The exceptions to this regularity are the two passages scanned above, portraying the phoenix, the image for Samson as regenerate proto-Christian hero. With three flutters of her wings in quinary rhythm (lines 1699–1701) the "self-begott'n bird" begins to rouse herself from the ashes; with two flutters in the final line of the ode she attains her lofty perch as "A secular bird" who lives for "ages of lives."

    Manoa follows this exalted moment with a solo recitation. It is a lyrical monody, not a piece of dialogue intended to reveal Manoa's personal character. He is here speaking—or perhaps singing in recitative, becoming more melodic for the lyrical section on Samson's monument planted round with laurel green—at any rate, he is here reciting as part of the concluding choral ensemble, of things that must be celebrated in a great hero. When he says, "Nothing is here for tears, nothing to wail / Or knock the breast, no weakness, no contempt," he means by "here" not in Samson's whole story but in the manner of Samson's death. And in the world of the play he is right. This note of affirmation and the promise of a famous tomb are essential elements of the concluding choral celebration of Samson as divinely inspired hero, not indications of paternal sentimentality; the concluding "hallelujahs and harping symphonies" are to wipe away the tears from our eyes, if Milton has followed his scriptural model of tragedy.

After Manoa's solo the chorus sings a final piece ("All is best"), which, as both Martz and Johnson note, has the length and rhyme scheme of a sonnet, though only four lines of it are pentameter, the rest being shorter.[63] We recall that, according to Doni, the sonnet was the modern equivalent of the ancient paean or hymn, which would be sung either as solo monody or by an ensemble in part-song. This hymn, then, concludes the final choral ensemble and therewith the play, an ensemble with the same three-part structure as that ending act 1, namely a choral ode (this time expanded by division into semichoruses), a solo response treating the same themes, and a final song or hymn of the reunited chorus.

I have not been arguing that Milton intended *Samson Agonistes* actually to be performed partly sung, but rather have been following his own statements about his aims and models for tragedy and thereby spelling out a likely imagined performance for readers, which can especially enrich our reading of the choral odes. We should imagine the suitable parts of *Samson* sung or chanted (the shorter monodies, *canzonetti*, and act-ending ensembles), just as Milton when he read the Apocalypse imagined "a sevenfold chorus" performing the suitable passages there. What was "still in use among the Italians" in monody and musical-dramatic chorus with their presumed classical basis has provided ample details for this task of imaginative reconstruction. Thus we can appreciate *Samson* not as a versified theological treatise but as the "stately image" of a drama of dark inner conflict, proposing, shaping, and exalting a piece of human experience, a loss and restoration of faith.

Italian Song and the Inset Lyrics of Paradise Lost

Lawrence of virtuous Father virtuous Son,
  Now that the Fields are dank and ways are mire,
  Where shall we sometimes meet and by the fire
  Help waste a sullen day, what may be won
From the hard Season gaining? . . .
. . . .

63. Martz, "Chorus and Character in *Samson Agonistes*"; Lee M. Johnson, "Milton's Blank Verse Sonnets."

What neat repast shall feast us, light and choice,
Of Attic taste, with Wine, whence we may rise
To hear the Lute well toucht, or artful voice
Warble immortal Notes and *Tuscan* Air?
(Sonnet 20, lines 1–5, 9–12)

Through this sociable sonnet to Edward Lawrence we see Milton, blind and middle-aged, enjoying Italian solo song to instrumental accompaniment, probably to the theorbo-lute popular by then. In earlier decades Milton had sung and taught his Phillips nephews to sing late sixteenth-century madrigals and other part songs (fa la la's and frottola) of Marenzio, Gesualdo, Vecchi, and Monteverdi.[64] But this later picture of him reflects the fact that musical taste by then in England, as earlier in Italy, had largely turned away from unaccompanied part singing to solo song, accompanied by an instrumentalist who could improvise a realization of the bass line (usually all that was written out for song accompaniment). Antonio Cifra, whose works Phillips also saw among Milton's music books, had published a book of solo, monodic songs. And of course Monteverdi contributed solo pieces to the monodic song of the time, besides his operatic works. In Italy the vogue of solo song was related to the growing popularity of music drama and its theoretical reinforcement by humanists who promoted monody.

While we do not know which Italian songs Milton favored on raw winter days, we can surmise an important point about them: they were mostly love lyrics. The strong emphasis on affective expression in monody had inclined its composers to choose texts devoted to direct analysis of emotions, and given the available lyrics, this meant overwhelmingly the plaints and fleeting joys of lovers—sometimes in pastoral, sometimes in courtly or epic contexts. In such song books as Sigismundo d'India's *Musiche da Cantar Solo* (1609), Antonio Cifra's *Scherzi et arie* (1614), Giovanni Francesco Anerio's *Arie Canzonetti e Madrigali a 1–3 voci* (1619), Gabriele Puliti's *Armonici accenti voce sola per cantar* (1621), Frescobaldi's *Arie musicali* (1630), or Monteverdi's *Madrigali guerrieri et amorosi* (1638), to take a representative sample from the second to fourth decades of the century, the predominant texts represent the kind of pastoral and courtly love lyric that was still vital enough to inspire the aging Milton's reproach. In *Paradise Lost* these tradi-

---

64. As Parker notes (*Milton*, 1:181), Milton shipped "a chest or two" of music books from Italy. Three of the five composers Edward Phillips remembered as well represented there were Doni's greatest favorites: Luca Marenzio, Gesualdo Prince of Venosa, and Claudio Monteverdi. Doni also mentions the other two several times, Orazio Vecchi and Antonio Cifra (see for example *Compendio del Trattato* . . . [Rome, 1635], p. 117). Except for Cifra (d. 1629), these were composers of the late sixteenth and turn of the seventeenth century (Monteverdi made his name then too, though his long career continued afterward). Milton's selection suggests that his taste at that time was similar to Doni's and focused on the decades just before and after 1600, and further that he bought not mainly organ music (his instrument) but vocal music of various kinds—madrigals, frottola, villanelles, as well as solo songs (Cifra and Monteverdi published monodic songs).

tions supply the natural lyric mode of Satan, and indeed the only lyric expression of which he is capable.

Besides independent monodic songs Milton could, as we have seen, hear famous lovers' monodies from music drama, and these often breathed a mixed air of pastoral and epic, a special ether produced by such musical theater, where Tancred and Aminta could cross paths singing gloriously in the woods of a *favola boschereccia*. Likewise Milton's Satan can leave a war council of devils to go sing a moonlit-window song at the wedded wood nymph Eve's bower, and no one minds. What he sings in Eden and its relationships to Italian monodic song will be one of our concerns in this section.

In the monodies and choral odes of *Samson* just discussed, we can note the progress up to their date (whenever that may have been) of what may be called the dramaticizing—the thorough, broad-based, and radical dramaticizing of English lyric through the course of the seventeenth century. In *Samson* we have seen Milton's Italianate version of "grand lyric," of what others would fashion into self-contained English odes in irregular meter, as they would soon be practiced by Cowley and Dryden, becoming the most fruitful lyric form of the Restoration. Then lyric would reach its apex of reliance upon dramatic effects: declamation, irregular pulsing rhythms, apostrophe, exaggerated gestures, posturing, the sense of the speaker as a theatrical persona. Vocal music and its evolving baroque techniques being imported to England would continue to play their part in this development of dramaticizing lyric, as music had done earlier in the century.

In another place besides *Samson*'s monodies and odes we can take a reading of the Miltonic achievement in dramatic/declamatory lyric, namely in the embedded lyrics of *Paradise Lost*. They occupy a position further along the spectrum toward pure declamatory lyric, by contrast with *Samson*'s mixed song and declamation. And they display more variety of lyric types and moods, having been devised for a greater variety of situations. These inset lyrics have not lacked commentators, but they require study in the context of monodic song.[65]

That epic verse in general might be intended for singing in recitative and aria is the first fact to be considered. Doni in 1635 had cited ancient precedent for such performance in Plato, Plutarch, and others (*Compendio*, p. 119); the ancients already knew recitative singing, he claims, citing the term *logikon melos* of Aristoxenus.[66] Epic should be performed in some academy, a brief epic such as Preti's "L'Oronta" in one sitting, a long one such as Tasso's "Gierusalemme" in several (*Compendio*, p. 118). The ideal

---

65. See, for example, David Parker, "The Love Poems of *Paradise Lost* and the Petrarchan Tradition."

66. "Trattato della Musica Scenica," *Lyra Barberina Amphichordos*, 2:35: Doni says that Aristoxenus speaks of *logikon melos*, "il canto sermocinatorio o parlaresco," as opposed to true song (*oedikon melos*), which has its "firm, determined composure," and says furthermore that Vitruvius alludes to such speech song in his chapter on harmony in book 5 of his works.

recitante would be a sonorous, graceful tenor such as Francesco Bianchi, though a bass or soprano could also serve, a singer skilled in reciting and gesturing as well as singing (p. 118)—thus portions of the work might be recited. An accompanying harp should be placed near the *recitante*, the harpist tapping the beats of each line with the foot. These details are reminiscent of the sort of performance at which Milton heard the famous Leonora Baroni singing to her mother's harp accompaniment. Varying the music, Doni says, the composer could sometimes follow the poetic meter in the melody against assorted bass rhythms, sometimes vary the melodic rhythm against a steady bass; he could use different harmonic modes to suit the mood of various passages; he could instruct the singer when to vary the tempo and tone of voice. In a Florentine lecture of 1641 or 1642 Doni promises to present such a performance of epic for the academicians soon.[67]

In 1651 the concept of epic sung in *stile recitativo* was propounded by William Davenant, who would soon produce "Recitations and Music after the Manner of the Ancients." His incomplete epic, *Gondibert*, begins with a preface justifying his four-line stanzas:

> I beleev'd it would be more pleasant to the Reader, in a Work of length, to give this respite or pause, between every *Stanza* (having endeavour'd that each should contain a period) then to run him out of breath with continu'd *Couplets*. Nor doth alternate Rime by any lowliness of cadence make the sound less Heroick, but rather adapt it to a plain and stately composing of Musick; and the brevity of the *Stanza* renders it less subtle to the Composer, and more easie to the Singer; which in *stilo recitativo*, when the Story is long, is chiefly requisite. And this was indeed . . . the reason that prevail'd most towards my choice of this *Stanza*, and my division of the main work into *Canto's*, my *Canto* including a sufficient accomplishment of some worthy design or action; for I had so much heat . . . as to presume they might (like the Works of Homer) . . . be sung at Village-feasts.[68]

Davenant goes on to plead, in humanist fashion, for heroic poesy and music on the stage to improve the morals, morale, and productivity of the people. Milton probably found this preface of interest. He would have known Davenant's work (would at least have had some of it read to him) before joining Bulstrode Whitelock in the rescue of the Royalist Davenant from the death sentence.[69]

Doni, like Davenant, remained within the mainstream of Renaissance tradition in regarding rhymed stanzaic verse as the usual medium for vernacular epic, but not so entirely as Davenant did. Epics in Italian are nor-

67. Lecturing "Sopra la Rapsodia," Doni says that on another occasion he hopes "to present in practice that which today we are considering" ("sî anco per riservare qualche cosa in altro luogo, dove spero . . . di farvi sentire in pratica quello, sopra che oggi ragioneremo" [*Lyra Barberina Amphichordos*, 2:181]).

68. *Gondibert: An Heroick Poem* (1651; facs., Menston, England: Scolar Press, 1970), pp. 25–26.

69. See Parker, *Milton*, 1:419.

mally in *ottava rima*, Doni says, bowing to Tasso; but some, such as Tris-sino's, have been written in blank verse ("Trattato della Musica Scenica," p. 19). Furthermore, in the section I have just cited on sung epic, Doni avers that monodic music must rise to the challenge of setting "poesie sciolte, e non legate in Stanze" (*Compendio*, p. 121—see note 55 above), and that monody is especially suitable for grave and heroic matter. Such views, which probably influenced Milton's thinking about epic meter, were no dissuasion from writing in blank verse or from considering it quite as suitable for music as was rhymed stanzaic verse.

Milton could hardly have imagined a work so long as *Paradise Lost* set and sung in its entirety, even one book at a sitting. But he consented later to Dryden's plan to "tag his verses" and make a semiopera based upon them,[70] and may all along have conceived of excerpt performances of mixed recita-tions and song. At any rate, in his conception of the dramatic scenes of the epic, certain portions were portrayed as sung, and we are to imagine them so in reading, just as Milton so imagined portions of the Apocalypse. "Reci-tations and Music" are part of the daily routine in paradise:

> Lowly they bow'd adoring, and began
> Thir Orisons, each Morning duly paid
> In various style, for neither various style
> Nor holy rapture wanted they to praise
> Thir Maker, in fit strains pronounct or sung
> Unmeditated, such prompt eloquence
> Flow'd from thir lips.
>   (*PL* 5.144–50)

Given the concept of "fit strains pronounct or sung unmeditated," let us see what mode of performance the text of Adam and Eve's duet implies.

In "tuneable" lines (that is, lines they sing together), they begin:

> These are thy glorious works, Parent of good,
> Almighty, thine this universal Frame,
> Thus wondrous fair; thyself how wondrous then!
> Unspeakable, who sit'st above these Heavens
> To *us* invisible.
>   (*PL* 5.153–57, my italics)

Echoes of Psalms and the angel choruses of the Apocalypse pervade this jointly sung hymn. The midsection of the ensemble then consists of a series of shorter or longer apostrophes to God's creatures, descending hierarchi-cally from angels to beasts.[71] The pronouns *I* and *my* in the final apostrophe, as opposed to *us* in both the opening and closing passages, substantiate the natural suggestion of the variable structure that these are improvised apos-

---

70. Ibid., p. 635.
71. Joseph Summers, *The Muse's Method*, pp. 74–82, suggested that these are separate strophes of the hymn.

trophes, alternately "pronounc't" by Adam and Eve individually—that is, spoken, or sung solo in improvised recitative. In accord with his natural pre-eminence Adam probably begins and, as the sequence turns out, concludes. He calls first to the angels:

> Speak yee who best can tell, ye Sons of Light,
> Angels, for yee behold him, and with songs
> And choral symphonies, Day without Night,
> Circle his Throne rejoicing, yee in Heav'n.

Eve then responds:

> On Earth join all ye Creatures to extol
> Him first, him last, him midst, and without end.

Adam:

> Fairest of stars, last in the train of Night,
> If better thou belong not to the dawn,
> Sure pledge of day, that crown'st the smiling Morn
> With thy bright Circlet, praise him in thy Sphere
> While day arises, that sweet hour of Prime.
> (*PL* 5.160–70)

Contrary to Milton's usual enjambed structure (with "the sense variously drawn out from one verse into another"), the beginning and end of each apostrophe to one kind of creature coincides with the beginning and end of a verse line, so that each is a segment of whole lines and a syntactic unit—suitably so for alternating singers. Continuing from where we left off, the apostrophes are Eve to the sun, Adam to the moon, Eve to the air and other elements, Adam to the mists and exhalations, Eve to the winds, Adam to warbling fountains, Eve to the birds, and Adam in conclusion to the fish and beasts:

> Ye that in Waters glide, and yee that walk
> The Earth, and stately tread, or lowly creep;
> Witness if *I* be silent, Morn or Even,
> To Hill, or Valley, Fountain, or fresh shade
> Made vocal by *my* Song, and taught his praise.

The two then sing together the concluding hymn verse:

> Hail universal Lord, be bounteous still
> To give *us* only good; and if the night
> Have gather'd aught of evil or conceal'd,
> Disperse it, as now light dispels the dark.
> (*PL* 5.200–208, my italics)

Since Adam and Eve are nowhere described as having extrasensory communication that would let them improvise in unison, we should assume that the "unmediated" eloquence here refers to the alternatingly improvised apostrophes, that is, to the "pronounced" strains, and perhaps to a harmonizing part one of them would sing in the duet passages. These parts jointly "sung" at beginning and end would be to a tune or tunes they have, with their prelapsarian, unimpaired musical abilities, easily invented and taught to each other, of which they would have a repertoire for twice-daily orisons. While one sings the known melody, the other could freely improvise a harmonizing part, for Adam shows them to be familiar with "full harmonic number" in describing the angelic music they hear from the celestial guards walking rounds (4.680–88). No such surmisals would be in order if this were music drama, where the unquestioned convention is that people sing together spontaneously; they are on stage appearing to do that. In epic or other narrative, however, if there is a joint performance we assume it has been rehearsed. Thus Milton must give us inconspicuous performance directions: "in various style . . . in fit strains pronounct or sung / Unmeditated," "in tuneable lines," or in another passage (4.736) "this said unanimous."

At the end of the orisons, Adam and Eve practice contrafactum, the singing of new words to a known tune, lines they must have just agreed upon as suitable for the event of the night past, namely Eve's dream prompted by Satan. There the married Eve has heard a music of the future. Satan has sung her an adulterous courtly window serenade, a kind of song and wooing about which the epic narrator has just expressed his unambiguous feeling in one of his own lyric moments, the expostulation to wedded love. Of marriage he says:

> Here Love his golden shafts imploys, here lights
> His constant Lamp, and waves his purple wings,
> . . . .
> . . . . [not] in Court Amours,
> Mixt Dance, or wanton Mask, or Midnight Ball,
> Or Serenate, which the starv'd Lover sings
> To his proud fair, best quitted with disdain.
>   (*PL* 4.763–64, 767–70)

Thus we know how Eve ought to respond to Satan's serenade: "with disdain." But Eve has never heard of disdain, and as she will soon do in waking daylight, she yields to Satan's lovely lyric:

> Why sleep'st thou *Eve*? | now is the pleasant time,
> The cool, the silent, save where silence yields
> To the night-warbling Bird, that now awake
> Tunes sweetest his love-labor'd song; | now reigns
> Full Orb'd the Moon, and with more pleasing light
> Shadowy sets off the face of things; in vain,
> If none regard; | Heav'n wakes with all his eyes,
> Whom to behold but thee, Nature's desire,
> In whose sight all things joy, with ravishment
> Attracted by thy beauty still to gaze.
>   (*PL* 5.38–47)

To seduce Eve, Satan is imitating courtly love lyric at its most appealing. Even dipping into its Platonic springs, he echoes the sense and the assonance of Plato's beautiful epigram, "Gazing at the stars, my Aster," in which the stars are eyes of heaven.[72] But the conventional role of the outcast, unsatisfied courtly lover, the lamenting, self-pitying nocturnal wanderer, was not merely a technical convenience for Milton, a handy source of recognizable lyric conventions: it was utterly germane to his concept of Satan. Voyeuristically Satan spies on Adam and Eve at their sexual play, aroused and shuddering with envy ("Sight hateful, sight tormenting!") as he remembers that in his damned condition no sexual release is possible, for "fierce desire / Among our other torments not the least, / Still unfulfill'd with pain of longing pines" (4.505–11).

In their all-encompassing prosopopeia and self-pity, Satan's soliloquies resemble those monodic plaints of the extramarital "starv'd lover." We at times almost expect him to break into something like the pieces of which such songbooks were full, for example #22 of d'India's *Musiche da cantar solo*, a monostrophic lyric in loose canzone form set in typical monodic style:

Da l'onde del mio pianto a dietro volti	From the waves of my weeping may they reverse
corrano i fiumi e i fonti,	their course, the streams and springs,
cadano svelti a' miei sospir i monti,	rapidly at my sighs may the mountains fall,
freni suo corso a' miei lamenti il cielo	at my laments may the heaven restrain its course
e di notturno velo	and by the nocturnal veil
pietoso al mio dolor s'ammanti il giorno,	piteous to my dolor may the day be covered,
né mai faccia ritorno	never may the sun return
piú dall'occaso in oriente il sole.	again from west to east.
	(lines 1–8 of 11)

But significantly Satan, for all his rhetorical powers, cannot break into such a song. His poignant soliloquies are not lyrics but circular, self-deceptive reveries. At times he begins with a lyric impulse, but is unable to bring it to fruition in a completed lyric; instead he smothers it in endless self-justification. A good example is his attempted acclamation to the sun, which Edward Phillips remembered his uncle's having composed in the 1640s for the planned music drama of the Fall:

Then much revolving, thus in sighs [he] began.
O thou that with surpassing Glory crown'd,

---

72. #669 of Sepulchral Epigrams in the *Greek Anthology*, ed. W. R. Paton, 2:356–57. The assonating words, transliterated, are "*aysathrays, aythe, genomayn, ays*," echoed by Milton's "eyes, desire, sight." I thank Anne Winters for showing me this allusion.

> Look'st from thy sole Dominion like the God
> Of this new World; at whose sight all the Stars
> Hide their diminisht heads; to thee I call.
>   (*PL* 4.31–35)

This promises to be a lyric of praise to the sun and an invocation of its aid in Satan's quest. But Satan can neither praise nor invoke aid genuinely, and his would-be acclamation dies away into the famous soliloquy of self-aggrandizement concluding "Evil be thou my Good":

> to thee I call,
> But with no friendly voice, and add thy name
> O Sun, to tell thee how I hate thy beams
> That bring to my remembrance from what state
> I fell, how glorious once above thy Sphere.
>   (*PL* 4.35–39)

Original and completed lyric utterance is a form of release, and Satan, again by contrast with unfallen Adam and Eve at their satisfying improvised orisons, is no more capable of lyric than of sexual release. His two full lyrics—the serenade and the "Proem tun'd" of the temptation scene (9.532–48)—are derivative and calculated. They are set pieces, composed as it were by human poets of the future and imitated by Satan, whose skill at mimicry is one of his leading traits. He can imitate such poetry when he adopts the role of wedded Eve's courtly lover.

Satan's serenade and "Proem," because they evoke a long line of lovers' serenades and greetings, show well what Milton's lyric style had become in his maturity, under the twin stars of oratory and dramatic song. In the serenade, the only brief and direct clause is the first, the question: "Why sleep'st thou Eve?" The rest of the ten-line lyric is composed of three long sentences (marked off in the passage as quoted above), in which instead of the flowing smoothness of earlier song lyric with its frequent end-stopped lines, brief syntactic units, and metrical patterning, Milton cultivates a sinuosity created through oratorical syntax, elaborate periodic balancing, and frequent "figures of sound."

"The sense variously drawn out from one verse into another" (Milton's phrase in the preface to the second edition of *Paradise Lost*) is of course a principle of his epic blank verse in general, not just of the lyric portions. Besides extending the scope of the sentence (as compared to most earlier verse in English), Milton consistently orders the verses so that the primary units the ear perceives do not correspond with the metrical units: as Davenant "endeavour'd that each [four lines] should contain a period," Milton endeavored that this should not happen. In the serenade, for example, sentence 2 begins on the third foot of a line, sentence 3 on the fifth, sentence 4 on the third; the displacement is deliberate, steady, and consistent with Milton's rejection of rhyme. The ear secondarily perceives the line unit of five iambic feet, but this unit is not reinforced by syntax or rhyme because the primary audible unit is the stately, ample, orator's period with its flexible, indefinitely expandable grammatical structure, superimposed as it were on a muted rhythmic unit of five iambic beats. The verse period generally overlaps and syncopates against the line unit.

When this oratorical blank-verse period, "drawing out the sense" from verse to verse, is put to work in an inset lyric, it remains itself; but the ear is offered a syntactically more patterned and conspicuous euphony than in Milton's epic verse generally, with period balanced against period, phrase against phrase. And furthermore the balancing is frequently underlined by anaphora and the other devices of word repetition so often used in song lyric. Here for example, besides the polyptoton of silent/silence, we note that the openings of the first and second sentences comprise an anaphora: they begin with "Now" followed by the verb. On the verb, in each case, the whole remainder of the sentence, by ellipsis, hangs: "Now is the pleasant time, [now is] the cool [time], [now is] the silent [time], save where silence yields . . . ." The second sentence reinforces this syntactic pattern: after "now" follows the verb again: "now reigns Full-Orb'd the Moon, and with more pleasing light Shadowy [the Moon] sets off the face of things; [it sets the face off] in vain, If none regard [the face of things]." The third sentence retains the structure, again putting the verb in the second position and hanging the rest of the sentence from it, with weight after weight of phrase and subordinate clause dropped softly, as it were, in alternation onto balance pans hanging from the verb: "Heaven wakes"—the basic sentence is complete. But "Heav'n wakes with all his eyes"—the independent clause with immediate modification is complete, and the sentence is set up to conclude "Heav'n wakes with all his eyes, thee to behold." But to make the next addition possible the "thee" is displaced to a later position by a relative pronoun, where in turn (in that later position) the "thee" can support two successive appositional or adjectival phrases, and so on: "Heav'n wakes with all his eyes, Whom to behold but thee, Nature's desire, [thee] In whose sight all things joy, with ravishment Attracted by thy beauty still to gaze." Twice here Milton uses the classical figure of synchysis (a "figure of sense"), what modern grammarians sometimes call a squinting modifier: in "shadowy" and in "with ravishment." Shadowy, for example, is both a postpositional adjective in the phrase "more pleasing light Shadowy" and an adverbial modifier of what follows: "Shadowy sets off the face of things."

Did Milton regard such unrhymed lyric verse with elaborate grammatical patterning as musical? He did, and the principle I have been invoking tells what he thought supplied its "musical delight." He knew that, despite more than a century of humanist disparagement of rhyme, such as Doni's comments (see p. 120 and note 55), most of his readers still regarded rhyme as a very important means of creating musicality in vernacular verse, in both the senses of verbal musicality and of suitability for setting: as Davenant said, it helps to make verse "adapted to a plain and stately composing of Musick." Milton, in the famous preface to *Paradise Lost*, argues that the advantages of rhyme, one device among many for creating musicality, have been greatly overestimated and its disadvantages greatly underestimated:

> Rime [is] no necessary Adjunct or true Ornament of Poem or good Verse, in longer Works especially, but the Invention of a barbarous Age . . . . Not without cause therefore some both *Italian* and *Spanish* Poets of prime note have rejected Rime both in longer and shorter Works, as have also long since our best *English* Tragedies, as a thing of itself, to all judicious ears, trivial and of no true musical delight; which consists only in apt Numbers, fit quantity of Syllables, and the sense variously drawn out from one Verse into another, not in the jingling sound of like endings, a fault avoided by the learned Ancients both in Poetry and all good oratory.[73]

The devices he considers better than rhyme for creating "musical delight" in verse are "apt numbers, fit quantity of Syllables, and the sense variously drawn out from one Verse into another." Prince has shown that the third principle derives especially from the heroic sonnets and other heroic and religious verse of della Casa and Tasso;[74] furthermore, as we have seen, their innovations in verse and verse drama were to a considerable degree continued in early Italian music drama. In a sense Milton's first and second principles bring us around once more to the efforts of English poets to find in the classical quantitative principle of verse measurement a source of rejuvenation for English poetry. The key to Milton's success in embodying his own idea of "fit quantity" is found here in the same sentence with his three principles of verse musicality: his primary model, he says, is "the learned ancients," and not in their poetry alone but in "all good Oratory" as well. Upon the iambic pentameter line established by the Elizabethans and Jacobeans, Milton syncopates, and gives preeminence to, a longer and more flexible unit: the expanded period of ancient and Renaissance oratory, complete with its heavy use of syntactic devices of pre- and post-positional modifiers, structurally functional ellipsis, and indefinite expansibility of periods through simple and delayed apposition, nonfinite clauses, and other forms of subordination. In the inset lyrics of *Paradise Lost* in this verse idiom, we have the ultimate in what I have called oratorical or declamatory mode in lyric.

In those lyrics, his three stated means of achieving "musicality" are ap-

73. Milton polemically overstates his case in claiming that rhyme is "a fault" and pleases "vulgar Readers." Even so, the paragraph does not seem to prove that he could never after this have used even occasional rhyme, and thus could not have written *Samson Agonistes* after this date (1674). The qualifications (such as "of no *true* musical delight") recognize the very link between rhyme and musicality which, as we have seen, Milton exploited in the occasional rhymes of *Samson*'s choruses, whether they were composed before or after this defense of blank verse.
74. *The Italian Element*, pp. 21–51.

plied to the greatest possible degree and in the most patterned way. The "apt numbers" and fitly numbered syllables of the pentameter lines become more conspicuously apt; that is, the meter becomes smoother and the lines more fluid through the traditional devices for such fluidity: alliteration, assonance, liquid consonants, relative avoidance of consonant clusters. The ample rhetorical periods drawn out across the verses become more regular in length (such as those in the serenade, each three to four lines long), often correspondent or parallel in grammatical structure, and frequently punctuated for the ear by the rhetorical "figures of sound," even by near rhyme or occasional rhyme.

Satan's "Proem tun'd" of the temptation scene displays these same features we saw in the serenade; I need not detail them again, but we should note Satan's rhetorical tactics here and the narrator's comment upon them:

> Wonder not, sovran Mistress, if perhaps
> Thou canst, who are sole Wonder, much less arm
> Thy looks, the Heav'n of mildness, with disdain,
> Displeas'd that I approach thee thus, and gaze.
> . . . .
>
> In this enclosure wild, these Beasts among,
> Beholders rude, and shallow to discern
> Half what in thee is fair, one man except,
> Who sees thee? (and what is one?) who shouldst be seen
> A Goddess among Gods, ador'd and serv'd
> By Angels numberless, thy daily Train.
> So gloz'd the Tempter, and his Proem tun'd.
>   (*PL* 9.532–35, 543–49)

Again Satan approaches Eve with the courtly lover's tropes and ploys: her looks are heaven in their mildness, she is nature's chief adornment and should have an angel train, she must not show him "disdain."[75] His rhetorical feat of burying Adam's love for Eve in three little subordinate words ("one man except") among three full lines on the inadequacy of her beastly admirers shows him richly endowed with the talent of his underling Belial, through smooth and elaborate speeches to make "the worse appear the better reason."

What kind of music was suitable for setting so oratorical a form of lyric? The kind that grew out of the conviction that music itself is akin to rhetoric, namely the *stile monodico* in its various forms. The *ut oratoria musica* trope of continental music theory[76] was well known in England also, as is seen in Peacham's *Compleat Gentleman*:

---

75. Satan's Proem has been discussed by D. S. Berkeley in "Précieuse Gallantry and the Seduction of Eve."

76. See Claude V. Palisca, "Ut Oratoria Musica: The Rhetorical Basis of Musical Mannerism." On Milton's reference to monody in "L'Allegro" see Sandra Corse, "Old Music and New in 'L'Allegro' and 'Il Penseroso.'"

Yea, in my opinion no rhetoric more persuadeth or hath greater power over the mind; nay, hath not music her figures, the same which rhetoric? What is revert but her antistrophe? her reports, but sweet anaphoras? her counterchange of points, but antimetaboles? her passionate airs but prosopopoeias? [77]

As proper verse for such rhetorically inspired song, Doni praised especially the *Rappresentazioni* of Giulio Rospigliosi, librettist of a work Milton, at that time, was soon to witness, "Chi soffre, speri." [78] For this reason and for another as well, we turn now to a passage from one of Rospigliosi's music dramas, "Erminia sul Giordano" (Rome, 1637, composer Michelangelo Rossi). Its temptation scene relates to Satan and his mimicry of conventional lyric, for such demonic imitation was not an invention of Milton's but was inspired by the practices of evil beings in music dramas, who put the conventions of literary flattery to work in their temptation ploys. [79] Their resulting monodies bear more than one relationship to Satan's serenade and "Proem tun'd."

The plot of "Erminia sul Giordano" is a pastoral episode; its characters are drawn mostly from Tasso's *Aminta*, but they are cast upon the epic scene of his *Gierusalemme*, with crusading and defending armies deployed around Jerusalem, including the famous lover/enemies Tancred and Clorinda. The arrival of Erminia, a female warrior, at the Jordan River gets only two lines in the *Gierusalemme*, but Rospigliosi creates a story for her. She carries Clorinda's arms, falls in love with Tancred, and in disguise as a shepherdess meets Selvaggio and Lidia (Aminta and Silvia renamed). Tancred is sought out by the beautiful sorceress Armida, who in a sylvan scene tempts him to leave his holy crusader's calling and go away with her.

This scene (act 2, scene 7) and Satan's temptation of Eve are similar not only in their pastoral setting but also in both the tempters' appeals to long-standing literary conventions that make the proposed choice seem powerfully right, and in their use of a lyric or monody as high point of the evil one's plea. In the "Erminia" this takes the form of a recitative, more impassioned that that of the dialogue in which it is embedded. Milton's Eve, described as lovelier than any wood nymph, is closely akin to all those fresh lasses out picking flowers who fall to the powers of "love in the form of a shepherd." [80] Tancred likewise is out in the woods engaged in the activity most germane to his nature—in the case of the male, knightly deeds of prowess. Correspondingly, as the tempter appeals to the female's renowned

---

77. Cited by Mortimer H. Frank, who explains Milton's references to musical modes in "Milton's Knowledge of Music," p. 89.

78. Doni, "Trattato della Musica Scenica," *Lyra Barberina Amphichordos*, 2:15.

79. Merritt Hughes (*John Milton*, p. 391) notes the similar approach of Satan in Andreini's "L'Adamo," II, vi.

80. *PL* 9.386–95 compares Eve to a wood nymph in the fields and to Pomona fleeing the enamored god Vertumnus. A favorite theme of monodic song is suggested in this picture of Eve alone and vulnerable, that of the nymph tempted and succumbing to love, as in Giovanni Francesco Anerio's "Tra fresch' herba tenerina," from *La bella clori armonica, Arie Canzonetti e Madrigali a 1–3 voci* (Rome, 1619).

beauty, the temptress appeals to the male's renowned prowess in combat, each proposing the right to supreme honor. Satan uses conventions of courtly love, the playful approach, the praise of beauty and mildness, the plea for favorable attention. Armida uses the convention of courtly romance that a knight must help a damsel in distress, claiming that she has been dispossessed of her lands by an "impious tyrant." Armida's monody is in loose, partly rhymed monostrophic canzone verse.

In answer to Tancred's questioning what has brought her to him, she sings the following[81]:

La fama, che di tè rapida vola,	To honor your fame, which rapidly flies abroad,
Et ogni gesto di Tancredi offerir:	And every deed of Tancred:
Con fortunato auuiso	Through fortunate communication
Mi fe sentir pur hoggi,	I learned only today
Ch'eri giunto improuiso:	That you unexpectedly arrived.
Io, che in loco vicino	I, who in this region
Con i franchi Guerrieri	With the French warriors
Seguitauo il camino,	Have followed the road,
Poiche la tua virtù, ch'in tè si speri,	Because of your virtue, which in you is expected,
Tosto quà volsi il passo,	I soon turned my steps here,
E sol con due Donzelle à te ne venni.	And alone with two damsels came to you.
Hor s'à pietà ti moue	Now a bitter misfortune
Una acerba suentura.	Moves you to pity,
Fà, ch'io riponga il piede	See to it that I replace my foot
Nell'antica mia fede,	In my old faithfulness,
E con luci più liete	And with light most blessed
Fà, ch'io torni à mirar l'amate mura.	See to it that I return to look on my beloved walls.
Contro all'empio Tiranno,	Against the impious tyrant,
Che del mio sangue horribilmente hà fete,	Who has horribly feasted on my blood,
Arma Signor la Mano,	Arm your hand, Sir,
La Man, che suol con memorandi esempi	The hand, which with memorable examples is accustomed
Riso levar gl'oppressi, abbatter gl'empi.	To raise up the oppressed, to cast down the wicked.

Like Eve, Tancred protests and is not immediately convinced, but as with Eve, the plea has won a favorable hearing. Rossi's setting for this temptation monody of flattery and challenge will suggest the most likely style of song in which Milton (and thus we) might imagine Satan "tuning" his Proem to Eve. Let us consider especially the second, more intense half of it, beginning "Hor s'à pietà ti moue." (The piece would now be signed with two flats, for the key of B♭.)

81. From *Erminia sul Giordano Dramma Mvsicale*, composer Michelangelo Rossi, pp. 93–94.

Armida's monody
from *Erminia sul Giordano*

Giulio Rospigliosi   Michelangelo Rossi

This form of recitative is not so lively and varied as operatic recitative would become in the next decade, but has motion enough to convey the long sentences quickly and smoothly to the listener. And it is true to the declamatory emphases of the text; the intensity of "Hor s'à pietà ti moue / Una acerba suentura," for example, is reflected in the extra interval range and motion. Or again, "abbatter gl'empi" ("cast down the wicked"), the high point and conclusion of Armida's plea, reaches the highest note of the piece and falls down from it abruptly to the final cadence.

Armida's evil power is evident soon thereafter in a scene where she appears at Hell's mouth, with Lucifer and a chorus of devils, conjuring furies to arise and trouble the crusaders' ranks. The set of this scene, represented in the 1637 printed score,[82] is typical of many operatic sets of the time showing Hell and demons and reveals the evil nature hidden beneath Armida's beautiful appearance; as Armida descends after the temptation and shows her true nature, the lovely seeming Satan descends to Hell immediately after seducing Eve, and the ensuing operatic scene with its devil chorus depicts in images of sight and sound the insidious nature of the conquering tempter.

From *Erminia sul Giordano*, Rossi/Rospigliosi, 1637 score. By permission of the British Library.

The tonal effect of Milton's soldier chorus of devils in Hell has often been appreciated. His conception was influenced by this very common kind of chorus in music drama, that of infernal gods or devils.[83] Doni stipulated what kinds of melodies and harmonies are appropriate when Jove or God sings (a musical version of the rhetorical problem of how to represent God speaking), and also when angels, human beings, or devils sing. One possibility is that, in contrast to diatonic human harmony, the devils should sing in frequently dissonant harmony, as of tritones or sevenths, the melody mov-

82. *Erminia sul Giordano*, engraving following p. 116.
83. For example, the famous Rospigliosi/Landi "San Alessio" (1634), performed at the Barberini Palace, featuring Demonio, a prince of hell, or Cavalli's "Nozze di Teti e Peleo" (1639), with its devil chorus holding a "concilio infernale." Milton would have heard about such productions and perhaps seen sets or reproductions from them, even if he did not attend any besides "L'Adamo."

ing roughly in steps of large intervals, their voices harsh or grating.[84] Milton makes his newly fallen devils (in 1.531–68 and 2.536–55), fresh from Heaven and still with many angelic powers, more euphonious, though "thir Song was partial." But in book 9, after Satan has multiplied their sin by seducing mankind, the choral hallelujahs he expects to hear acclaiming his triumphant return to Hell become instead the hissing of a throng of snakes, a scene Merritt Hughes finds especially "operatic."[85] The first scene just mentioned (1.531–68) is equally operatic in effect, with its soldier chorus of the still luminous fallen angels marching in battle array to the sound of flutes and horns in Dorian mode and sending up "A shout that tore Hell's Concave, and beyond / Frighted the Reign of Chaos and old Night." Such effects are not surprising, since Milton first planned this portion of his work as a partly sung drama.[86] His infernal setting evokes operatic stage sets of the lower world such as the one just shown from "Erminia."

In Armida's temptation piece we note a number of features similar to those of Milton's inset lyrics, many of which are equally suitable for recitative. After a brief opening address to the listener (five lines) comes a long period, constructed upon delayed apposition and subordinate clauses, which extends over the next six lines ("Io, che in loco vicino / Con i franchi Guerrieri / Seguitauo il camino, / Poiche la tua virtù, ch'in tè si speri, / Tosto quà volsti il passo, / E sol con due Donzele à te ne venni"). The second and more impassioned half of the appeal also uses extended periods, now built on parallel structures of imperatives falling regularly, every three lines ("Fà . . ." "Fà . . ." "Arma . . ."), punctuated by anaphora ("Fà . . . Fà") and anadiplosis ("Arma, Signor la *mano*, / La *man*, che suol . . ."), and climaxing with the forceful parallelism of "levar gl'oppressi, abbatter gl'empi."

Besides a straight recitative setting, the other sort of song we might imagine for Satan's "Proem tun'd" is a cheerful pastoral monodic song of Maytime seduction such as Frescobaldi's "Se l'aura spira."[87] This at any rate is

---

84. "Trattato della Musica Scenica," *Lyra Barberina Amphichordos*, 2:89: ". . . assegnando il Diatonico agli uomini, si potrebbe pure in qualche modo differenziare da essi gli Spiriti infernali; non solo con darli le peggiori voci, e più false, ma con fare anco, che il loro canto fosse più duro, e spiacevole, quale sarebbe togliendoli le grazie, e accenti (se pure i Cantori potessero astenersene) e mettendovi spessi intervalli duri, e difficili, come Tritoni, Semidiapente, e Settime."

85. *John Milton*, p. 173. For other stage sets of Hell besides the one reproduced above, see Hellmuth C. Wolff, *Oper: Szene und Darstellung von 1600 bis 1900*, pp. 24–25.

86. Hughes, *John Milton*, p. 175, quotes most of the final sketch: Gabriel descends and speaks to a chorus of angels, who then "prepare resistance at his [Lucifer's] first approach. At last, after discourse of enmity on either side, he departs; whereat the Chorus sings of the battle and victory in Heaven against him and his accomplices, as before, after the first Act, was sung a hymn of the Creation. . . . Justice cites him [Man] to the place whither Jehovah called for him. In the meantime the Chorus entertains the stage and is informed by some Angel of the manner of his Fall. Here the Chorus bewails Adam's fall . . . ."

87. Frescobaldi, *Arie Musicali*, pp. 26–27.

the effect Satan would like to produce, though lighthearted and harmless he can never be.

Se l'aura spira tutta vezzosa,	If the breeze blows all charming,
La fresca rosa ridente sta,	The fresh rose stands smiling,
La siepe ombrosa di bei smeraldi	The shady hedge of beautiful emerald,
D'estivi caldi timor non ha.	Of summer heat has no fear.
A' balli, a' balli liete venite,	To dancing, to dancing gentle ones come,
Ninfe gradite, fior di beltà.	Admired nymphs, flowers of beauty.
. . . .	. . . .
Al canto, al canto, Ninfe ridenti,	To song, to song, smiling nymphs,
Scacciate i venti di crudeltà.	Chase away the winds of cruelty.
	(lines 1–6, 13–14)

End rhyme here has been replaced by a few near rhymes at the line ends and by regular internal rhymes in the pattern of anadiplosis in every pair of lines (*vezzosa*/*rosa*, *smeraldi*/*caldi*, *venite*/*gradite*, and so on). The first period of the singer's plea is extended by apposition and by ellipsis: "[if] the fresh rose stands." The music displays the combination of qualities monodic song composers aimed for in such arioso pieces of the time: a lively melody over chordal harmony, careful correlation of words and melody to make good articulation possible, and limitation of ornamentation to the concluding word of a phrase so that it does not reduce comprehensibility.

from Se l'aura spira

Girolamo Frescobaldi

D'e - sti - vi cal - di ti - mor non ha. A' balli' a bal - li, lie -

- te ve - ni - te, Nin - fe gra - di - te, fior di bel - tà.

(measures 1–24)

Like the singer here, Satan attempts the role of happy, playful seducer, beginning by entertaining the lady with snaky gambols, just as the lover of the song dances and sings, then calls the nymph to join him:

> Oft he bow'd
> His turret Crest, and sleek enamell'd Neck,
> Fawning, and lick'd the ground whereon she trod.
> His gentle dumb expression turn'd at length
> The Eye of *Eve* to mark his play; he glad
> Of her attention gain'd . . .
> . . . .
> His fraudulent temptation thus began.
> Wonder not, sovran Mistress, . . .
> (*PL* 9.524–32)

It seems likely that, given the depth of Satan's character, his absolute egotism, and his penchant for bombast, he would sing a high-flown recitative in the manner of Armida, perhaps with a contrasting arioso passage on "Fairest resemblance of thy Maker fair, / Thee all things gaze on, all things thine / By gift, and thy Celestial Beauty adore." I have suggested the examples from Rossi and Frescobaldi as illustrating each end of the range of musical possibilities within which we can imagine a likely monodic song setting for any of the embedded solo lyrics of *Paradise Lost*: either recitative, arioso song, or some combination of the two such as was also common in music drama and in monodic songbooks.

We now expand our perspective and survey the embedded lyrics. The length of Satan's Proem (17 lines) represents the scope Milton most often needed for the inset solo lyrics of *Paradise Lost*. Some readers have looked for sonnets in the epic,[88] but a survey of lyric passages without a preformed notion of what their length should be reveals that 16 to 24 lines is the favorite arc for the lyric flights of the oratorical muse. Thus we find Eve's love lyric "With thee conversing I forget all time" (4.639–56) has 18 lines, the apostrophe "Hail wedded Love, mysterious law" (4.750–73) has 24; Messiah's battle song "Stand still in bright array ye Saints, here stand / Ye Angels arm'd" (6.801–23), 23; Satan's seduction Proem just discussed (9.532–48), 17; Eve's apostrophe to the tree of knowledge, "O Sovran virtuous precious of all trees" (9.795–810), 16; Adam's lament for fallen Eve "O fairest of Creation, last and best" (9.896–916), 21; Eve's penitence lyric "Forsake me not thus, *Adam*" (10.914–36), 23; Eve's lament for paradise "O unexpected stroke, worse than of Death!" (11.268–85), 18; and Adam's lament for the devastation of the Flood "O Visions ill foreseen!" (11.763–84), 22 lines. This is a favorite length for monostrophic arias and other brief monodies in music drama, though Milton may not have consciously imitated their length. It is also roughly the length Doni had in mind when he said that the "shorter" and highly emotive (*affettuosi*) monodies of drama—and only those—should be sung.[89]

Two more types of brief lyric occur in *Paradise Lost*, as well as a few lengthy passages implying hymnic or choral ensemble. First, some lyrics follow the model of one stanza of a stanzaic song. Thus we have Adam's and Eve's jointly sung evening hymn "Thou also mad'st the Night, / Maker Omnipotent" (4.724–35); Adam's aubade "Awake / My fairest, my espous'd" (5.17–25); Satan's midnight serenade to Eve (5.38–47); Adam's pastoral lament of despair "Why comes not Death" (10.854–62); and his *felix culpa* hymn "O goodness infinite, goodness immense!" (12.469–78). Besides these

88. See Johnson, "Milton's Blank Verse Sonnets," and A. K. Nardo, "The Submerged Sonnet as Lyric Moment in Miltonic Epic."

89. In performance of tragedy and comedy, Doni says (*Lyra Barberina Amphichordos*, 2:13), soliloquies (monodies) should be sung when they are "affettuosi, e non troppo lunghi" ("emotive, and not very long"), as in ancient theater. While Doni does not here specify what he means by long, we can surmise it from other things he says. The usual length of monodies that occupied whole scenes in entirely sung music dramas was fifty to eighty lines, divided into several parts (such as in Monteverdi's Arianna monody). This modern multisectioned, whole-scene, entirely sung monody is what Doni meant by a "long" one. Doni observed correctly that the tendency to excessive length in entirely sung productions was forcing librettists to reduce the length of dramas from the ancient standard of some 1500 verses to about half that in three acts (*Lyra Barberina Amphichordos*, 2:172, 198–201). Thus while long meant 50–80 lines (a whole scene in a 250-line act), short would mean something on the order of 12–30, if most of the scene were to be spoken, as Doni argued the dialogue should be. Milton most probably heard short sung monodies in partly spoken productions such as "L'Adamo" (see note 5).

traditionally brief solo forms (9–12 lines) of hymn, serenade, aubade, and lament, there are choral and ensemble passages that vary greatly in length, the former being modeled primarily on the choruses of the Apocalypse. The angels' chorus to God and Messiah (3.372–415) lasts 43 lines, while other choruses, serving as response after some proclamation of God, may be brief, like that beginning "Hallelujah, Just are thy ways" (10.642–48). We studied the ensemble scene of Adam's and Eve's orisons; a much larger ensemble appears when God and Messiah return to Heaven after the Creation. They are celebrated with an oratorio of sorts, opened by an orchestra of ten thousand harps (7.557–632), similar to the heavenly music of 3.365–415. These festal oratorios are parodied by the "dismal universal hiss" of Satan's subjects when he returns victorious to Hell after seducing man (10.504–77).

Significantly, not one of the many embedded lyrics, neither solo nor ensemble, occurs in Hell. Satan himself becomes capable of completed lyric utterance—and even then it is derivative—only when he is, for the moment, "stupidly good" in the presence of unfallen Eve. In the opening scene in Hell, as we noted, the fallen angels retain a limited musical ability. But as their degeneration proceeds, their music becomes reduced to mere despicable parody. This loss of lyric and musical, as of sexual, capabilities is a crucial element in the psychological realism of Milton's portrayal of damnation: the damned are utterly alone, locked in, cut off, disabled for any genuine expressive flow of selfhood from within to outside. Only by becoming in Eden "stupidly good" enough to mimic these forms of expression could Satan—and we with him—recognize the full pathos of his loss.

We close this consideration of the embedded lyrics in relation to Italian dramatic song with a look at Eve's penitential plea to Adam (10.914–36). In her subsequent greeting poem to him (12.610–23, the only sonnet-length lyric I find in *Paradise Lost*), she will cast herself as prototype of her distant justified daughter the Virgin Mary, just as Adam is prototype of his redeemer offspring Christ, the second Adam. But first she is suitably cast as another distant daughter, Mary Magdalene. In creating this scene and Eve's lyric for it, Milton was inspired by a much-loved kind of *canto spirituale* of monodic and of earlier spiritual song, that on the theme of "Maddalena alla Croce." (Mary Magdalene, by traditional interpretation, was the "woman of ill repute" who washed the feet of Jesus with her tears and wiped them with her hair, as well as one of the Marys who watched at the cross.) Milton introduces Eve's "plaint" to Adam as follows:

> but *Eve*
> Not so repulst, with Tears that ceas'd not flowing
> And tresses all disorder'd, at his feet
> Fell humble, and imbracing them, besought
> His peace, and thus proceeded in her plaint.
> (*PL* 10.909–13)

The argument of Eve's lyric, as of Magdalene's in the *canti spirituali*, is a plea not to be deserted, but rather to be allowed to suffer and die with or for the beloved Adam/Christ. The lines following the lyric are also strongly reminiscent of this favorite story—loved especially by male clerics and delighted painters through the ages, and prototype of Thais legends of converted prostitutes—the story of the beautiful, submissive, enticing prostitute weeping in penitence and kissing the feet of Jesus. Milton's Adam likewise cannot resist this "creature so fair":

> She ended weeping, and her lowly plight,
> Immovable till peace obtain'd from fault
> Acknowledg'd and deplor'd, in *Adam* wrought
> Commiseration; soon his heart relented
> Towards her, his life so late and sole delight,
> Now at his feet submissive in distress,
> Creature so fair his reconcilement seeking.
> (*PL* 10.937–43)

Eve's penitence lyric, like her earlier love song, is most affecting: one cannot say of Milton's depiction of woman that he gave to Eve any less lyric power than he did to Adam. In that respect at least, they are equals.

> Forsake me not thus, *Adam*, witness Heav'n
> What love sincere, and reverence in my heart
> I bear thee, and unweeting have offended,
> Unhappily deceiv'd; thy suppliant
> I beg, and clasp thy knees; bereave me not,
> Whereon I live, thy gentle looks, thy aid,
> Thy counsel in this uttermost distress,
> My only strength and stay: forlorn of thee,
> Whither shall I betake me, where subsist?
> While yet we live, scarce one short hour perhaps,
> Between us two let there be peace, both joining,
> As join'd in injuries, one enmity
> Against a Foe by doom express assign'd us,
> That cruel Serpent: On me exercise not
> Thy hatred for this misery befall'n,
> On me already lost, mee than thyself
> More miserable; both have sinn'd, but thou
> Against God only, I against God and thee,
> And to the place of judgment will return,
> There with my cries importune Heaven, that all
> The sentence from thy head remov'd may light
> On me, sole cause to thee of all this woe,
> Mee mee only just object of his ire.
> (*PL* 10.914–36)

Again we have a lyric suitable in its length, its dramatic qualities, and its declamatory verse form of enjambed, extended periods to serve as text for

an *affettuoso* monody of music drama. The flexibility of impassioned recitative, with its ability to subsume long subordinate sentence elements in
flights of rapid yet comprehensible phrases and then by retardation and in-
creased interval size to supply strong emphasis to the emphatic portions,
such as the several repetitions of "me" in lines 27–36—this flexibility would
just fit Eve's lyric, which would probably be set with an intermixture of
more tuneful passages on especially emotive lines, such as "While yet we
live, scarce one short hour perhaps, / Between us two let there be peace."
With the pleas that she was deceived into sin and that she cannot live without Adam's love and aid, she has led up to this center and high moment of
her lyric.

The portions most reminiscent of the Magdalene songs are the plea
"Whereon I live, thy gentle looks, thy aid"; the question "forlorn of thee, /
Whither shall I betake me?"; and the offer to go to the judgment place and
"importune Heaven, that all / The sentence from thy head remov'd may
light on me." Frescobaldi's "Maddalena alla Croce" (*Arie Musicali*, I, #6)
illustrates those features:

A piè della gran croce, in cui languiva	At the foot of the great cross, on which
Vicino a morte il buon Giesu spirante,	Near to death the good Jesus, expiring, was suffering,
Scapigliata così pianger s'udiva	[She] Was heard to lament, dishevelled,
La sua fedele adolorata amante;	His faithful dolorous lover;
E dell'umor che da' begli occhi usciva,	And as for the liquid which flowed from the beautiful eyes,
E dell'or della chima ondosa, errante,	And as for the wavy, errant golden hair,
Non mandò mai, da che la vita è viva,	India and Atlantis never sent forth, ever since life began,
Perle ed oro più bel l'India o l'Atlante;	Pearls and gold more beautiful;
"Come far," dicea, lassa, "O Signor mio	"What shall I do," she said, wretched, "O my Lord,
Puoi senza me quest' ultima parola?	Can you speak this last word without me?
Come, morendo tu, viver poss'io?	How, you dying, can I live?
Che se morir pur vuoi, l'anima unita	If you must die, I have united my soul
Ho teco (il sai, mio Rendentor, mio Dio),	With you (you know that, my Redeemer, my God),
Però teco aver deggio e morte, e vita."	Yet with you I must have both death, and life."

As Magdalene does in the passion story, Eve recognizes that Adam/Christ is
suffering in part for her sin. In asking to bear the whole suffering for sin, Eve

outdoes the humble Magdalene. This excess, however, is immediately corrected by Adam: "Unwary and too desirous . . . who desir'st / The punishment all on thyself; alas, / Bear thine own first, ill able to sustain / His full wrath." While Milton's Eve is theologically more sophisticated than Mary Magdalene, mentioning that the serpent was her fated foe and that she has sinned against both Adam and God, but Adam against God only, the dishevelled hair, weeping and foot clasping, and the basis of their penitential pleas are the same: you are suffering for my sin, how can I live without you? I want to be with you in suffering and death.

Just as the overtones of adulterous courtly love were appropriate to Satan's character, the allusions to the formerly promiscuous Magdalene are appropriate for Eve here. Her original sin with Satan, both in its presaging dream and in the event, has taken the form of a sexual experience. In the dream, she soars above the clouds with the lyric serenader. In the event, having eaten the fruit, she and Adam feel as if it has given them "wings / Wherewith to scorn the Earth" and the pleasure of "things to us forbidden," as they become fiercely passionate in a way they have not known. This new guilty sex, unlike the earlier good sex, "inflames the senses" to painful extremes of stimulation, overrules reason and reverence, and brings on afterward a restless, unhealthy sleep "with unkindly fumes" and nightmares "encumber'd." They arise from the nap like Samson and the harlot Delilah, the narrator concludes, with Adam "shorn of his strength." Since Eve has "played the harlot," as it were, what better model can there be for her penitence lyric than songs of Mary Magdalene?

In this case I believe Milton was actually thinking of some "Maddalena" song or songs, and if Eve were to sing her penitence, the setting might be something like Frescobaldi's, translated above.[90]

from Sonetto Spirituale: Maddalena alla Croce

Girolamo Frescobaldi

"Co - me far," di - ce - a, las - sa, "O Sig - nor

90. *Arie musicali*, ed. Spohr, pp. 10–11.

(measures 23–47)

This monodic setting displays the qualities Milton had in mind in praising Lawes for imitating Italian monodic song: clear articulation of words through careful accentuation and the limiting of ornamentation (here to the final two measures); reinforcement of the dramatic high moments of the text through limited repetition and other devices of emphasis (the lines "Come, morendo tu, viver poss'io?" and "Però teco aver deggio e morte, e vita" are the only words repeated); and expression of the emotional depths of the text through chordal harmony, that is, through rhythmically simple chord progressions that leave text and melody preeminent in the listener's consciousness. Milton's mode of verse in the inset lyrics was the culmination of many years of ear training in such music.

If Milton had written and published his epic in the late 1640s or 1650s while he was politically ascendant, some of his inset lyrics might well have been set in similar fashion by declamatory composers like Henry Lawes or Charles Coleman. By the time he did publish it, not only was he politically one of the least desirable poets for composers to flatter with settings, but also the midcentury declamatory song style had become passé. The Royalist Lawes, rewarded at the Restoration with his old post in the King's Music, had been well in the rear of musical development and was now dead. Restoration composers such as Matthew Locke, Pelham Humfrey, John Blow, and soon Henry Purcell, under the influence of French as well as Italian music,

were developing a rhythmically and harmonically more complex song style
that often broke texts into brief, repeatable phrases and thus required a different form of lyric with shorter periods. So it happened that Milton's lyric
texts, so much influenced by an Italian song style that found strong echoes
in his own England, had to wait until the eighteenth century for setting,
then in the larger forms of cantata and oratorio.[91] But the musical-dramatic
elements in *Paradise Lost* and *Samson Agonistes*, deriving from his experience of Italian monody and music drama, are in themselves so rich, adding
so much depth to his greatest works, that we need not much lament the absence of English musical response to them in Milton's own lifetime.

91. See note 18.

VI.   Cowley and Restoration Song

Though no man hear't, though no man it reherse,
Yet will there still be *Musick* in my *Verse*.
(*Davideis*, 1.467–68)[1]

The Davideis and *The Mistresse*
in Relation to Music

ven though Milton's oratorical lyric did not find musical response until the next century, the stream of interacting lyric practice and song setting flowed on into the Restoration with currents that we saw evidenced in Milton's lyric verse. The notable poet riding high on this stream was Abraham Cowley, a Royalist who like many others did not enjoy all the favor he had expected from Charles II.[2] But his poems were highly favored by Restoration composers, in number of extant settings surpassed only by those of D'urfey, a prolific theatrical versifier, and the nobleman Stanley, who sent his poems to composers for setting. Not only in quantity but also in quality and sensitivity the settings of Cowley texts are noteworthy; many were done by the best-known Restoration composers, Pelham Humfrey, John Blow, and Henry Purcell.

England's popular song poets of the Restoration were D'urfey, Shadwell, and Scheidt, humming and strumming purveyors of triple-time songs for concert hall or playhouse. Such lyrics can have their beauties, especially in the hands of Dryden, and I would not discredit them all, though humming through the settings of them quickly becomes tedious. They are a strain

---

1. *The Poems of Abraham Cowley*, vol. 1 of *The English Writings of Abraham Cowley*, ed. A. R. Waller, p. 253. Subsequent citations of Cowley are also from the Waller edition.
2. Arthur H. Nethercot, *Abraham Cowley: The Muse's Hannibal*, pp. 194–208.

apart from the ode, the line of "grand lyric" development I am tracing in Crashaw, Milton, and Cowley, but are also related to it in a certain way, as we shall see in Chapter VII.

Cowley, so far as we know, was not a musician. But he was interested in music as it related to poetry, and his ears were attuned to what the new forms of extended dramatic song would require for lyric texts. Texts well suited for setting are not necessarily, on that account, good poems, but Cowley's efforts to create "musical Numerosity" would prove remarkably stimulating to him. His incomplete epic the *Davideis*, mostly of the early 1650s it seems,[3] rather extensively cites a current musical compendium, Athanasius Kircher's *Musurgia Universalis sive Ars Magna Consoni et Dissoni* (Rome, 1650).[4] There Cowley could find, amid more practical information, the long-standing humanist commonplaces on the powerful effects of music, the musical origins of poetry, and modern revival of close relations between text and music.

Such topoi were inevitable for an epic of David, the archetypal poet-singer, and we might suppose they had no practical bearing on Cowley's poetry but for three facts: first, in Kircher's *Musurgia* he was citing one of the newest and most reputable general works on music and not merely repeating commonplaces; second, he invented special verse forms for David's songs in the epic (otherwise in pentameter couplets), in his notes pointing out the novelty of this procedure (Waller, 1:277); and finally, in notes with his pindaric odes he indicated that musically based considerations about rhythm were central to his verse experimentation:

> We must consider in *Pindar* the great Difference of Time betwixt his age and ours, . . . the no less difference betwixt the *Religions* and *Customs* of our countrys . . . . And lastly (which were enough alone for my purpose) we must consider that our Ears are strangers to the *Musick* of his *Numbers*, which sometimes (especially in *Songs* and *Odes*) almost without anything else, makes an excellent *Poet*. (preface, "Pindarique Odes")

In translating Pindar's poetry, Cowley continues, he seeks "to supply the lost Excellencies of another *Language* with new ones in [our] own." Prime among these is "the Musick of his Numbers," and in the *Davideis* notes to a passage on the nature of poetry he shows what he means by that phrase when he explains how song can cure disease:

3. Frank Kermode, in "The Date of Cowley's *Davideis*," argues convincingly for this dating, though one may still follow Sprat so far as to suppose that Cowley began the epic in his student years.

4. In a series of notes (nn. 32–37) to book 1 of the *Davideis*, Cowley cites Kircher several times, concluding, "See at large *Kercherus* in his 10. Book *de Arte Consoni & Dissoni*" (Waller, 1:274–76). Cowley does not literally believe in the music of the spheres, but sees it as a figure for the proportion and harmony in all things. He declares some reports about music's powers to be "so false, that I wonder at the negligence or impudence of the *Relators*," but believes indeed that music can be therapeutic for emotional illness; he then works out a way to affirm even "that it should cure settled Diseases in the Body."

In the same manner as *Musical* sounds move the outward air, so that [the outward air] does the *Inward*, and that the *Spirits*, and they the *Humours* (which are the seat of *Diseases*) by *Condensation, Rarefaction, Dissipation,* or *Expulsion* of *Vapours*, and by Vertue of that *Sympathy* of *Proportion*, which I express afterwards in Verse. For the producing of the effect desired, *Athan. Kercherus* requires . . . *Harmony, Number* and *Proportion,* [and] *Efficacious* and pathetical *words* joined with the *Harmony* (which by the way were fully and distinctly understood in the *Musick* of the *Ancients*). (*Davideis*, 1, note 32)

Thus Cowley considered the musically defined rhythms of ancient lyric verse to be a structurally constitutive feature, not to be copied, but their place somehow to be "supplied" with comparable "excellencies." We must discover what comprised that comparable musical "Numerosity" in his mature lyric verse and why the best English composers of the Restoration found it so congenial. Cowley's rhythms were not simply idiosyncratic and undefinable.

The Mistresse (1647), mostly in speech mode, supplied texts for many songs, but most of those were done by only two relatively obscure composers who were fond of the midcentury speech-mode lyric and the ideals of monodic song, namely William King and Pietro Reggio (a naturalized Italian), respectively in *Poems of Mr. Cowley And Others. Composed into Songs and Ayres* (Oxford, 1668) and *Songs Set by Signior Pietro Reggio* (London, 1677–1680). These works contain thirty-nine of the fifty-one *Mistresse* settings listed by Day and Murrie.[5] The musical ideals behind most of them are suggested by Shadwell in an encomium to Reggio's volumes. It condemns the new "jog-trotting" song composers (dutifully and oddly, since he himself was one of their best suppliers and since many of Reggio's songs were in triple-time!) and repeats the musical humanist ideals: preservation of the poet's sense, word-based special rhythms for each song, sparing use of ornamentation (though in fact Reggio was hardly less fond of it than his contemporaries), and evocation of the emotional *effetti*:

The Author's sense by Thee is ne'r perplext,
Thy MUSICK is a Comment on his Text.
. . . .

   But the Pretenders of this Quacking Age,
Who, (with their *Ditties*,) plague the Town and Stage;
. . . .

Still in their Beaten Road, they troll along,
And make alike the sad and cheerful *Song*:
. . . .

Each *Shake* and *Grace* so harshly too, th'express
A *Horse's Neighing* does not please me less.
. . . .

5. Others were by Piggott, R. King, Banfield, Barrett, Forcer, Blow, and Purcell. See Cyrus L. Day and Eleanore Murrie, *English Songbooks: 1651–1702; A Bibliography*.

Thou to each Temper canst the Heart engage,
To Grief canst soften, and inflame to Rage.
. . . .
Great COWLEY's Virtues thou dost understand.
Thou on each Excellence of His canst hit,
On every Master-stroak of his Unbounded Wit.
   (Thomas Shadwell, "To my Much Respected Master,
    . . . Signior Pietro Reggio")

But by 1650 Cowley had for the most part left speech-mode lyric behind
for experimentation in the free-swinging ode and other imitations of the
classics. In this later vein he has often been censured, from Dryden to our
own time, for roughness of meter. Even his friend and biographer Sprat declared that the fine thing about Cowley's pindaric verse was its close prox-
imity to prose.[6] (Sprat's remark accords with the idea that Cowley's odes are
largely oratorical in mode.) Yet it was just this prosy rhetorical vein of lyric
that proved most interesting to Blow and Purcell, who did not choose actual
prose for their nonliturgical settings.

Certainly neither Cowley's early speech mode nor his later odic vein was
suitable for the popular, triple-time theatrical song of the early Restoration.
Consider the transformation one of his *Mistresse* lyrics had to undergo to
become a Royalist drinking song:

Well then; I now do plainly see,
 This busie world and I shall ne're agree;
The very *Honey* of all earthly joy
 Does of all meats the soonest *cloy*,
 And they (methinks) deserve my pity,
Who for it can endure the stings,
The *Crowd*, and *Buz*, and *Murmurings*
 Of this great *Hive*, the *City*.

 Ah, yet, e're I descend to th'Grave
May I a *small House*, and a *large Garden* have!
And a *few Friends*, and *many Books*, both true,
 Both wise, and both delightful too!
    ("The Wish," lines 1–12)

Fountains, fields, woods, murmuring winds, and a mistress are to complete
the happy place, with pride and ambition to appear there "Only in *far fecht
Metaphors*." "The Wish," one of Cowley's best-known poems, is part of the
tradition of *integer vitae*, rural retreat poetry inspired by Horace, Martial,
and others, and subsequent lyrics in that vein were not necessarily influenced by Cowley. But Walter Pope's "The Wish" or "The Old Man's Wish"

 6. Thomas Sprat, "The Life and Writings of Mr. Abraham Cowley," p. xxii: "If the irregularity of the number disgust them [readers] they may observe that this very thing makes that
kind of poesy fit for all manners of subjects: . . . But that for which I think this inequality of
number is chiefly to be preferred, is its near affinity with prose: from which all other kinds of
English verse are so far distant."

does appear to be a song-mode version or imitation of Cowley's poem, related to it as Dowland's "To ask for all thy love" was to Donne's "Lovers infinitenesse" (see Chapter I) and as Herrick's song "To Musick" was to his *Hesperides* version.

Pope's "Wish" became a popular Royalist song in a setting by John Blow in 1685.[7] Cowley, now dead and exalted in Royalist eyes, here appears genially parodied in the country retreat of his last two years. His "small house" has become a "warm house," his murmuring winds a "murmuring brook," his "mistress moderately fair" a "cleanly young Girl to rub my bald Pate"; his many true books are now "Horace and Plutarch" (in some versions "Petrarch"!) "and one or two more," his "few" choice friends are the vicar and other rural gentry, whom the old man welcomes on Sunday with "remnants of Latin" and "stout humming liquor." The ending, that he "leaves not behind him his fellow," reflects King Charles's funeral statement that "Mr. Cowley has not left a better man behind him in England." The piece proved so likable as to inspire ever more raucous parody texts, such as "The Old Woman's Wish," a bawdier "Old Woman's Wish," and even "Jack Presbyter's Wish."

The Old Man's Wish

Walter Pope   John Blow

If I live to be old, for I find I go down, let

this be my fate in a coun - try town; may I have a warm

house with a stone at the gate, and a cleanly young girl to

7. For this setting, see Playford and Carr, eds., *The Theatre of Music*, 1:50–51. Its first printed appearance as verse was in Pope's *The Wish* of 1697, but it had already been printed in songbooks, one of which dates it: *A Choice Collection of 180 Loyal Songs . . . Written since*

rub my bald pate. May I go - vern my pas - sion with an ab - solute

sway, and grow wi - ser and bet - ter as my strength wears a - way; without

gout   or   stone, with - out gout   or   stone,   by a

gen - tle de - cay, by a   gen   -   tle de -

cay.

In this lyric hardly any speech-mode characteristics are left: no more "Well then; I now do plainly see" or "methinks," fewer syntactic interruptions, as in "shall I / My self, eas'd of unpeaceful thoughts, espy?" or exclamations ("Oh Fields!"), and far less metrical roughness (like "Mǎy Ì ǎ *smǎll Hóuse*, ǎnd ǎ *lǎrge Gǎrděn* háve! / And ǎ *féw Fríends*"). Instead of Cowley's speech-mode stanzas in variable line lengths, we have the song lyricists'

---

the *Two late Plots* (Viz) *the Horrid Salamanca Plot in 1678 and the Fanatical Conspiracy in 1683* (1685). This book also contains parody versions of the text.

smooth triple-meter tetrameters. The distance between Cowley's "Wish" and this Royalist song is a measure of the distance between midcentury speech-mode lyrics, which were usually settable in declamatory song, and the triple-time song-mode lyrics of the Restoration, which so abruptly replaced the declamatory as the dominant style of brief lyric. The larger explanation and result of this replacement will be considered in Chapter VII. Here we note that it explains why the Restoration settings of Cowley's *Mistresse* texts are to be found mostly in two specialized volumes.

Cowley's Mature Odes and the Settings of Blow and Purcell

We return now to consideration of music in relation to Cowley's later lyric vein, evolved in the years pivotal for his poetic development, the 1650s, when he wrote his anacreontics, pindarics, some occasional odes, and most of what we have of the *Davideis* with its inset songs. In this verse he was attuned to what most Restoration composers would find amenable once the "jog-trotting" craze had died down. John Blow set several later lyric texts of Cowley's, displaying such sensitivity to the verse that the music historian Percy Young is inspired to say, "The temperament of [Cowley's] verse shows marked affinities with that of Blow's music."[8]

In order to explore what Cowley's odes could mean to composers, we begin with his smooth, isometric, primarily song-mode lyrics, his tetrameter "anacreontics." Day and Murrie record fourteen Restoration settings of ten of these, the most popular being "Love" (three settings):

> I'll sing of *Heroes*, and of *Kings*;
> In mighty Numbers, mighty things,
> Begin, my *Muse*; but lo, the strings
> To my great *Song* rebellious prove;
> The strings will sound of nought but *Love*.
> I broke them all, and put on new;
> 'Tis this or nothing sure will do.
> These sure (said I) will me obey;
> These sure *Heroick Notes* will play.
> (lines 1–9 of 17)

Cowley's anacreontics are in the vein of Ben Jonson's songs, metrically smooth, mostly isometric, yet with a distinct dramatic element, and, even while smooth, able to evoke vivid speech at times: "The strings will sound of nought but Love. / I broke them all, and put on new; / 'Tis this or nothing sure will do." Thus Cowley teaches the fabled Anacreon to lyricize in English, "supplying" the untranslatable excellences of verbal musicality in the Greek with this seventeenth-century combination of smoothness and informal speech. Again we hear this strain in the cruel/kind remarks of Ana-

8. *A History of British Music*, p. 245.

creon's lady loves: "Oft am I by the Women told, / Poor *Anacreon* thou grow'st old. / Look how thy hairs are falling all; / Poor *Anacreon* how they fall." The suggestions of garrulity, mock sympathy, and the coy playing of a young girl with a middle-aged lover are achieved by word repetition, rhythm, and suggested raised intonation on "Poor" and "Look."

The setting of "I'll sing of heroes" by John Jackson (1687)[9] illustrates how Restoration composers could treat this playful, gently mocking jollity with musical-dramatic devices. The melody begins like some stately recitative or fanfare opening, with ascending fourths, fifths, and octaves in G major, leading up to a high G on "Begin, my Muse," suggesting that some lofty theme will be treated. But instead of continuing in G major, the "Muse" goes to D♯ and thus to the relative minor (E) for a passage that humorously suggests a tug of war between the singer and his lyric strings. He holds out for high, heroic notes; they pull the song loose, down to the low, lascivious tones of love: in two step-wise descending measures the melody repeats each note before being pulled down to the next tone, then the last phrase of the passage is repeated softly as an echo, to make the effect unmistakable, on "the Strings will sound of nought but Love" (measures 11–13).

from I'll sing of heroes

Abraham Cowley   John Jackson

9. *The Theater of Music: A Choice Collection of . . . Songs Sung at the Court, and Public Theaters* (London, 1687), 4:54–55.

nought but Love. I broke them all and put on new, 'tis this or nothing

sure will do; these sure, said I, will me o-bey, these sure hero - ic

notes will play. Straight I be-gan with thun -

dring Jove, and all th'immor - tal pow'rs but Love.

(measures 1–25)

The colloquial quality of the next lines ("I broke them all . . ."), with their repetitions of "sure" for what is not sure—today we would say "definitely"— is matched with a declamatory melody to contrast with the succeeding unprepared, humorously overblown run on "Thundring Jove." After that last effort at lofty song, the singer gives in to his "enfeebled Lyre" and sings of "melting Love" in a tuneful lyrical passage ("farewel then Hero's, farewel Kings"), which the composer extends by repeating it in three parts as an ensemble conclusion to the song. This extension is musically effective, creating a lyrical second half of the song to balance with the musical declamation and humorous foolery of the first half.

Cowley's anacreontics are primarily song-mode verse in smooth isometric rhyming lines—a vein that turns up in his irregular odes as well, not as their overall verse form but as a kind of songlike core for the usual irregular, as

Milton said "allaeostrophic," odic stanza. Such a stanza for Cowley is built around a core of two or more rhyming lines, usually short and isometric, which become the stanza's focal point or climax. Song mode in his century, as we have seen, encompasses much more than smooth, isometric rhyming lines, but such lines are characteristic and suggestive of so many songs that they evoke a feeling of song when they occur in the midst of a rhythmically irregular passage. Around the songlike core Cowley's irregular lines are slower and faster, shorter and longer, freely varied to range with the sense. In the following examples the song-mode core will be marked with a bracket.

The core can be as short as a couplet, for example in stanza 3 of "The Praise of Pindar":

Whether at *Pisa*'s race he please
To *carve* in polisht *Verse* the *Conque'rors Images*,
Whether the *Swift*, the *Skilful*, or the *Strong*,
Be crowned in his *Nimble*, *Artful*, *Vigorous* Song:
Whether some brave young man's untimely fate
In words worth *Dying for* he celebrate,
    Such *mournful*, and such *pleasing* words,
As *joy* to'his *Mothers* and his *Mistress grief* affords:
  { He bids him *Live* and *Grow* in fame,
  { Among the *Stars* he sticks his *Name*:
The *Grave* can but the *Dross* of him devour,
So *small* is *Deaths*, so *great* the *Poets* power.

Cowley here celebrates a favorite Pindaric theme, the power of poetry to immortalize, coming to a forceful climax in the tetrameter couplet that puts up the poet's as well as the young man's name among the stars.

Or the stanzaic core can be as long as the miniature song in the midst of the next, quite long stanza (#4) of "The Praise of Pindar," an isometric segment eventually halted by a shorter penultimate line:

[Pindar sails high in the clouds] . . .
    / Whilst, alas, my *tim'erous Muse*
    | *Unambitious* tracks pursues;
    | Does with weak unballast wings,
    | About the *mossy Brooks* and *Springs*;
    { About the *Trees* new-blossom'ed *Heads*,
    | About the *Gardens* painted *Beds*,
    | About the *Fields* and flowry *Meads*,
    | And all *inferior beauteous things*
    | Like the laborious *Bee*,
    \ For little drops of *Honey* flee,
And there with *Humble Sweets* contents her *Industrie*.
        (stanza 4, lines 5–15 of 15)

Rhyme helps to mark off these song-mode passages for the ear, whether it be couplet rhyme or the irregular but prominent rhyme of the example just cited.

The core can occasionally be in, or include a segment in, some nonisometric meter traditionally used for songs, such as fourteeners, as in stanza 4 of the Pindaric ode "Destinie":

> With *Fate* what boots it to contend?
> Such I *began*, such *am*, and so must *end*.
> { The *Star* that did my *Being* frame,
> { Was but a *Lambent Flame*,
> { And some small *Light* it did dispence,
> { But neither *Heat* nor *Influence*.
> No Matter, *Cowley*, let proud *Fortune* see,
> That *thou* canst *her* despise no less then *she* does *Thee*.
>   (lines 1–6 of 16)

Occasionally, as in the stanza just cited in part, a very long odic stanza can contain two core passages for emphasis or focus. Another such double-core stanza is #1 of "Christ's Passion," to be considered shortly.

The core passages in Cowley's odic stanza structure not only resemble song but also originated in song meters, as is evident in David's stanzaic wooing serenade in mixed line lengths in the *Davideis* (set by Blow for performance at an Oxford occasion in 1678, as well as by King and Reggio). Just such song stanzas had been perfected by the lutenist song poets and used by Herbert and Herrick.

> Awake, awake my *Lyre*,
> And tell thy *silent Masters* humble tale,
> In sounds that may prevail;
> Sounds that gentle thoughts inspire,
> { Though so *Exalted* she
> { And I so *Lowly* be,
> Tell her such *diffe'rent Notes* make all thy *Harmonie*.
>   (*Davideis*, III, Waller, p. 344)

"Though so *Exalted* she / And I so *Lowly* be" sounds the keynote of the country lad's serenade beneath the princess's window and makes a penultimate rhythm signaling to the ear the coming end of the stanza, just as a slow passage followed by a pause does in a song. Having thus defined a rhythmic pattern in stanza 1, Cowley then repeated it for four stanzas, as lute-song lyrics usually had done.

In the *Davideis*, repeated lute-song stanza structure seemed fitting for inset songs to the hero's lyre, but Cowley's Pindaric experiments led him to write odes in which each of the stanzas or strophes could evolve its own length and metric shape, no two of them alike. To Cowley this "allaeostrophic" structure seemed a good English equivalent for what he perceived as Pindar's inspired metrical freedom: varied metrical lines within each opening strophe and each opening epode. And as an English equivalent of what was originally a mode of verse for musical setting (Pindar's odes), it was in fact quite suitable for Restoration styles of through-composed setting, in

which metrically identical stanzas were of no value and the composer simply selected as much of a text as he wanted for the song's length and emphases. Musicians of Cowley's later years had the means and the inclination to
set just such dramatic lyric verse treating lofty themes.

We need not suppose that Cowley was ignorant of Pindar's dithyrambic
structure of strophe-antistrophe-epode,[10] with the antistrophe duplicating
the metric pattern of the strophe, the epode then having a different pattern,
and this whole tripartite structure being repeated if the ode continues beyond three strophes. Ben Jonson had followed it in his Cary-Morrison ode.
Milton, as we saw, for his *Samson* odes chose modified canzone form and
explicitly rejected dithyrambs, which he said were designed by the Greeks to
fit "the music then used" for choruses, meaning a tune sung AAB, AAB, and
so on.[11] Cowley had already rejected it, and Milton perhaps admired him for
that reason, among others.[12] In the preface to the Pindaric odes, Cowley
says, "Though the Grammarians and Criticks have labour'd to reduce his
[Pindar's] Verses into regular Feet and Measures . . . yet in effect they are
little better than Prose to our Ears." As his next sentence shows, he does not
mean by this that he cannot recognize the overall dithyrambic structure, but
that he cannot hear the meter grammarians find in each line (indeed it was
not understood till the nineteenth century) and that their translation is simply prose "to our Ears." For, he continues, "I would gladly know what Ap-
plause our best Pieces of English Poesie could expect from a Frenchman or
Italian, if converted faithfully, and Word for Word, into French or Italian
Prose." Thus Cowley thought that Pindar's meters could not be reproduced
in translation and apparently saw no reason to imitate the dithyrambic
structure if one's odes were not to be for stanzaic setting.

Cowley was especially challenged by the task of translating poetry, the
effort to carry across or to recreate in another language something akin to
the achievement of the original. His comments on the task reveal one of the

10. John Heath-Stubbs, *The Ode*, p. 40: "It would appear that Cowley was unaware of the
true structure of the Pindaric ode." This notion, originating with Gosse, had already been dis-
credited by, among others, George Shuster, in *The English Ode from Milton to Keats*, pp.
109–10.

11. G. B. Doni, the musical humanist we studied in Chapter V, discusses the Greeks' own
eventual rejection of this structure for odes. He speculates that stanzaic song to a repeatable
tune was used in early times because the choristers were aristocrats honoring the occasion
by their participation [as in Renaissance masques] and thus could not learn long, through-
composed settings like those sung later by trained singers. See *Lyra Barberina Amphichordos*,
2:20–21: ". . . ne' tempi antichissimi, quando i Ditirambi erano rappresentati da persone no-
bili, avevano gli antistrofi (cioé, erano divisi in stanze all' usanza delle canzoni, che ripetono la
medesim' aria in tutti) perché non si trovavano facilmente uomini di quella fatta, che potessero
continuare a mente un canto molto lungo, e vario; ma che poi quanto s' introdusse di farli
cantare a persone vili, e mercenarie, si lasciarono gli antistrofi; perciocchè allora si poteva fare
un canto variato sempre, e prolisso quanto si voleva."

12. William R. Parker, in *Milton: A Biography*, 1:584, says Milton's wife Elizabeth re-
ported that Cowley was one of his three favorite English poets.

ways in which his mind was modern, for like a comparatist of our own time, he knew that much of poetry's power depends on the aural qualities and resources of the particular language in which it was composed. His aim was not to reproduce words, meter, and structure but, as he says, to stick to the poet's "Subject" (theme), to suggest "what was his way and manner of speaking," and "to supply the lost Excellencies of another Language with new ones in [our] own."

Cowley's was a bookish muse, with her "lambent flame" at its brightest when he was translating, annotating, puzzle-solving, making fine adjustments to relate his words and rhythms to those of a source or model, perhaps of different models at once. His elaborate notes to the *Davideis* and to the Pindaric imitations proper (Odes 1 and 2) reveal the process and display his reverence for rational study of the ways of nature, God, and poetry. When an intense effort at such scholarly response coincided with absorption in his favorite kind of theme, his muse became "kindled at a hint so great" and poured out pulsing metric units, each a new variant of his ode stanza with its song-mode core. The themes that brought his verse to life involved vast or strong forces in motion or cosmic energies at work: resurrection and doomsday, thousands of people crossing the Red Sea (the stanzaic psalm in the *Davideis*), Drake's world explorations, Hobbes's vast philosophy, momentous scientific discovery, the immortal-making power of poetry—even its power over the "nice tenets" of faith (ode to Crashaw). With such themes a talent came to the fore that had rarely found expression in the pastoral and amatory verse of his juvenilia and *Mistresse*.

Translating a neo-Greek ode on Christ's passion could inspire him to his lively fashion of energized cosmic galloping, for it treats the passion in terms not of quiet, Good Friday mourning but of universal change brought about by the act of redemption. John Blow did a duet setting of stanza 1 of this work: "Christ's Passion, Taken out of a Greek Ode, written by Mr. Masters." [13]

> Enough, my Muse, of Earthly things,
> And inspirations but of wind,
> Take up thy Lute, and to it bind
> Loud and everlasting strings;
> And on 'em play, and to 'em sing,
>   The happy mournful stories,
>   The Lamentable glories,
>   Of the great Crucified King.
> Mountainous heap of wonders! which do'st rise
>   Till Earth thou joynest with the Skies!
> Too large at bottom, and at top too high,
>   To be half seen by mortal eye.

---

13. John Blow, "Enough, my Muse, of earthly Things," in *Harmonia Sacra* (London, 1688), pp. 47–49.

{How shall I grasp this boundless thing?
{What shall I play? what shall I sing?
I'll sing the Mighty riddle of mysterious love,
Which neither wretched men below, nor blessed Spirits above
        With all their Comments can explain;
How all the whole Worlds Life to die did not disdain.

As Blow's treatment reflects, this stanza too has such segments of isometric lines as we have noted, contrasting with the longer, mostly irregular lines and presenting their theme *in nuce.* Cowley has varied his practice here with a relatively long opening song-mode passage, inspired by the image of lute stringing, that shifts rhythmically in the middle into a short-lined core section. These trimeter lines in emphatic rhythm present the traditional oxymoron of blessed suffering, "The happy mournful stories," while the second isometric core passage (a couplet) emphasizes the question "How shall I grasp . . . ," and brings the motion of the stanza to a climactic halt with its symmetry, simplicity, and sharp caesura. Blow's treatment shows his sensitivity to these contrasting passages in song and declamatory modes.[14]

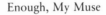

Enough, My Muse

Abraham Cowley   John Blow

14. "Enough my muse," *Harmonia Sacra* (1688), pp. 47–49.

and e - verlasting strings, and on them play and to them sing the happy

and e - verlasting strings, and on them play and to them sing

mourn - ful sto - ries, the lamen — table glories of the great

the happy mournful sto - ries, the lamen - table glories of the great

— cru - cified King: mountainous heaps of won - ders which doth

— cru - cified King: mountainous heaps of won - ders which doth

rise, till earth thou joinest with   the skies,   too large at bottom and at top   too

rise,   till earth thou joinest with   the skies,   too large at bottom and at top   too

high to be half, to be half seen by mortal eye. How shall I grasp this bound-

high to be half seen by mor - tal eye.

— less thing? What shall I play? What, what shall I sing?

I'll sing the mighty riddle of myster - ious love, which neither wretched men be - low nor blessed

I'll sing the mighty riddle of myster - ious love, which neither wretched men be - low nor blessed

spirits above with all their com - ments can explain:

spirits above with all their com - ments can explain:

Blow's rhetorical handling of the text shows him no longer bound by mid-century subservience to it but still responding to it and preserving its major units of statement. He sometimes has the two voices diverge in their textual underlay, but only very briefly and in such a way as to keep the words clear, and only at the beginnings of syntactic units: "Enough my muse," "take up thy lute," and so on. These close-spaced voice entries create a fitting sense of extra breath and motion for "inspirations but of wind." Otherwise the two voices move together, even in elaborated figures, as on "everlasting" and "die." Indeed, such parallel motion is so frequent as to give much of the song an odd quality of fauxbourdon, loosely defined—perhaps Blow conceived such archaic-sounding harmony to be appropriate for a neo-Greek ode. In contrast with it, expressive voice division reflects the opposing qualities comprising the oxymoron of "happy mournful," where the phrase is in one voice major in mode, while in the other it veers into G minor, the disjunction giving stress to one of the core passages we have noted. The pain suggested by "Lamentable" is expressed in a sonority created by two non-harmonic tones (treble suspension and échappée in the bass) over the instrumental F.

Again, but by different means, Blow gives strong emphasis to the other isometric segment, the couplet: "How shall I grasp this boundless thing? / What shall I play? what shall I sing?" These are the only words in the piece sung solo. The tenor declaims them, introducing the song's concluding section about the paradoxical "Riddle" of "Life" willing to die, with its echo repetition on "die." As here, Cowley's song-mode core passages do not necessarily suggest to composers a musically lyrical treatment; rather they may connote the rhythmic clarity and forceful simplicity of short-lined passages used for emphatic climax in earlier song lyrics of variable lines (see Chapter II). Thus an appropriate musical texture for them can be declaimed solo over homophonic accompaniment, by contrast lifting them out of the surrounding musical texture of duet with more varied accompaniment. Blow seems to be well attuned to Cowley's verse, as Percy Young has suggested. While the song is no masterpiece, it has its interest and shows Blow responding to Cowley's verse in an original harmonic idiom.

Blow's pupil Henry Purcell did a lengthy, concert-style setting of most of Cowley's pindaric ode "The Resurrection." [15] What he omitted, as well as his treatment of the text, shows him to have been well aware of the ode's structure, rhythms, and emphases, though he adapts them to suit his dramatic music. He omits the first stanza, recognizing that it is a kind of proem, from a dramatic perspective detachable, a ceremonious mounting of the muse's Pindaric horse in preparation for the intense depiction of resurrection day, the ode proper, which Purcell can make into music. The starting point for the depicted scene is the opening chord struck for stanza 2, "Begin the *Song*, and strike the *Living Lyre*," and there Purcell begins.

Stanza 1 is, however, integrally related in theme to the rest of the ode, for it has posed the unusual question that shapes this dramatic meditation: on doomsday what will become of our poetry, which we have believed "never will decay"? The answer: all the long and glorious poetry-making of our race will be obliterated in consuming fire. Pindar's beloved theme, the immortal-making power of poetry, is challenged in this best of Cowley's pindarics. The poetry of the virtuous ancients, which they thought as essential to human life as winds are to sailors, as rains to growing plants, will, along with the heavens and the earth, "melt away, / And nought behind it stay." Of course there will be poetry in the resurrected life of the saints, but it will sing, the meditator assumes, not of Odysseus Raider of Cities, nor of pious Aeneas, much less of "melting Love and soft desires," nor "of May-poles, Hock-carts, Wassails, Wakes," but all of God and his angels—fine themes doubtless, but how can one conceive of a glorious life without Virgil? What a strange perspective. In a cataclysmic destruction of all that we have and are, who would think to lament first the works of Virgil? Though Purcell omits the introductory stanza on the death of human poetry, he has not missed the theme: the ground tone of his melody, the only occurrence of low E in the solo line, falls on the "die" of " *Virgil's* sacred *work* shall dy" (measures 42–43).

from The Resurrection

Abraham Cowley

Henry Purcell

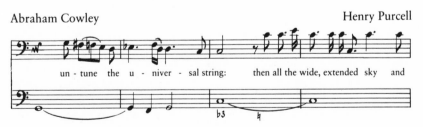

un - tune the u - niver - sal string: then all the wide, extended sky and

15. Henry Purcell, "The Resurrection, out of Mr. Cowley's Pindaricks," in ibid., pp. 12–17. For the modern performing edition see *The Works of Henry Purcell*, ed. Anthony Lewis and Nigel Fortune (London: Novello, 1965), 30:18–27.

all th'harmo - nious worlds on high and Virgil's sa - cred work shall die;

(measures 36–43)

Cowley's image of all the future years till doomsday as a smooth, elegant dancing line of choristers becomes Purcell's descriptive opening, set to dotted-note dance rhythms on "smooth and equal," appropriately echoing and drawing out the same rhythm on "my music's voice shall bear it [the dance] company":

from The Resurrection

Abraham Cowley   Henry Purcell

Begin the song, and strike the living lyre!

Lo! how the years to come, a nu - merous and well fit - ted choir,

all hand in hand do de - cently ad - vance, do

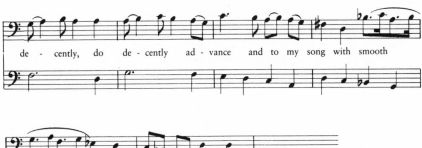

(measures 1–17)

In this disembodied *carpe diem* image, poetry vows to sing, dance, and be merry while it may:

> Begin the *Song*, and strike the *Living Lyre*;
> Lo how the *Years to come*, a numerous and well-fitted *Quire*,
> All hand in hand do decently advance,
> And to my *Song* with smooth and equal measures *dance.*
> Whilst the *dance* lasts, how long so e're it be,
> My *Musicks* voyce shall bear it companie.
>   Till all *gentle Notes* be drown'd
>   In the *last Trumpets* dreadful sound.
> That to the *Spheres* themselves shall *silence* bring,
>   Untune the *Universal String.*
>   Then all the wide extended *Sky,*
>   And all th'*harmonious Worlds* on high,
>   And *Virgils* sacred *work* shall dy.
> And he himself shall see in one *Fire* shine
> Rich *Natures* ancient *Troy*, though built by *Hands Divine.*

To the beats of mortal poetry all the years of human time have danced. But now the doom trumpet breaks in for good, to dominate the rest of the ode. The slowly dancing chorus line of alexandrines, pentameters, and four-teeners of the opening six lines is suddenly over, "drown'd." The untuning of the "*Universal String*" (borrowed later by Dryden for his famous Cecilia ode) Purcell naturally sets to a descending chromatic phrase (see above), as of a string being loosened and thereby lowered in pitch. But he quickly re-tightens the pegs for the triple-rhyme isometric lines immediately following (lines 23–25), which as we have seen proclaim the holocaust of the stars and of poetry, when the resurrected Virgil himself will have to stand by and see consumed, in one fire, both the natural Troy of the Dardanelles (what is left from its ancient firings) and the depicted Troy of his epic.

Ars longa vita brevis. If even our long-held-immortal art cannot stand on that fiery day, how will the flames feel to the newly reconstituted flesh and bones of ordinary mortals? Without this transition, the meditator's thoughts turn naturally to the fleshly fuel for the fire, and as the Pindaric Pegasus feels it burning his shanks, he gallops with ever more wild agitation. "This Ode is truly *Pindarical*," Cowley says in his notes, "falling from one thing into another, after his *Enthusiastical manner*." Indeed the links between stanzas are not spelled out but are easily sensed once we begin following the meditator's chain of thoughts, from the "immortality" of poetry to the holocaust of poetry, and then to the annihilation of flesh and of all that mind and flesh have clung to. Thus Cowley could evoke the terror of a moment when newly raised bodies beg the mountains to fall on them and when even the mountains "shake and run about." Cowley builds to this climax with a long, gradual increase in intensity, and Purcell does the same.

> Whom *Thunders* dismal noise,
> And all that *Prophets* and *Apostles* louder spake,
> And all the *Creatures* plain *conspiring voyce*,
>   Could not whilst they *liv'ed*, awake,
>   This mightier sound shall make
>   When *Dead* t'arise,
>   And open *Tombs*, and open *Eyes*
> To the long *Sluggards* of five thousand years.
> This *mightier Sound* shall *make* its *Hearers Ears*.
> Then shall the scatter'ed *Atomes* crowding come
>   Back to their *Ancient Home*,
> ⎧ Some from *Birds*, from *Fishes* some,
> ⎪ Some from *Earth*, and some from *Seas*,
> ⎨ Some from *Beasts*, and some from *Trees*.
> ⎪ Some descend from *Clouds* on high,
> ⎩ Some from *Metals* upwards fly,
> And where th'*attending Soul* naked, and shivering stands,
>   Meet, salute, and joyn their hands.
> As disperst *Souldiers* at the *Trumpets* call,
>   Hast to their *Colours* all.
>   *Unhappy* most, like *Tortur'ed Men*,
> Their *Joynts* new *set*, to be new *rackt* agen.
>   To *Mountains* they for *shelter* pray,
> The *Mountains* shake, and run about no less *confus'd* then *They*.
>   (stanza 3, lines 28–51)

In Purcell's setting, Cowley's repeated phrase "mightier sound" (lines 32 and 36) becomes the doom trumpet fanfare, dominating this section of the piece, down to "shall make its Hearers Ears": Purcell repeats it three times to stirring runs on "sound." Then for the indented isometric core passage he switches, for the first time, from common to triple measure, and to make sure we do not miss the introductory phrase, the music slows down, stops, and repeats it (measures 70–76).

high, some from metals up-ward fly, some de-scend   from clouds on

high,   some from met-als   up   -   ward fly.

(measures 64–93)

Cowley's seventeenth-century atomism here gives scientific definition to the still moment in Ezekiel's valley of bones when the joints start reconnecting, and Purcell's setting dances a little jig of the gathering atoms before going back to the sounding trumpet and some sour chords for the torture of newly reset joints. The image of people and mountains together running about in terrified confusion might defy a painter's representational ability, but for Purcell's music it is highly suitable. Motion and emotion are what music, insofar as it is representational, can best depict.

from The Resurrection

Cowley   Purcell

To   moun-tains they for shelter   pray;   the mountains shake and run

—   about   no   less con-fused   than they, the mountains

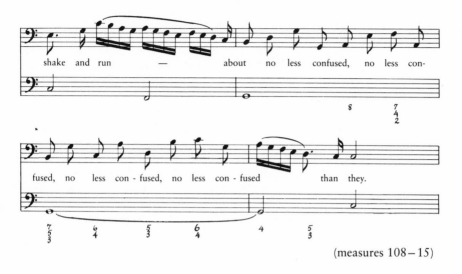

shake and run — about no less confused, no less con-fused, no less con-fused, no less con-fused than they.

(measures 108–15)

With different treatment, this line could have ended the setting, since it concludes the dramatic vision proper. But the vision is more broken off than concluded when Cowley's meditator reaches his peak of excitement, as in a nightmare one awakes when the fall from the cliff begins. "Stop!" the poet shouts to his mounted muse, "your horse has gone wild!" Purcell sets the first two lines in quasi-recitative.

Stop, stop, my *Muse*, allay thy vig'orous heat,
    Kindled at a *Hint* so Great.
Hold thy *Pindarique Pegasus* closely in,
    Which does to *rage* begin,
And this steep *Hill* would gallop up with violent course,
'Tis an unruly, and a *hard-Mouth'd Horse*,
    { Fierce, and unbroken yet,
    { Impatient of the *Spur* or *Bit*.
Now *praunces* stately, and anon *flies* o're the place,
Disdains the *servile Law* of any settled *pace*,
Conscious and *proud* of his own *natural force*.
    'Twill no *unskilful Touch* endure,
But flings *Writer* and *Reader* too that *sits* not *sure*.

Purcell continues through this final stanza of the meditator's recovery from his vision. The lively verbs are perfect for his musical conclusion: *rage, gallop up, prances, flies, flings*. A Pindaric Pegasus that "disdains the servile law of any settled pace" is an especially apt subject for a composer with Purcell's rhythmic versatility.

Cowley's "Resurrection" is a remarkable imaginative achievement and not because Purcell set it so well, though he has been our model reader here.

It has not received due notice, probably because his other Pindaric pieces, as whole poems, fall well short of the standard it sets up. His calling it "truly Pindarical" shows that he knew it was his best ode of the experimental group. The traditional idea of doomsday—of an all-consuming fire on a day of terror and agony to be succeeded by some unknown mode of resurrected life—supplied the conservative Cowley with the artistic material to express the intensity with which, even in exile and without the time and materials for his work, he still clung to humanist values: the love of poetry and oratory, of the mind's powers to understand and admire the natural world, of the arts, architecture, and ideals of past civilizations. In the 1650s these things appeared to English Royalists to be threatened from all sides, by religious sectarianism and fanaticism, by decline of institutions of learning, and by political revolution.

"A warlike, various, and a tragical age," Cowley wrote, "is best to write of, but worst to write in" (preface to *Works*, 1668). Friend and appreciator of notable artists, scientists, and philosophers (Crashaw, Van Dyke, Harvey, Hobbes), Cowley spent much of his poetic effort in celebrating what he saw as threatened. But only when he was attempting to "supply" an equivalent to the untranslatable musical rhythms of Pindar was he able to make, out of such effort, a new mode of English lyric poetry. And it was the musicians of the Restoration who best appreciated his art.

Crashaw, Milton, and Cowley had all begun their work with song forms by writing metrically smooth, flowing song-mode verse, Crashaw in English song forms of variable line length, Milton mainly in Italian canzone form, Cowley in lute-song style of variable lines and in the isometric, dramatic song mode of Jonson. All three went on to incorporate the features of traditional song forms into their own versions of ode or "grand lyric." Crashaw's hymnic odes alternated a lyric mode of liturgical declamation and speech with that of chant or song, as in a liturgy of spoken prayers mixed with chants and hymns. Milton and Cowley too created their versions of grand lyric primarily in what I have called oratorical mode, dominated by passages of pulsing, swinging, irregular rhythm that give way periodically (more regularly in Cowley than in Milton) to metrically smooth, ear-soothing passages evocative of traditional song rhythms. These were English embodiments of the humanist ideal for grand lyric, expressed for example by Scaliger and Doni, that the divine poet should follow the Psalms and ancient Greek odes in using irregular verses to express a *furore divino* or divine inspiration. In these attempts, the poets kept in mind that such verse, whatever its metrical irregularities, is by nature suitable to be sung, in through-composed, monodic setting. Developments in both the theory and the practice of music in their own times let them suppose that music was ready for such verse. The connection of the English irregular ode with Restoration music has been noted but little explored by historians of the ode, and further work is needed.[16]

In his Pindaric pieces Cowley had developed a primarily oratorical mode of grand lyric. Having that mode at his command, he was then able, for the rest of his life, to write occasional odes with a great variety of verse textures, from his inspired oratorical "Ode on the Death of Mr. Crashaw" (1656), mostly in pentameter couplets but with each long grammatical period ending in an alexandrine, to "The Complaint," with its smooth verses of variable length and its conceptually defined irregular stanzas, usually with terse core passages of song mode. He could intermingle oratorical and song modes for suitable effects. And as in the "Ode. Sitting and Drinking in the Chair . . . [from] Sir Francis Drake's Ship" (set by Pelham Humfrey), he could even occasionally intermingle speech mode as well in passages of his free-swinging odes, when the dramatic context called for it. Composers found these modal mixtures, it seems, more stimulating than trying. And Cowley's conscious experiments with creating them had made him a far better poet than he would otherwise have been.

16. See, for example, Heath-Stubbs, *The Ode*, pp. 44–45 and Shuster, *The English Ode*, pp. 12–13, 101, 115–16, and 133–34.

VII. Interacting Stylistic Changes in Lyric and Song Setting through the Century

hoever reads English poetry from 1580 to 1690 and listens to songs of the same period senses that the parallel processions of different styles in both lyric poetry and vocal music—from Sidney and Shakespeare to Dryden, from Morley to Purcell—are related in some fashion. When we think of Campion and Herbert tuning their instruments and setting their own lyrics, of Dowland revising lyrics and writing commendatory verses, of Herrick's poems sung before Charles I, of Milton teaching his nephews part singing, playing his organ, and planning music dramas, of Henry Lawes and John Wilson writing each other verses to commend their literary tastes, of John Gamble doggedly "setting" his way through eighty-six poems sent him by Thomas Stanley, of Dryden "tagging" Milton's epic verses to make them the text for a semiopera—when we think of this century of musical poets and literate composers, a synthetic approach to the history of style in the two arts seems in order. We moderns may believe with Susanne Langer that in song a poem is "swallowed hide and hair," but seventeenth-century poets and composers did not think so, and their beliefs influenced their poetry and their songs.[1]

In conclusion we now consider relationships between lyric text and music in two representative songs and review the interactions between the two arts, whereby we can see each affecting stylistic developments in the other. Our sample texts will be poems by Jonson and Dryden, with settings respectively by Ferrabosco and Purcell. The composers' treatment of these texts

---

1. *Problems of Art*, p. 84. As noted in Chapter I, Elise Jorgens in *The Well-Tun'd Word* has done valuable work on such holistic study for seventeenth-century England.

will help us to illustrate two things: the shifts in English song style from Jacobean lute song to Caroline continuo song to Restoration songs and cantatas; and the stylistic shifts in the lyric of the same periods, from Jonson's smooth and isometric but dramatic song mode to the midcentury prominence of speech mode and finally to the Restoration's lyric combinations: song, and sometimes combined song and declamatory modes for dancing and the theater (a large proportion in triple meter), and the mixed verbal modes of its great odes.

The subject of parallel stylistic shifts in lyrics and song settings of the period was discussed almost two decades ago by Wilfrid Mellers, who demonstrated the feasibility of joint literary-musical analysis of songs and made useful observations about seventeenth-century song styles.[2] Mellers notes, for example, that in Henry Lawes's declamatory songs,

> the music serves to point the verbal rhythm of the poem, to underline the shifts in the argument. We do not find here, as we do in Dowland, a poem metamorphosed into lyricism: nor as later in Purcell, a poem that becomes musical drama. We find a musically unobtrusive setting that exaggerates the manner in which a reciter would declaim the poem before an initiated audience. By giving relatively long notes to the important words Lawes clarifies the complicated syntax . . . the music is the servant of the poetry in a manner that is remote from Dowland, or even Campion.[3]

Unfortunately Mellers worked from the notion that while Donne and Herbert (whom he repeatedly links with Campion, Dowland, and Daniel) wrote personal, sincere lyrics of deep emotion, the Cavalier poets Herrick, Suckling, and Carew wrote polished, superficial, insincere lyrics, which usually inspired similarly superficial song settings by Lawes and others. The Cavalier poets, however, had their own depths and serious concerns. Mellers's application of the metaphysical versus Cavalier distinction led him to link poets and composers of the lute-song era subjectively. But so far as we know, Campion, Dowland, and Daniel never set any lyrics by Donne, much less any by Herbert (who wrote too late for them). The closest Dowland came to setting a poem of Donne's was in "To ask for all thy love," the text of which appears to be a paraphrase of one stanza of "Lovers infinitenesse."[4] The difference between Donne's stanza and this filled-out, metrically regu-

2. Mellers's *Harmonious Meeting: A Study of Music, Poetry, and Theatre in England, 1600–1900* is primarily about seventeenth-century vocal music. Another work related to my topic, Paula Johnson's *Form and Transformation in Music and Poetry of the English Renaissance*, is more abstract and its generic scope much broader than mine (including plays, prose romance, and instrumental music), so that the present study has little relation to it.
3. *Harmonious Meeting*, p. 115.
4. On this text see Chapters I and II above. For "Lovers infinitenesse," see *John Donne: The Complete English Poems*, ed. A. J. Smith, p. 64; for Dowland's "To ask for all thy love," see Edmund Fellowes, ed., *The English School of Lutenist Song Writers*, 12:12.

larized paraphrase is a measure of the distance between Donne's speech mode and the fluid, metrically patterned lyrics preferred by Jacobean composers.[5]

Elise Jorgens, in a recent study of Jacobean and Caroline song and poetry, avoids such an inappropriate linkage, noting that the Jacobean composers usually chose texts from "poets in the generation just before their own" or from "their conservative contemporaries."[6] Recounting the features of what has long been called metaphysical poetry—the tone of private or personal speech, rough meter, obscure diction, irony, syllogistic argument, and extended figural complexity—she observes that it took time for composers to respond to such lyrics. They did assimilate and respond to poems with such features, to a remarkable degree, in midcentury declamatory and semideclamatory song (the English form of monody), a development we shall review shortly.

For concluding illustrations to span the century, we begin now with Ben Jonson's song-mode lyric "Come my Celia, let us prove" and the lute-song setting of it by Alfonso Ferrabosco the Younger, which are similar in many ways to Campion's texts and songs. But Jonson, working in the context of the theater, gives the seduction poem a dramatic particularity that sets it apart from Campion's timeless lyric versions of the theme (such as "My Sweetest Lesbia") and allies it, in that respect, with the speech-mode lyric. (The "few poor household spies" and the husband's "easier ears" make us feel like eavesdroppers amid intrigues, even if we do not place the song in its context in *Volpone*.) The similarity to Campion as musician that I especially want to point out is the composer's sensitivity to selected rhythms of the text.

> Come, my Celia, let us prove,
> While we may, the sweets of Love.
> Time will not be ours for ever;
> He at length our good will sever.
> Spend not then his gifts in vain;
> Suns that set may rise again,
> But if we once lose this light,
> 'Tis with us perpetual night.
> Why should we defer our joys?
> Fame and Rumour are but toys.
> Cannot we delude the eyes
> Of a few poor household spies?
> Or his easier ears beguile
> Thus removed by our wile?
> 'Tis no sin Love's fruits to steal;
> But the sweet theft to reveal,

5. So many texts are anonymous that we cannot say for certain what poets they liked best. Two often chosen were Fulke Greville and Sidney. See the author index to Edmund Fellowes, ed., *English Madrigal Verse 1588 to 1632*, 3d ed.

6. *The Well-Tun'd Word*, pp. 11–14.

To be taken, to be seen,
These have crimes accounted been.[7]

Jonson is using the crisp, seven-syllable or truncated trochaic line imported by Sidney (see Chapter I), varied by one regular trochaic couplet. "Come my Celia" is isometric until the penultimate line. There we have, indeed, the same number of syllables as in the other lines but in a very different metrical arrangement: two anapests separated by an extra syllable and a caesura.[8] Until this point the tetrameter lines have danced along so energetically that this broken penultimate line, like many in Campion and other lutenist poets, serves as a conclusion rhythm, a climactic signal that the end is near. Ferrabosco picks up its rhythm most effectively (see Example 2 following).

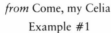

from Come, my Celia

Example #1

---

7. For the complete score of the song, see Fellowes, ed., *English School of Lutenist Song Writers*, ser. 2, vol. 16, pp. 10–12.

8. This line might be otherwise described with less common terms from classical scansion; at any rate the patterns of emphasis are clear.

(measures 1–11)

Example #2

Jonson   Ferrabosco

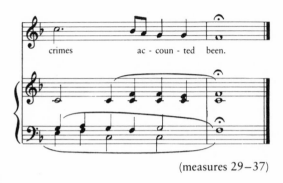

(measures 29–37)

Besides this anapestic conclusion rhythm, Ferrabosco follows another less obvious feature of verbal rhythmic structure, a division of the poem into sections which, in the text, are defined by a pattern of speed variation. According to whether a line is (a) metrically regular, (b) has a spondee, or (c) has a group of lightly stressed syllables and no spondee, we may designate its motion, respectively, either standard, slower, or faster, with the result that the poem divides into three rhythmic sections. Lines 1 to 8, except for the name Celia (three syllables), are regular, establishing the standard speed of a smooth, truncated trochaic tetrameter. Thus Ferrabosco could repeat the melody for lines 1–4 on 5–8, effectively correlating the climactic figure for the section with "good will" and "perpetual," and correlating a rising interval with "rise again" and "sweets of love." Lines 9 to 14 then follow a pattern of line-by-line variation—each line is a different speed from both the one before it and the one after. The concluding section, by contrast after the lighter, quicker line 14, begins with the two heavier lines ("'Tis no sin . . .") containing the spondees "Love's fruits" and "sweet theft." After these images in their slowed, climactic lines have capped the seduction argument, the dancing anapestic line I described above ("to be taken, to be seen") serves as a penultimate conclusion signal before the final line returns to metric regularity.

In the middle section (lines 9–14) we note an effective imitation of verbal rhythm: the music for "Ŏf ă féw pòor hóusehòld spíes" echoes Jonson's anapest and seems rhythmically to reflect the speaker's feelings of frustration and urgency.

Example #3

Jonson   Ferrabosco

Can - not we   de - lude the eyes   of a few poor household spies?

(measures 16–20)

Furthermore, in the repeated concluding section, the spondees "Love's fruits" and "sweet theft" get expressive emphasis, the first by constituting the high point of an ascending phrase, the second by getting the full length of two half-notes. For a very slow phrase ending to contrast with what is coming next and thereby to give an effect of penultimate rhythm comparable to that of the textual spondees before anapests, Ferrabosco follows these half-notes with two whole notes on "reveal." Having thus slowed the song to a complete halt, the composer has prepared us for the sudden lively anapestic motion of the melody for "To be taken, to be seen," which he continues through the nonanapestic final line because of its musical effectiveness. Thus this rhythmic figure dominates the concluding section, forcing even "These have crimes," which is not anapestic, into its pattern. The verbal rhythm of a line has been the seed of a musical idea; and in this style of composition, its musical value as an expression of seductive, frisky vitality, so suitable for the song's ending, outweighs its failure to reflect the last line's implied speech rhythms of contrastive stress: "*These* have crimes *accounted* been."[9] To summarize, Ferrabosco has imitated the poem's three-part rhythmic division and only in single lines the most striking rhythmic effects, thus including a few declamatory touches but creating his own rhythmic/melodic conception for each section. He gave his musical invention relatively free play, not allowing the flow of melody to be impeded by constant imitation of verbal rhythm, but reflecting only the poem's most emphatic rhythms.

A midcentury declamatory composer would have scrupulously stressed

9. John Hollander, *Vision and Resonance*, pp. 49–50, rightly makes this point. But I do not find Ferrabosco's stress pattern so inappropriate as he does. The doubled note length on the repeat does give "These" a positional stress. Furthermore, sins and crimes are not identical, and the contrastive stress reading thus not unequivocal. This song has also been discussed briefly by Mary Chan in *Music in the Theatre of Ben Jonson*, pp. 90–98, and by Elise Jorgens in her review of Chan's book, *Renaissance Quarterly* 35 (1982): 339–43. I agree that Chan needed further illustration for her praise of its "serious ideals for setting words to music" and hope I have supplied some of that illustration.

"These" over "crimes," but would thereby have lost the vitality of Ferrabosco's ending. Solo song composers of the Caroline and interregnum periods, under the influence of Italian monodic style and of musical humanism,[10] would do close musical readings of the poems, would allow poetic meter, syntax, and speech inflections, as well as mood and imagery, to shape the melody, musical organization, and rhythm in as many ways as possible. We have examined samples of their song style—by John Wilson and the Lawes brothers—in the chapters on Herbert, Herrick, and Crashaw. These composers' faithfulness to the sounds of the text has earned them the censures that their songs usually lack melodic interest, are "lapidary," and show "logogenic inflexibility."[11] These were the English versions of Italian *aria parlante* and other forms of monodic song intermingling, or sometimes striking a half-way vein between, recitative and tuneful songs. At their worst they have neither the lively, vivid motion of good recitative nor the tunefulness of arioso pieces. But the best of them do achieve vitality of subtle declamation and a measure of melodic interest.[12] As with Continental monody, such songs often give abundant evidence of careful textual interpretation and thus are valuable for literary scholars. As was mentioned in Chapter II, they can be enjoyed by people who already know the poems and thus have an extramusical dimension to their listening pleasure. Henry Lawes and Wilson, in commendatory poems for songbooks, praised each other for judiciousness in selecting fine poems and for reading them well:

> . . . . thy choice of lines are good
> Not like to those, who get their food
> As Beggars Raggs from Dunghills take,
> (Such as comes next) ill Songs to make;
> Who by a witty blind pretense
> Take words that creep half way to sense;
> . . . .
>
> These with their brave *Chromaticks* bring
> Noise to the Ear, but mean No-thing:
> . . . .
>
> Shew Them good lines, They cannot read.
> 　　　　(Wilson, in Henry Lawes, *Ayres and Dialogues*, 1655)

10. D. T. Mace, in "Musical Humanism, the Doctrine of Rhythmus, and the Saint Cecilia Odes of Dryden," appears to assume that Continental musical humanism was little known in England until the Restoration. But it certainly infuenced English composers' ideas earlier as well.

11. Pamela Willets, in *The Henry Lawes Manuscript*, p. 8, contrasts Lawes's Ariadne (Arianna) monody with Monteverdi's famous monody on the same theme. Lawes's close following of textual detail, she says, causes him to lose dramatic power and unity of mood; and his "assignment of rhythmic values to the words" results in rhythmic poverty. Franklin Zimmerman, in "Sound and Sense in Purcell's 'Single Songs,'" pp. 54–55, applies the term *lapidary* to the "Lawes school."

12. Among recent musical scholars who find a few such pieces to praise are Curtis Price, Ian Spink, and Elise Jorgens. See Chapter II, n. 45.

How would Tobias Hume, with his murky lyrics, have stood up to this standard! In his time the brother and sister arts had had a different relation with each other.

Midcentury composers responded to lyrics with prominent features of speech and declamatory modes. To take irony, for example, William Lawes, with his inset triple-time section in a song in common time, could reflect the witty irony of the disabused lover in Herrick's "He that would not love" (see Chapter III); and later John Jackson, with well-paced declamation and clever melodic word-painting, could catch the likewise ironic mood in Cowley's anacreontic "Love" (see Chapter VI), in that case spoken by a lover who pretends to be struggling for higher themes but is actually delighted with his tumble into "melting love." Nor was rough meter an insoluble problem for midcentury song, though as the century advanced, poets needed rather less metrical irregularity to evoke colloquial speech than Donne had used, thus coming part way to meet musical requirements, even in lyrics of speech and declamatory modes—Carew and Cowley are examples. For dealing with obscure diction, intricate step-wise logic, or figurative language too complex for comprehensibility in song, the composer's best friend was editing, the practice of picking out an excerpt text that would work for either through-composed or stanzaic setting. Thus Wilson took four stanzas from Herbert's "Content" for a through-composed setting, out of several conceits keeping only the "fire in flints" image, which he could treat musically in the climactic passage of his song, along with the didactic, nonfigural stanzas. Ian Spink has said that when Lawes and Wilson responded to metaphysical verse in such ways, their "expressive devices" were parallel to "metaphysical wit." [13]

Sometimes, incidentally, composers edited so judiciously that one wishes poets had turned over to them some of the more prolix poetic efforts: Purcell's cantata text of Cowley's "The Complaint" ("In a deep Vision's intellectual scene"), to take a later example, makes a more readable and forceful ode than is the full poem, containing all the strongest passages and bringing out its dramatic debate structure.

The challenge of setting lyric dialogues, popular in the late 1620s and 1630s with such composers as Nicholas Lanier, Robert Ramsey, and Henry Lawes, must have been an impetus to experimenting with declamation, thus furthering declamatory trends in song. The alternation of singers, suggesting dramatic interchange, would have encouraged poets and composers alike to notice the potential and the requirements of musical "speech" in declamation or recitative. (In Chapters I–IV we noted how the dialogue form was rhythmically stimulating for Watson, Herbert, Herrick, and Crashaw.) Lanier, who set some of Herrick's dialogues among others for perfor-

---

13. *English Song, Dowland to Purcell*, p. 126.

mance at court, composed the earliest surviving piece of recitative in English, his "Hero and Leander" monody of about 1630.[14] Perhaps partly inspired by dialogue writing, Herrick was later inclined to revise his almost pure song-mode lyrics of the 1620s and 1630s in the direction of speech mode, reflecting both the popularity of speech mode and the accompanying declamatory trends in song setting between 1630 and 1647, when he prepared *Hesperides* for print.

Of course not all song texts were stimulating to composers, nor were all settings noteworthy for poets. Composers could draw from a store of smooth, usually song-mode lyrics of conventional sentiment that left the composer strictly to his musical resources, offering neither inspiration nor hindrance. Such were those generally preferred by, say, Robert Jones, William Lawes, or later the prolific theatrical composers like Samuel Ackeroyd, who were especially well supplied by the dramatists Shadwell, Motteux, and D'Urfey. These comprise many of the strictly tuneful songs of the century, or as Jorgens calls them, the "musically oriented" as opposed to the "textually oriented" songs. Since musical beauty can indeed exist independently of literary merits in a text, these include some fine pieces. But composers of the age generally took a literary interest in their texts, and changing styles in the two arts interacted. The major shifts in the styles of vocal music, to the extent that they are related to lyrics, can be viewed in terms of composers' changing uses of song, speech, and oratorical modes.

We observed Crashaw, Milton, and Cowley experimenting with song-related verse textures as they developed their versions of "grand lyric," of monody, ode, and hymnic or choral ode. They followed the humanist ideal of imitating the ancients in expressing a "furore divino all' improviso," a sense of unbounded high inspiration, through free-swinging meters in long and variable lines, mostly in declamatory mode but with frequently intermingled evocations of song mode. Crashaw and Cowley achieved this result by interspersing allusive passages reminiscent of the fluid, rhythmically versatile Jacobean song mode, either isometric or in variable line lengths. Crashaw used inset song passages, of the usual Jacobean solo-song length and style, to evoke a sense of singing at moments thematically appropriate for it in his depictions of earthly and heavenly prayer, meditation, or ecstasy. Cowley by contrast, in attempting to domesticate the hoary and ill-fathomed verse sounds of Pindar in seventeenth-century England, constructed a type of variable verse stanza or "allaeostroph" (in Milton's term), mostly in declamatory mode but built around a song-mode core passage: a few metrically smooth lines, either isometric or in common song meters, expressing the stanza's theme in condensed fashion. Crashaw and Cowley, then, drew upon English song tradition for their versions of "grand lyric." But Milton, as

14. Vincent Duckles published its score with his paper "English Song and the Challenge of Italian Monody."

Spenser had, drew instead mainly upon Italian song, using a modified canzone form to give a songlike texture to primarily declamatory verse in portions of "Lycidas" and the monodies and odes of *Samson Agonistes*.

Thus the two song traditions we saw influencing Sidney, Watson, and other Elizabethans had continued to affect English lyric. In the inset lyrics of *Paradise Lost*, inspired by the extreme rhythmic flexibility of recitative, Milton achieved lyric-verse musicality purely in declamatory blank verse, mainly through the devices of figures of sound, syntactic balancing, and measured syncopation of extended syntactic units against the pentameter line. *Ut oratoria musica* as a literary ideal there reached full fruition.

In these different fashions, all three poets could combine a large measure of figural and conceptual complexity with some measure of verse musicality, giving themselves a capacious scope for large lyric forms. Such verse, they knew, would not be settable and singable in the earlier compositional styles of brief Renaissance song forms, which had flowered in England so late and so richly under Elizabeth and James, though some of it would be suitable for midcentury declamatory song if carefully excerpted; it would be eminently settable in the new, larger-scale dramatic vocal forms then emerging in Continental music drama and church music: monodies short and long, operatic chorus, cantatas, extended anthems, and the component pieces of oratorios. For in such pieces the composer's range of word treatment choices, from recitative to air and all shadings in between, made it possible to treat with success any mixture or alternation of the verbal lyric modes, if the composer were skillful enough. In the Restoration era, Cowley's odes were thus frequently set in through-composed songs and cantatas by Humfrey, Blow, Purcell, and others. Milton's lyric passages were set later, as we noted at the end of Chapter V.

Cowley, especially, had developed a style of verse in his odes that was amenable to English composers' early baroque usage of brief, detachable phrases as musical units for sequential repetition and other forms of musical development. This was so because, even while writing in a mainly declamatory mode of lengthy clauses and sentences, he provided frequent partial closure (in traditional terms, used little extended periodicity). With Milton's verse, in order to encompass the lengthy periods, composers would more often have to turn to the recitative treatment that had inspired it. Crashaw was almost as musically accessible as Cowley in these terms, and probably the scarcity of late-century settings of his texts was due mainly to his Catholicism. If he had written secular songs it would have made no difference, but his was a higher muse. Cowley could boldly declare that though Crashaw "in some nice tenents [*sic*] might be wrong, his *Life*, I'm sure, was *in the right*" ("Ode on the Death of Mr. Crashaw"), but his hymnic odes were too distinctly Catholic, even Marian, to be sung as anthems in Anglican churches. There is more to tell of musico-poetic interaction in the Restoration than Cowley's ascendance there, and we shall return to it shortly.

Because the declamatory style focused on interpreting various modes of poetry, it helped prepare the way for the eventual English adoption of baroque declamatory and arioso styles after the Restoration.[15] It seems likely, for example, that the Caroline composers' urge to find ever more precise ways of reflecting lyric personae and complex textual meanings gave added impetus to progressive harmonic practices.[16] John Wilson's harmony, in his "Content" setting and elsewhere, illustrates new directions in midcentury English music, for it shows English song on the way to modern ditonal harmony.[17] Ian Spink points to Charles Coleman as a more successful midcentury harmonic progressive than Wilson, instancing Coleman's effective chord progressions, full recognition of the harmonic minor, and figured basses; Wilson, Spink says, "has forsaken the modes but is not yet at home in the tonal system."[18] Discussing Wilson's innovative harmony, Vincent Duckles points out that the lute fantasias that begin Wilson's Oxford Manuscript (containing "Peace, mutt'ring thoughts") comprise a sort of "well-tempered lute," possibly "the earliest effort at systematic composition in all keys."[19] In *A Proposal to Perform Music in Perfect and Mathematical Proportions* (1688), one of the first English theoretical works to formulate the ditonal system, Thomas Salmon stated that he had clearly observed the principle in the works of "the most Eminent Masters for these last Twenty years." Thus he saw it in works of the 1660s—presumably of court musicians such as Matthew Locke and Pelham Humfrey. And we should expect to see earlier midcentury composers already moving in that direction.

The changing lyric styles of the midcentury can be illustrated by Thomas Stanley, gentleman classicist and translator, whose *Poems* of 1647 and 1651 might be classed thematically as Cavalier lyrics but make more use of speech mode than Lovelace or Herrick did. Stanley is thus sometimes enrolled in the school of Donne. He sent a batch of his poems to the composer John Gamble, who eventually set them all. In a dedicatory epistle for the resulting songbook, the composer says, "It was not in my ambition, or hope to mend the least Accent or Emphasis which they [the poems] received from your own numerous Soul, but to essay, how neer, a whole life spent in the study

15. See n. 7 above; Zimmerman, "Sound and Sense," p. 70; and Henry Davey, *History of English Music*, p. 328.

16. I suggest this as possibly of interest for a music historian to pursue, since I do not have the expertise to prove it.

17. The Wilson Manuscript was catalogued at Oxford in 1656. If its pieces are in chronological order, "Peace, mutt'ring thoughts" would presumably have been composed in the 1640s.

18. *English Song*, pp. 107–16.

19. Duckles, "The 'Curious' Art of John Wilson." Salmon is cited for his formulation of ditonality in John Harley, *Music in Purcell's London*, p. 164.

of Musical Compositions, could imitate the flowing and natural Graces, which you have created by your fancie." [20] This devotion to the primacy of the text is quite evident in Gamble's settings.

The poem discussed below may be considered primarily a speech-mode lyric because of its strongly enjambed syntactic periods, frequent spondees, and closely defined dramatic nature as a humorously exaggerated, macabre, contrived, but still private address of lover to lady. It looks toward the characteristic Restoration dramatic lyric in its theatrical posturing and exaggeration and in its relative metrical smoothness. For in the Restoration era, theatrical poets, like Ben Jonson before them, can at times convey some sense of a speaking voice with only a little metrical irregularity. As Eldred Revet said of Stanley's poems in verses for the Gamble volume, "No Crowded words in Huddle meet, / That *shuffle* on *uneven Feet*, / And struggling labour in their Pains; / As if the *Verse* were *pac'd* in *Chains*."

> The Cold Kisse
> Such icie kisses Anchorites that live
> Secluded from the world to dead sculls give;
> And those cold Maids on whom Love never spent
> His flame, nor know what by desire is meant,
> To their expiring Fathers such bequeath,
> Snatching their fleeting spirits in that breath.
> The timorous Priest doth with such fear and nice
> Devotion, touch the holy sacrifice.
> Fie *Chariessa*, whence so chang'd of late,
> As to become in love a reprobate?
> Quit, quit this dulnesse, fairest, and make known
> A flame unto me equall with mine owne.
> Shake off this frost for shame that dwells upon
> Thy lips, or if it will not so be gone
> Let's once more joyn our lips, and thou shalt see,
>   That by the flame of mine 'twill melted be.[21]

Gamble's setting of "Such icie kisses" is, like other such songs we have considered, a good example of the midcentury declamatory style in its duple meter, limited use of mannerist word painting, frequent fourth and fifth steps in the melody line, frequent rests and cadences to mark syntactic units, and imitation of verbal pitch and poetic meter in its melody and rhythms. While such poets as Quarles (in his *Divine Fancies*), Herbert, Vaughan, Stanley, and Cowley (in *The Mistresse*, 1647) explored the possibilities of speech-mode lyric in the 1630s and 1640s, song composers alternately practiced the declamatory and the tuneful styles of homophonic continuo song. The period of Gamble's well-received settings of Stanley's poems, published

---

20. *Ayres and Dialogues* (London, 1657), dedicatory epistle.
21. From *The Poems and Translations of Thomas Stanley*, ed. Galbraith M. Crump, p. 240.

in 1656–1657 though they were apparently begun a decade earlier,[22] may be considered the high moment of popularity of declamatory style. From 1652 through the next decade, John Playford's music-publishing enterprise enabled these songs to reach a wide audience.

In the 1660s both lyric and song setting took new directions. The following collage of facts and trends will suggest some influences that helped transform the styles of the 1640s and 1650s. Cowley was publishing the much-admired metrical experiments that he dubbed anacreontics and Pindarics, and other poets were using varied verse forms for odes and other extended lyric forms. Captain Henry Cook and the skillful, Italianate Matthew Locke were organizing the reinstated Chapel Royal. Pelham Humfrey was studying in France, apparently with Lully, and would return (1667) to introduce Continental declamatory recitative in his anthems, and sometimes to write his own words for secular songs.[23] Charles II was importing French musicians, reopening the playhouses, and creating a broad market for dance-tune songs in triple meter. Playgoers, like the new public concert audiences to come in the 1670s, were expecting more and more of the lively rhythms and vocal ornamentation popularized by Italian-style singers: as Playford lamented in 1666, "All Solemn and Grave Musick is much laid aside, being esteemed to heavy and dull for the light Heels and Brains of this Nimble and wanton Age." [24]

The immediate result was a spate of triple-time, or as detractors called them "jog-trotting," lyrics and songs for court and theater through the late 1660s and early 1670s. As Ian Spink observes, this fad reached its peak in Playford's *Choice Ayres* of 1676 and then gave way to a returning preference for airs in common time.[25] The fad submerged secular song in dance conventions (symmetrical phrasing, stylized rhythms, and harmonically ordered cadences), Spink continues, and this submergence was necessary to free English song from what had now become a "declamatory bondage" to the midcentury style. Here too poetry may have helped push along musical progress, once the fad had produced this needed result; the tedium of these lyrics as verse for reading was such that the fashion passed quickly into self-parody. Soon the composers had to turn to the new dramatic lyric in duple or mixed meters.

Growing out of diverse traditions and influences, the late Restoration song lyric sometimes achieves a blend of all three lyric modes, speech, song, and declamation, for its own form of expression especially suited for the

---

22. Crump (p. xxxi) says that Stanley had given Gamble the poems in the late 1640s, and then, annoyed at his procrastination, gave John Wilson nine of them to set.
23. See Davey, *History of English Music*, p. 311.
24. Preface to *Harmonia Sacra: Divine Hymns and Dialogues* (London, 1688).
25. *English Song*, p. 152.

theater of heroic adventure and courtly comedy. It was influenced by the metrical experimentation of the ode, by the midcentury speech mode we saw illustrated in Stanley, and by the triple-time fad. From speech mode it has frequent partial closure and a modicum of metrical roughness; from song mode, frequent emphatic assertions, use of triple meters, metrical patterning, and songlike repetition of brief phrases; from declamatory mode, frequent enjambment, the theatricality of lofty oratorical declarations, verbal posturing and gesturing, and the sense of the speaker as stage persona. To Dryden, Cowley's great successor in metrical experimentation, we turn for our concluding example.

Besides to the traditions just mentioned, Dryden's lyrics hark back, in their smoothness and rhythmic delicacy, to the earlier English song mode of lyric we focused on in Chapters I–III. This slightly old-fashioned quality, as compared to the average lyric verse of his contemporaries, was no accident for Dryden; it was based on his commitment to the same humanist ideals that had been held up to poets and composers for over a century. As D. T. Mace has shown, Dryden was inspired by the Continental scholar Isaac Vossius's presentation (in *De poematum cantu et viribus rhythmi*, 1673) of the long-standing idea that the *effetti* of ancient music could be achieved in modern song through neoclassical meters—that is, "if words and music together observed precisely in appropriate combinations the rhythmical proportions of the classical feet."[26] If Dryden did suppose this possible, he must have been, in the early part of his theatrical career at least, far out of touch with current music. Imagine Purcell sitting down with a text to fill in notes to words in exact rhythmic proportion to the poetic feet. (Campion, following Ronsard and the Pleiade, had attempted something like that eighty years earlier and soon given it up as too constraining.) Dryden in the preface to his opera *Albion and Albanius* (1685), for which he chose the French composer Louis Grabu, expresses an old-fashioned admiration for song-mode lyric, saying that the poet should "make words so smooth, and numbers so harmonious, that they shall almost set themselves. And . . . there are rules for this in nature." He continues, "It is my part to invent, and the musician's to humor that invention."[27] Dryden was used to Lawes's and Gamble's ideal of music's total subservience to the text. But the younger composers had left it behind. Perhaps it took him a while to adjust his expectations. It was not until *Amphitryon* (1690) that he commissioned Purcell, who had composed for the theater since 1679, to do theatrical music for him.[28] If Dryden was somewhat out of touch with musical progress, he was nevertheless able to

---

26. Mace, "Musical Humanism," p. 261.
27. See *John Dryden*, ed. George Saintsbury, pp. 228–29.
28. For a list of Purcell's theatrical compositions (1679–1696) see *Songs from the Restoration Theater*, ed. Willard Thorp, pp. 91–92. On Dryden and Purcell see "A Note on Purcell's Music" in *Dryden: The Dramatic Works*, ed. Montague Summers, 1 : cxxxi–cxxxiv.

write eminently settable lyrics. His song lyrics, with their leading traits of smoothness, theatricality, and simple syntax, proved to be perfect material for Purcell's settings. For even though his song lyrics looked back in some ways to the earlier, predominantly song-mode style, they were musically suggestive with a difference. The dramatic quality of terse, situation-defining declarations is dominant; and the syntax, even while comprising extended units, avoids strong enjambment and, as Cowley did in his odes, provides frequent partial closure, creating a texture of smoothly interlocked but discrete and detachable phrases, perfect for musical declamation and development in the style of the time.

To be suitable for heroic drama, Restoration songs needed these qualities of declamatory syntax as well as natural English word order to proclaim their high and dignified sentiments. In such songs of plays and semioperas, English composers found suitable material for introducing some of the newest Continental styles and devices. There Cowley's skill with rhythmic and forceful declamation stood Dryden in good stead, even while the latter retreated into greater metric regularity. The composers knew what to make of stylized gestures, challenging direct addresses, or abrupt and somber declarations that define a dramatic situation, such as "I look'd and saw within the Book of Fate, / Where many days did lower," the opening of Dryden's Kalib song (set by Purcell for a revival of *The Indian Emperour*). They knew how to evoke a sense of gesture and action in music through rhythmic and harmonic conventions, largely Italian, which midcentury composers either were unaware of or had only begun to use. (Matthew Locke was an important forerunner.[29]) Our final example will be Purcell's Kalib song.

Kalib is an Indian priest to whom the Emperor Montezuma comes for divination, to learn that in his gloomy future "one happy hour" or opportunity stands out—as we later understand, the brief time when Cortez will be his captive:

> I look'd and saw within the Book of Fate,
> > Where many days did lower,
> > When lo one happy hour
> Leapt up, and smil'd to save thy sinking State;
> > A day shall come when in thy power
> > Thy cruel Foes shall be;
> > Then shall thy Land be free,
> > And thou in Peace shalt reign.
> But take, O take that opportunity,
> Which once refus'd will never come again.[30]

Dryden's lyric is patterned and metrically smooth with purposefully varied line lengths and a rhyme scheme interlocking the sections of the lyric. Lines

29. See Percy Young, *A History of British Music*, pp. 234, 261.
30. Dryden, *The Dramatic Works*, 1:290.

1 through 4, a 5-3-3-5 unit rhymed a-b-b-a, complete the rapid, emphatic statement of the poem's dramatic situation. Their drumming monosyllables, exclamation ("lo"), and active verbs lay out for us, in one firm stroke, the emperor's "lowering" future and slight hope. Then the indented midsection, lines 5–8 (a fourteener and a trimeter pair), functioning like the song-mode cores in Cowley's ode stanzas (see Chapter VI), moves smoothly, depicting a moment of repose. It suggests the visionary or tentative quality of the seer's description of possible happiness, because after its smooth flow has created the feeling that the happy vision will continue in trimeter lines, it is instead abruptly cut off by the shift to a pentameter couplet for the conclusion. Purcell's setting preserves these sectional divisions. After a declamatory opening with sustained single-note bass and concluding descriptive melismata, he treats the midsection and its vision of peace with point-imitative, mostly note for note accompaniment, then turning to extensive sequential development with multiple word repetition for the final section.[31]

I look'd and saw within the Book

John Dryden

Henry Purcell

I look'd, I look'd,   and saw within   the Book   of Fate where

many   days   did   low'r,   when   lo!   when   lo!   one happy, happy

hour leap't up,   leap't up and smiled,   leap't up and smiled   to save thy

31. This represents a typical structure of word-setting contrasts for Purcell. As another example, Zimmerman ("Sound and Sense," p. 58) describes "Fair Cloe my breast so alarms" by saying, "Purcell followed his customary procedure, employing alternately solo, point-imitative, and duo-homophonic settings of the lines, the resultant texture animated and cadentially articulated by descriptive melismata."

gain, will never, never, never, never, never, never, never come a - gain.

In Purcell's setting of the song, his expressiveness focuses especially on single emphatic phrases ("I look'd," "leapt up and smiled," "Oh take," "never").[32] Dryden's metrically smooth lines of such detachable phrases are malleable, readily absorbed in musical rhythms. Purcell's patterns of intensity and relaxation are purely musical, using the devices of sequential repetition (for example on "Oh! Oh!" and "foes shall be"—"Land be free"), long rapid runs, harmonically elaborated cadences, and others, while also stretching out short word groups through repetition (as in "thou in peace"). Word repetitions in sections 1 and especially 3 are so extensive that the rhythms of the text as poem are mostly obscured. After hearing the song we are left with that sense of driving irrepressible energy characteristic of baroque rhythms and harmonic motion. This energy in Purcell's use of ditonal harmony derives, as Percy Young says, from "the calculated disposition of activating dissonance."[33] Thus its materials are purely musical; they work the same way in instrumental music.

This is not to say that Purcell has neglected pictorialisms or ignored the poem's overall structure. The notion of a visible, fixed fate with its "lowering" days is well figured in the echoing quality of the held bass note under the first line. The "sinking" state descends sequentially in an extended run. The gentle relief of that one "happy hour" or day is reflected in the musical calm, as of an image in a wind-still lake, of his slow phrase for "A day shall come when in thy pow'r / Thy cruel foes shall be." To this whole indented passage, as we noted, Purcell gives a more lyrical or arioso treatment after the suitably declamatory treatment of the text's first four lines with brief, forthright, and energetic ornamentation. Thus Purcell retains the overall sectional organization of the text though not the particular rhythms of its words. For the conclusion, plenteous word repetition allows the poem's simple plea ("take that opportunity") to be built into a highly emotional warning of doom to come. The rhythmic treatment of "never" here illustrates, as well as other more complex features do, how thoroughly Purcell

32. For the modern edited score, see *The Works of Henry Purcell*, vol. 25.
33. *History of British Music*, p. 261.

subordinates verbal to musical rhythm: he reverses the relative syllable lengths on "never" for the sake of the effect of combined speed and expressive emphasis on the element of warning.

I have called attention to two representative seventeenth-century songs in order to recapitulate our intermittent observations of stylistic changes in both song and lyric during the century. The result may be summarized as follows. Composers of the madrigal and lute-song era preferred smooth, patterned, end-stopped, song-mode lyrics of simple syntax, with conventional, sensuously immediate imagery; those texts allowed the greatest play for their mood painting and melodic inventiveness. In Jonson's "Come my Celia" we have such a song-mode lyric, but one that in its dramatic quality and hint of speech mode looks forward to later styles, as does Ferrabosco's setting of it, with a few declamatory touches but primarily in the tuneful lute-song style of symmetrical phrase lengths and sectional melodic repetition. From the 1620s through the 1640s speech-mode lyrics became quite popular among both poets and composers. At the same time, composers developed a highly literary mode of song composition capable of setting such lyrics in both dialogues and solo songs. The popularity of speech-mode lyric intensified these declamatory trends and seemingly encouraged innovative harmony, while in turn the declamatory style influenced poets who were alert to musical fashion.

In the middle decades of the century, Milton, Cowley, and others were inspired by contemporary dramatic music and by musical humanism in their experiments with new lyrical meters, primarily in oratorical modes, for monodies, odes, and other longer lyric forms. Meanwhile a new generation of composers was becoming active who would welcome the Restoration versatility in amalgamating speech, song, and oratorical modes, as in Cowley's and Dryden's odes and in the heroic declamation of the later theatrical song lyrics. Influenced by the dramatic declamation and the syntax of accumulated discrete phrases practiced in odes and other "grand lyrics," poets writing lyrics for brief song also sometimes incorporated these theatrically useful qualities, transfering them to the smaller scale of brief lyric, as we saw in Dryden's Kalib song. They were aided in that transference by composers' frequent practice of excerpting one "allaeostroph" or irregular odic stanza for setting as a brief solo song, as Pelham Humfrey did with Cowley's "Ode. Sitting and Drinking."

Thus a style of lyric evolved that was suitable for the word-setting techniques of late Restoration composers such as Blow, Robert King, and preeminently Purcell. The mixture of song, speech, and declamatory modes, often in irregular stanzas, accorded with the composers' inclination to vary their word-setting approaches within each song and to ignore or subsume verbal patterns of rhythm (beyond those of the single brief phrase) and verbal pitch patterns, in songs that brought the complexities of Continental baroque music to England. In English song, "the tendency of the century as a whole," as Ian Spink concludes, "had been towards increasing dramatization." [34] The trend in spoken lyric had been just the same, and throughout the century each art had periodically reinforced it in the other.

34. *English Song*, p. 259.

Select Bibliography

Songbooks and Other Early Printed Sources

Allison, Richard. *The Psalmes of David in Meter*. London, 1599.

———. *An Howres Recreation in Musicke*. London, 1606.

Anerio, Giovanni Francesco. *La bella Clori armonica, Arie Canzonetti e Madrigali a 1–3 voci*. Rome, 1619.

Bandini, Angelo M. *Commentariorum de vita et scriptis Ioannis Bapt. Doni libri quinque*. Florence, 1755.

Butler, Charles. *The Principles of Musick in Singing and Setting: with The Two-fold Use thereof, Ecclesiasticall and Civil*. London, 1636.

Byrd, William. *Songs of Sundrie Natures*. London, 1589.

Campion, Thomas. *Observations in the Art of English Poetry*. London, 1602. Rpt. London: Bodley Head, 1925.

———. *Two Bookes Of Ayres . . . To be sung to the Lute and Viols*. London, 1613.

———. *Third Book of Ayres*. London, 1617.

Campion, Thomas and Philip Rosseter. *A Book of Ayres*. London, 1601.

A Choice Selection of 180 Loyal Songs. Compositor "N.T." 3d ed. London, 1685.

Cifra, Antonio. *Scherzi et Arie*. Rome, 1614.

Clifford, James. *The Divine Services and Anthems Usually Sung in His Majesties Chappell*. 2d ed. London, 1664.

Coprario, Giovanni [John Cooper]. *Funeral Teares. For the death of the Right Honorable the Earl of Devonshire*. London, 1606.

Doni, Giovanni Battista. *Compendio del Trattato de' Generi e de' Modi della Musica Con un Discorso sopra la Perfettione de' Concenti*. Rome, 1635.

———. *Annotazioni sopra il Compendio de' Generi, e de' Modi della Musica*. Rome, 1640.

———. *De praestantia Musicae Veteris*. Florence, 1647.

———. *Lyra Barberina Amphichordos*. 2 vols. Ed. Antonio Gori and G. B. Passeri. Florence, 1763.

Dowland, John. *The First Booke of Songes or Ayres of fowre partes with Tableture for the Lute*. London, 1597.

———. *The Second Booke of Songs or Ayres*. London, 1600.

———. *The Third And Last Booke of Songs Or Aires*. London, 1603.

———. *A Pilgrimes Solace. Wherein is contained Musical Harmonie of 3. 4. and 5. parts*. London, 1612.

205

Dowland, Robert. *A Musicall Banquet.* London, 1610.

Gamble, John. *Ayres and Dialogues.* London, 1657.

Gascoigne, George. *Certeyne Notes of Instruction.* London, 1575.

Hatton, J. L. and E. Faning, eds. *The Songs of England.* London: Boosey & Hawkes, 1888.

Hilton, John. *Catch that Catch Can.* London, 1652.

Hume, Tobias. *The First Part of Ayres, French, Pollish and Others.* London, 1605.

———. *Captaine Humes Poeticall Music, Principally made for two Basse-Viols.* London, 1607.

Hunnis, William. *Seven Sobs of a Sorrowfull Soule for Sinne.* London, 1583.

Kircher, Athanasius. *Musurgia Universalis sive Ars Magna Consoni et Dissoni.* Rome, 1650.

Lachrymae Musarum . . . Elegies upon the death of Henry, Lord Hastings. London, 1649.

Lawes, Henry. *Ayres and Dialogues, For One, Two, and Three Voyces.* Ed. John Playford. London, 1652.

Marenzio, Luca. *Madrigali a 4 Voci.* Venice, 1585.

———. *Il Primo Libro di Madrigal: a 4, 5, e 6. Voci.* Venice, 1588.

Parker, Archbishop Matthew. *The Whole Psalter Translated into English Metre.* London, 1567.

The Passionate Pilgrim. W. Jaggard, Compositor. London, 1599.

Pembroke, William Herbert, Earl of. *Poems Written by the . . . Earl of Pembroke.* London, 1660.

Playford, Henry, ed. *Harmonia Sacra: Divine Hymns and Dialogues.* London, 1688.

Playford, Henry and Richard Carr, eds. *The Theatre of Music: Or, A Choice Collection of the newest and best Songs Sung at the Courts, and Public Theaters.* 4 vols. London, 1685–1687.

Playford, John, ed. *Select Musicall Ayres and Dialogues.* London, 1659.

———. *The Treasury of Music.* 2d ed. London, 1669.

———. *Psalms & Hymns in Solemn Musick.* London, 1671.

Reggio, Pietro. *Songs Set by Pietro Reggio.* London, 1677.

Rossi, Michelangelo. *Erminia sul Giordano Dramma Mvsicale,* Rome, 1637; facs., vol. 12. *Bibliotheca Musica Bononiensis IV.* Bologna: Forni Editore, 1969.

Speght, Thomas, ed. *The Works of Chaucer.* London, 1598.

The Tears of Fancie, by "T. W." London, 1593.

Ward, John. *The First Set of English Madrigals.* London, 1613.

Watson, Thomas. *The Hekatompathia.* 1582; facs., ed. S. K. Heninger, Jr. Gainesville, Fla.: University of Florida Press, 1964.

———. *Italian Madrigals Englished, not to the Sense of the Original Ditty, but after the Affection of the Note.* London, 1590.

Modern Works

Alvarez, A. *The School of Donne.* London: Chatto & Windus, 1961.

Arthos, John. *Milton and the Italian Cities.* London: Bowes, 1968.

———. "Milton, Andreini, and Galileo," in *Approaches to Paradise Lost.* Ed. C. A. Patrides. London: Arnold, 1968.

Attridge, Derek. *Well-weighed Syllables: Elizabethan Verse in Classical Metres.* Cambridge: Cambridge University Press, 1974.

Auden, W. H. Introduction to "The Sonnets," in *The Complete Signet Classic Shakespeare.* Ed. Sylvan Barnet. New York: Harcourt, Brace, 1962.

Bennett, Joan. "Liberty under the Law: The Chorus and Meaning of *Samson Agonistes.*" *Milton Studies*, 12 (1978), 141–63.

Berkeley, D. S. "Précieuse Gallantry and the Seduction of Eve." *N & Q*, 196 (1951), 337.

Bontoux, Germaine. *La Chanson en Angleterre au Temps d'Elisabeth*. London: Oxford University Press, 1939.

Bottrall, Margaret. *George Herbert*. London: Murray, 1954.

Brennecke, Ernest. "Dryden's Odes to Draghi's Music." *PMLA*, 49 (1934), 1–36.

Brik, Osip. "Contributions to the Study of Verse Language," in *Readings in Russian Poetics*. Ed. Ladislav Matejka and Krystyna Pomorska. Cambridge, Mass.: M.I.T. Press, 1971.

Campion, Thomas. *Works*. Ed. P. Vivian. Oxford: Oxford University Press, 1909.

———. *The Works of Thomas Campion*. Ed. Walter Davis. New York: Doubleday, 1967.

Chan, Mary. *Music in the Theatre of Ben Jonson*. Oxford: Oxford University Press, 1980.

Charles, Amy. *A Life of George Herbert*. Ithaca, N.Y.: Cornell University Press, 1977.

Chute, Marchette. *Two Gentle Men: The Lives of George Herbert and Robert Herrick*. London: Secker & Warburg, 1969.

Corse, Sandra. "Old Music and New in 'L'Allegro' and 'Il Penseroso.'" *Milton Quarterly*, 14 (1980), 109–13.

Cowley, Abraham. *The Poems of Abraham Cowley*. Ed. A. R. Waller. Vol. 1. *The English Writings of Abraham Cowley*. Cambridge: Cambridge University Press, 1905.

Crashaw, Richard. *The Poems in English Latin and Greek of Richard Crashaw*. Ed. L. C. Martin. 2d ed. Oxford: Clarendon Press, 1957.

———. *The Complete Poetry of Richard Crashaw*. Ed. George W. Williams. New York: Doubleday, 1970.

Crum, Margaret C. "Notes on the Texts of William Lawes's Songs in B. M. MS Add. 31432." *The Library*, 9 (1954), 122–27.

———. "A Manuscript of John Wilson's Songs." *The Library*, 10 (1955), 55–57.

———. "An Unpublished Fragment of Verse by Herrick." *RES*, n.s., 11 (1960), 186–89.

Cunnar, Eugene R. "Richard Crashaw and the Hymn Tradition." Ph.D. diss., University of Wisconsin, 1973.

Cutts, John P. "British Museum Additional MS. 31432: William Lawes' Writing for Theatre and Court." Vol. 7. *The Library*, 5th Series, 7 (1952).

———. "A Bodleian Song-Book: Don. c. 57." *ML*, 34 (1953), 192–211.

———. "'Mris. Elizabeth Davenant 1624' Christ Church MS. Mus. 87." *RES*, n.s., 10 (1959), 26–37.

Davey, Henry. *History of English Music*. 1921. Rpt. New York: DaCapo, 1969.

Day, Cyrus L. and Eleanore Murrie. *English Songbooks: 1651–1702; A Bibliography*. London: Bibliographical Society, 1940.

Demaray, John. *Milton's Theatrical Epic*. Cambridge, Mass.: Harvard University Press, 1980.

Dickey, Franklin M. "Forgeries in the Stationer's Register." *SQ*, 11 (1960), 39–47.

Dobrez, Livio. "The Crashaw-Teresa Relationship." *Southern Review, Adelaide*, 5 (1972), 21–37.

Donne, John. *The Poems of John Donne*. Ed. H. J. C. Grierson. London: Oxford University Press, 1929.

————. *John Donne: The Complete English Poems.* Ed. A. J. Smith. New York: St. Martin, 1971.

Doughtie, Edward, ed. *Lyrics from English Airs, 1596–1622.* Cambridge, Mass.: Harvard University Press, 1970.

Dryden, John. *John Dryden Works.* Ed. George Saintsbury. London: Fisher Unwin, n.d.

Duckles, Vincent. "The 'Curious' Art of John Wilson." *JAMS,* 7 (1954), 92–112.

————. "John Jenkins's Settings of Lyrics by George Herbert." *Musical Quarterly,* 48 (1962), 461–75.

Duckles, Vincent and Franklin Zimmerman. "English Song and the Challenge of Italian Monody" (with score of Lanier's "Hero and Leander") and "Sound and Sense in Purcell's 'Single Songs'" in *Words to Music.* Los Angeles: Clark Lib., 1967.

Eccles, Mark. *Christopher Marlowe in London.* Cambridge, Mass.: Harvard University Press, 1934.

Einstein, Alfred. "The Elizabethan Madrigal and 'Musica Transalpina.'" *Music and Letters,* 25 (1944), 66–77.

Ejxenbaum, Boris. "The Theory of the Formal Method," in *Readings in Russian Poetics.* Ed. Ladislav Matejka and Krystyna Pomorska. Cambridge, Mass.: M.I.T. Press, 1971.

Emslie, MacDonald. "Three Early Settings of Jonson." *Notes & Queries,* (1953), 466–68.

————. "Milton on Lawes," in *Music in English Renaissance Drama.* Ed. John H. Long. Lexington: University of Kentucky Press, 1969.

England, Martha W. "John Milton and the Performing Arts." *Bulletin of the New York Public Library,* 80 (1970).

Erlich, Victor. *Russian Formalism, History-Doctrine.* The Hague: Mouton, 1965.

Evans, C. "Cartwright's Debt to Lawes," in *Music in English Renaissance Drama.* Ed. John H. Long. Lexington: University of Kentucky Press, 1969.

Evans, Willa. *Ben Jonson and Elizabethan Music.* 1929. Rpt. New York: DaCapo Press, 1965.

————. *Henry Lawes: Musician and Friend of Poets.* London: Oxford University Press, 1941.

Fabry, Frank. "Sidney's Poetry and Italian Song-Form." *ELR,* 3 (1973), 233–48.

Fellowes, E. H., ed. *English Madrigal Verse: 1588–1632.* 3d ed. rev. Sternfeld and Greer. Oxford: Clarendon Press, 1967.

————. *The English School of Lutenist Song Writers.* Series 1 and 2. 1920–25; 2d ed. London: Stainer & Bell, 1959.

Finney, Gretchen. *Musical Backgrounds for English Literature, 1580–1650.* New Brunswick, N.J.: Rutgers University Press, 1962.

Fletcher, Angus. *The Transcendental Masque.* Ithaca, N.Y.: Cornell University Press, 1971.

Frank, Mortimer H. "Milton's Knowledge of Music," in *Milton and the Art of Sacred Song.* Ed. J. Max Patrick and Robert H. Sundell. Madison: University of Wisconsin Press, 1979.

Fraunce, Abraham. *The Lamentations of Amyntas* (1585). Ed. Walter F. Staton, Jr., and Franklin M. Dickey. Chicago: University of Chicago Press, 1967.

Freer, W. Coburn. *Music for a King: George Herbert's Style and the Metrical Psalms.* Baltimore: Johns Hopkins University Press, 1972.

Frescobaldi, Girolamo. *Arie Musicali* (1630). Ed. Helga Spohr. Mainz: Schott, 1960.

Greenberg, Noah, W. H. Auden, and Chester Kallman, eds. *An Elizabethan Song Book.* Garden City, N.Y.: Anchor Books, 1955.

Haas, Robert. *Musik des Barocks.* Potsdam: Athenaion, 1929.

Harley, John. *Music in Purcell's London.* London: Dobson, 1968.

Hart, E. F. "Caroline Lyrics and Contemporary Song-books." *The Library,* 8 (1953), 89–110.

Hatton, J. L., and E. Faning, eds. *The Songs of England.* London: Boosey & Hawkes, 1888.

Hayes, Albert M. "Counterpoint in Herbert." *SP,* 35 (1938), 43–60.

Heath-Stubbs, John. *The Ode.* London: Oxford University Press, 1969.

Herbert, George. *The Works of George Herbert.* Ed. F. E. Hutchinson. Oxford: Clarendon Press, 1945.

Herrick, Robert. *Herrick's Poetical Works.* Ed. L. C. Martin. Oxford: Oxford University Press, 1956.

――――. *The Complete Poetry of Robert Herrick.* Ed. J. Max Patrick. New York: New York University Press, 1963.

Hollander, John. *The Untuning of the Sky: Ideas of Music in English Poetry, 1500–1700.* Princeton, N.J.: Princeton University Press, 1961.

――――. *Vision and Resonance: Two Senses of Poetic Form.* New York: Oxford University Press, 1975.

Hunt, Clay. *"Lycidas" and the Italian Critics.* New Haven: Yale University Press, 1979.

Ing, Catherine. *Elizabethan Lyrics.* London: Chatto & Windus, 1951.

Ingram, R. W. "Words and Music," in *Elizabethan Poetry.* Ed. John R. Brown. New York: St. Martin's, 1960.

Jacobus, Lee A. "The Musical Duel in 'Musicks Duell,'" in *Essays on Richard Crashaw.* Ed. Robert M. Cooper. Salzburg: University of Salzburg Press, 1979.

Johnson, Lee M. "Milton's Blank Verse Sonnets." *Milton Studies,* 5 (1973), 129–53.

Johnson, Paula. *Form and Transformation in Music and Poetry of the English Renaissance.* New Haven: Yale University Press, 1972.

Jorgens, Elise B. "On Matters of Manner and Music in Jacobean and Caroline Song." *ELR,* 10 (1980), 239–54.

――――. *The Well-Tun'd Word: Musical Interpretations of English Poetry, 1597–1651.* Minneapolis: University of Minnesota Press, 1982.

――――. "Review of *Music in the Theatre of Ben Jonson.*" *Renaissance Quarterly,* 35 (1982), 339–43.

Kastendieck, Miles. *England's Musical Poet, Thomas Campion.* 1938. Rpt. New York: Russell, 1963.

Kerman, Joseph. *The Elizabethan Madrigal.* London: Oxford University Press, 1962.

Kermode, Frank. "The Date of Cowley's *Davideis.*" *RES,* 25 (1949), 154–58.

Kime, Mary W. "Lyric and Song: Seventeenth Century Musical Settings of John Donne's Poetry." Ph.D. diss., University of Denver, 1969.

Langer, Susanne K. *Feeling and Form.* New York: Scribner's, 1953.

――――. *Problems of Art.* New York: Scribner's, 1957.

Lawes, William. *Six Songs.* Ed. Edward H. Jones. London: Schott, 1971.

Lefkowitz, Murray. *William Lawes.* London: Routledge, 1960.

Le Huray, Peter. "The Fair Musick that All Creatures Made," in *The Age of Milton: Backgrounds to Seventeenth-Century Literature.* Ed. C. A. Patrides and Raymond B. Waddington. Totowa, N.J.: Barnes and Noble, 1980.

Lewalski, Barbara. "*Samson Agonistes* and the 'Tragedy' of the Apocalypse." *PMLA,* 85 (1970), 1050–62.

Lewalski, Barbara and Andrew J. Sabol, eds. *Major Poets of the Earlier Seventeenth Century.* New York: Odyssey Press, 1973.

Lowbury, Edward, et al. *Thomas Campion, Poet, Composer, Physician.* London: Chatto & Windus, 1970.

Mace, D. T. "Musical Humanism, the Doctrine of Rhythmus, and the Saint Cecilia Odes of Dryden." *JWCI*, 27 (1964), 251–92.

Mandel, Leon. *Robert Herrick: The Last Elizabethan*. Chicago: University of Chicago Press, 1927.

Martz, Louis L. *The Poetry of Meditation: A Study in English Religious Literature of the Seventeenth Century*. New Haven: Yale University Press, 1954.

———. *The Wit of Love*. Notre Dame: University of Notre Dame Press, 1969.

———. "Chorus and Character in *Samson Agonistes*." *Milton Studies*, 1 (1969), 115–34.

———. "The Action of the Self," in *Metaphysical Poetry*. Ed. M. Bradbury and D. Palmer. Bloomington: Indiana University Press, 1971.

Maynard, Winifred. "The Lyrics of Wyatt: Poems or Songs, I & II." *RES*, n.s., 16 (1965), 1–13, 245–57.

Mellers, Wilfrid. *Harmonious Meeting: A Study of Music, Poetry, and Theatre in England, 1600–1900*. London: D. Dobson, 1965.

Milton, John. *The Works of John Milton*. Ed. Frank Patterson et al. New York: Columbia University Press, 1931.

———. *Complete Poems and Major Prose*. Ed. Merritt Hughes. Indianapolis: Bobbs-Merrill, 1957.

———. *Complete Prose Works*. Ed. Don M. Wolfe. New Haven: Yale University Press, 1953–1971.

Miner, Earl. *The Metaphysical Mode from Donne to Cowley*. Princeton, N.J.: Princeton University Press, 1969.

———. *The Cavalier Mode from Jonson to Cotton*. Princeton, N.J.: Princeton University Press, 1971.

———. *The Restoration Mode from Milton to Dryden*. Princeton, N.J.: Princeton University Press, 1974.

Morley, Thomas. *A Plain and Easy Introduction to Practical Music*. Ed. R. Alec Harman. London: Dent, 1952.

Morris, Brian. " 'Not without Song': Milton and the Composers," in *Approaches to Paradise Lost*. Ed. C. A. Patrides. Toronto: University of Toronto Press, 1968.

Nardo, A. K. "The Submerged Sonnet as Lyric Moment in Miltonic Epic." *Genre*, 9 (1976), 85–117.

Nethercot, Arthur H. *Abraham Cowley: The Muse's Hannibal*. London: Oxford University Press, 1931.

Ostriker, Alicia. "Song and Speech in the Metrics of George Herbert." *PMLA*, 80 (1965), 62–68.

Palisca, Claude V. "Ut Oratoria Musica: The Rhetorical Basis of Musical Mannerism," in *The Meaning of Mannerism*. Ed. Franklin W. Robinson and Stephen G. Nichols, Jr. Hanover, N.H.: University Press of New England, 1972.

Parker, David. "The Love Poems of *Paradise Lost* and the Petrarchan Tradition." *Ariel*, 3 (1972), 34–43.

Parker, William R. *Milton: A Biography*. Oxford: Clarendon Press, 1969.

Paton, W. R., ed. *Greek Anthology*. New York: Putnam, 1917.

Pattison, Bruce. *Music and Poetry of the English Renaissance*. 1948. 2d ed. London: Methuen, 1970.

Petrarca, Francesco. *Petrarch's Lyric Poems*. Ed. Robert M. Durling. Cambridge, Mass.: Harvard University Press, 1976.

Poulton, Diana. *John Dowland*. Berkeley: University of California Press, 1972.

Praz, Mario. *The Flaming Heart: Essays on Crashaw, Machiavelli and Other Studies*. Garden City, N.Y.: Doubleday, 1958.

Prince, F. T. *The Italian Element in Milton's Verse*. Oxford: Clarendon Press, 1954.

Quirk, Randolph and Sidney Greenbaum. *A Concise Grammar of Contemporary English*. New York: Harcourt Brace, 1973.

Richardson, David A. "The Golden Mean in Campion's Airs." *CL*, 30 (1978), 108–32.

Ringler, William A., Jr. "Master Drant's Rules." *PQ*, 29 (1955), 70–74.

Rollin, Roger B., and J. Max Patrick, eds. *"Trust to Good Verses": Herrick Tercentenary Essays*. Pittsburgh: University of Pittsburgh Press, 1978.

Saintsbury, George. *History of English Prosody from the Twelfth Century to the Present Day*. 3 vols. London: Macmillan and Co., 1906–1910.

Schleiner, Louise. "Herbert's 'Divine and Morall' Songs." Ph.D. diss., Brown University, 1973.

———. "The Composer as Reader: A Setting of George Herbert's 'Altar.'" *Musical Quarterly*, 61 (1975), 422–32.

———. "Seventeenth-Century Settings of Herbert: Purcell's 'Longing,'" in *Too Rich to Clothe the Sunne*. Ed. Claude Summers and Ted-Larry Pebworth. Pittsburgh: Pittsburgh University Press, 1980.

———. "Milton, G. B. Doni, and the Dating of Doni's Works." *Milton Quarterly*, 16 (1982), 46–52.

Schleiner, Winfried. "Jaques and the Melancholy Stag." *ELN*, 17 (1980), 175–79.

Selig, Edward. *The Flourishing Wreath: A Study of Thomas Carew's Poetry*. New Haven: Yale University Press, 1958.

Shakespeare, William. *The Riverside Shakespeare*. Ed. G. Blakemore Evans et al. Boston: Houghton Mifflin, 1974.

Shawcross, John. "The Poet as Orator," in *The Rhetoric of Renaissance Poetry*. Ed. Thomas Sloane and Raymond Waddington. Berkeley: University of California Press, 1974.

———. "Herbert's Double Poems: A Problem in the Text of *The Temple*," in *Too Rich to Clothe the Sunne*. Ed. Claude Summers and Ted-Larry Pebworth. Pittsburgh: Pittsburgh University Press, 1980.

Shuster, George. *The English Ode from Milton to Keats*. Gloucester, Mass.: Peter Smith, 1964.

Sidney, Philip. *The Poems of Sir Philip Sidney*. Ed. William A. Ringler, Jr. Oxford: Clarendon Press, 1962.

Smith, G. Gregory, ed. *Elizabethan Critical Essays*. London: Oxford University Press, 1904.

Smith, Hallett. *Elizabethan Poetry*. 1952. Ann Arbor: University of Michigan Press, 1968.

Souris, André, ed. *Poèmes de Donne, Herbert et Crashaw mis en musique par leurs contemporains*. Paris: Centre National de la Recherche Scientifique, 1961.

Spink, Ian. *English Song, Dowland to Purcell*. New York: Scribner's, 1974.

Sprat, Thomas. "The Life and Writings of Mr. Abraham Cowley," in *Cowley's Prose Works*. London: William Pickering, 1826.

Stanley, Thomas. *The Poems and Translations of Thomas Stanley*. Ed. Galbraith M. Crump. Oxford: Clarendon Press, 1962.

Stevens, John. *Music and Poetry in the Early Tudor Court*. London: Methuen, 1961.

Summers, Joseph. *George Herbert: His Religion and Art*. Cambridge, Mass.: Harvard University Press, 1954.

———. *The Muse's Method*. London: Chatto & Windus, 1962.

Summers, Montague, ed. "A Note on Purcell's Music," in *Dryden: The Dramatic Works*. 1932. Rpt. New York: Gordon, 1968.

Swinburne, Algernon C. *Studies in Prose and Poetry*. London: Chatto & Windus, 1894.

Thibault, G. "Musique et Poésie en France au XVIe Siècle Avant les 'Amours' de Ronsard." Ed. Jean Jacquot. *Musique et Poésie au XVIe Siècle.* Paris: Centre Nationale de la Recherche Scientifique, 1954.

Thorp, Willard, ed. *Songs from the Restoration Theater.* Princeton, N.J.: Princeton University Press, 1934.

Tillyard, E. M. W. *The English Renaissance.* Baltimore: Johns Hopkins University Press, 1952.

Traugott, Elizabeth and Mary Pratt. *Linguistics for Students of Literature.* New York: Harcourt Brace, 1980.

Tuve, Rosemond. "Sacred 'Parody' of Love Poetry, and Herbert." *SR,* 8 (1961), 249–90.

Tynjanov, Jurij. "Rhythm as the Constructive Factor of Verse," in *Readings in Russian Poetics.* Ed. Ladislav Matejka and Krystyna Pomorska. Cambridge, Mass.: M.I.T. Press, 1971.

Wallerstein, Ruth. *Richard Crashaw: A Study in Style and Poetic Development.* Madison: University of Wisconsin Press, 1935.

Walton, Izaak. *Lives of Donne and Herbert.* Ed. S. C. Roberts. 1929. 2d ed. Cambridge: Cambridge University Press, 1949.

Warren, Austin. *Richard Crashaw: A Study in Baroque Sensibility.* Baton Rouge: University of Louisiana Press, 1939.

Watson, Thomas, *Amyntas,* and Abraham Fraunce, *The Lamentations of Amyntas.* 1585. Ed. Walter F. Staton, Jr., and Franklin M. Dickey. Chicago: University of Chicago Press, 1967.

Willets, Pamela. *The Henry Lawes Manuscript.* London: British Museum, 1969.

Williams, George. *Image and Symbol in the Sacred Poetry of Richard Crashaw.* Columbia: University of South Carolina Press, 1963.

Winn, James. *Unsuspected Eloquence: A History of the Relations between Poetry and Music.* New Haven: Yale University Press, 1981.

Winters, Yvor. *Forms of Discovery.* New Mexico: Alan Swallow, 1967.

Wolff, Hellmuth C. *Oper: Szene und Darstellung von 1600 bis 1900.* Leipzig: VEB Deutscher Verlag Für Musik, 1968.

Young, Percy. *A History of British Music.* New York: Norton, 1967.

Zimmerman, Franklin. *See* Duckles, Vincent.

Index